MEASURING YOUR MEDIA PROFILE

MEASURING YOUR MEDIA PROFILE

Dermot McKeone

Gower

Published by
Gower Publishing Limited
Gower House
Croft Road
Aldershot
Hampshire GU11 3HR
England

Gower
Old Post Road
Brookfield
Vermont 05036
USA

Dermot McKeone has asserted his right under the Copyright, Designs and Patents Act 1988 to be identified as the author of this work.

British Library Cataloguing in Publication Data
McKeone, Dermot
  Measuring Your Media Profile
  I. Title
  659.2

ISBN 0–566–07578–4 ✓

Library of Congress Cataloging-in-Publication Data
McKeone, Dermot H.
    Measuring your media profile / Dermot McKeone.
      p.   cm.
    Includes index.
    ISBN 0–568–07578–4
    1. Mass media–Methodology.   2. Mass media criticism.   3. Public relations.   I. Title
P91.M374   1995
302.23'01–dc20   95–12172
                                                   CIP

Typeset in Century Old Style by Raven Typesetters, Chester
Printed and bound in Great Britain by
Biddles Ltd, Guildford and King's Lynn

Contents

List of Figures   vii
List of Tables   ix
Preface   xi
Acknowledgements   xiii

Part I   Principles of Media Analysis

1   The Context   3
2   What is a Media Profile?   11
3   What Should be Measured?   19
4   The Concept of Target Audience   31
5   The Concept of Message   41
6   Collecting and Sampling   53
7   Who Should Evaluate?   63

Part II   Media Analysis in Action

8   The Communications Audit   73
9   Deciding Your Analysis Technique   83
10   Corporate Profile and the Media   101
11   Analysing Coverage of Products, Services and Brands 109
12   Media Analysis and Sponsorship   123
13   Analysing Adverse Coverage   131
14   Analysing Crisis Coverage   141
15   Values, Costs, and Advertising Value Equivalents   145
16   Positional Data   151
17   The Role of the Picture   157
18   The Corporate Environment   161

Part III   Media Analysis in Perspective

19 Direct Measurement of Opinions, Perceptions, Reputation and
    Behaviour   171
20 The Feedback Process   181
21 Trouble Shooting   189
22 Building an Influencer Database   201
23 Budgeting for Media Analysis   209
24 Media Analysis and the Board   215

References and Further Reading   227
Index   229

List of Figures

1.1   Simplified structure of the communications function of a
typical large corporation   7

3.1   Company media analysis: volume analysis, June   24

3.2   Company media analysis: namechecks, June   25

3.3   Company media analysis: message point totals for all media, June   27

4.1   Media analysis for a manufacturing company: volume analysis, June   34

5.1   Message point readership for 'management strength' message
in adults, aged 30–60, June   50

5.2   Message pressure chart: trend report 1995, adults aged 30–60   51

9.1   BRT: total number of press cuttings received during May–June   86

9.2   BRT: positive press cuttings received during May–June   87

9.3   BRT: total press cuttings received during May–June   88

9.4   Anglian Water: volume analysis, June 1993   90

9.5   Anglian Water: message point totals for all media, June 1993   91

9.6   Amex TRS: favourability (by volume), January–December 1993   92

9.7   Amex TRS: proactive communications trend analysis (by volume),
January–December, 1993   93

9.8   Amex TRS: leading arguments in 1993 (by volume), October–
December 1993   94

9.9   ICL: message density for the 'Systems integrator' message in 1994   96

11.1   Volume analysis for imaginary company Promofiz for a single
month   112

11.2   Message point totals for Promofiz: all media for a single month   114

11.3   Volume of coverage by story source for Promofiz: all media for a
single month   115

11.4   Message delivery by story source for Promofiz: all media for a
single month   116

11.5   Message delivery by type of coverage for Promofiz: all media for a
single month   118

11.6   Message delivery by type of coverage for one of Promofiz's
competitors: all media for a single month   119

20.1   A simple feedback process for PR programme management   185

20.2   Line-of-best-fit trend analysis for namechecks in a particular
       media category over a year   186
20.3   Line-of-best-fit trend analysis for message delivery in a
       particular media category over a year   187
24.1   Comparative volume trend analysis over a year for Michele's
       company and two competitors   219
24.2   Comparative volume trend analysis over a year for Michele's
       company and two competitors, using lines-of-best-fit   220
24.3   How Michele's company has delivered the 'quality' message
       in the UK trade and vertical market press over a year, with a
       line-of-best-fit trend graph superimposed on the comparative
       bar chart   221
24.4   Bar chart comparing message delivery scores for the 'quality'
       message with the number of enquiries received for one of
       Michele's company's products   223
24.5   How Michele's company has delivered the 'customer service'
       message in the UK trade and vertical market press over a year,
       with a line-of-best-fit trend graph superimposed on the comparative
       bar chart; the chart shows a gradual deterioration in message
       delivery over the year   224
24.6   Bar chart comparing the different elements of the coverage
       which contribute the 'customer service' message scores:
       Michele's proactive PR has delivered a stable and positive
       element; the other bars in the chart highlight a deteriorating
       standard of customer service   225

List of Tables

4.1   A target media list for a manufacturing company: a starting point   33
5.1   Message point readership for 'management strength'
      message in adults, aged 30–60, June   49
7.1   Example of a media analysis brief   68
9.1   Report of media coverage for BRT and its competition (May–June)   85
10.1 Relevance of IBM's key messages to its key organizations   107
15.1 Message scores for five key messages in a single month   149
16.1 How media analysis data can be adjusted for varying editions, page
      number and position on page   155
22.1 Influencer data – analysis of a single cutting   205
22.2 Table of data produced as a result of media analysis of a particular
      issue over an extended period   205
23.1 Choosing a media analysis bureau. By completing the whole table,
      an accurate idea of annual costs can be obtained   211

Preface

At the time of writing this book, media analysis is a very fashionable subject. There are articles and supplements on it in the trade press, and modules concerning it on university courses. Rather more importantly, PR people are using media analysis techniques in the management of their communication programmes. It's nevertheless a trendy, glossy subject on which PR people like to hold forth. What a great subject to pontificate about!

Media analysis could now go in one of two directions. It could go the way of the skateboard and the hula hoop and be consigned to oblivion in a year or two, or it could lose a little of its gloss and evolve into an essential working tool, becoming a requirement of an increasingly professional PR business. I sincerely hope that the latter occurs.

There have also been a good many letters and articles written (in the PR trade press) and more than a few words spoken (in PR seminars and conferences) on the subject of the professionalism of the PR business. I'd like to add just this: in the minds of many of our audiences, PR is still almost synonymous with 'gloss', superficiality, lack of substance, or worse. PR people no longer even bother to react when they hear that something '... was just a PR exercise' on the radio or television. Public relations is being beaten to death by the media – the same media its practitioners are supposed to have such a profound influence over.

So it seems to me that by using media analysis and other evaluation techniques, PR people can reach a number of goals. First, they can gain respect from those who work in professions in which measurement is demanded; second they can learn to come to terms with the forces which have given public relations its current reputation. And of course, they'll also be able to do a better job for their clients – but then, that is what this book is all about.

Dermot McKeone, Autumn 1994

Acknowledgements

My thanks are due to all who have helped in the production of this book including Tony Peck and all my colleagues on the board at the Infopress Group, and the people who comprise IMPACT, the media analysis service offered by my own company Infopress Communications Limited.

Many of the case studies (and anecdotes) in the book are based on work that I have shared with this team. They are Rob Walker, Suzanne Rose, Penny James, Dennis Cunningham, John Hymas, Kate Davis, Emma Newman, Mandy Sinnott, Audrey Winterbottom, Penny Sucharov, Jonathan Rush, Yvonne Wilcox, Anne Haley, Andrea Bensusan, Fiona Baird, and Linda Beardmore.

Thanks are also due to a number of professional communicators and the companies they represent, each of whom have let me use some of their material for case studies. They include Edmund King (The RAC), Robert Goodsell (ICL), Mandy Wilkins (BR Telecommunications), John McAngus (Anglian Water), David Jones (Courage).

I'd also like to say a special word of thanks to Pete Cape of Audience Selection who helped with Chapter 19, Sandra Stroud of FT-Profile who provided valuable resources for Chapter 6, and Sandra Macleod of CARMA and Jill Ury of Delahaye who provided information for case studies in Chapter 9.

Part I
Principles of Media Analysis

1 The Context

This chapter introduces the concepts of media analysis and evaluation and explains their role within the frameworks of PR programme evaluation and corporate communications strategy.

'Of course it's right! It was in the newspaper this morning!' Comments like these deserve to be scoffed at, but they are still heard when people are striving to convince.

A statement carried in a newspaper, or heard on radio or seen on television undoubtedly carries authority. In addition to the fact that the media reach large numbers of people, it is this authority which makes the media so important to those who need to communicate with large numbers of people.

INFLUENCING THE MEDIA

People have been trying to influence the media almost since the publication of the first mass-circulation newspapers in the eighteenth century. But it is only relatively recently that the influencers have started attempting to analyse their content and to measure the effect they have on readers, listeners and viewers.

It has been a matter of regret to some, and a source of solace to others that since the birth of the public relations business in the years immediately after the Second World War, the effectiveness of PR has been one of the great imponderables. And in the debate about the professionalism (or otherwise) of public relations the inability to measure the effectiveness of PR has been both a talking point and a sticking point.

In the 1960s and 1970s, there were practitioners around who planned programmes carefully, agreed objectives and devised communication strategies to meet them. These practitioners thought of themselves as being PR professionals and, within the context of the industry at the time, they undoubtedly were. They were surrounded by operators who carried out short-term promotional and press relations work under the tactical control of sales and marketing and other senior managers (who also had other, perhaps weightier responsibilities) and could lay no claim to any kind of strategic or professional responsibility.

What the early professionals lacked was any kind of formal management information to convey to their managers how effective they had been in carrying out their work. PR people then were operating like a gunner bombarding a target from behind a range of hills. The gunner has no information on range or direction from his position: he needs a scout located on the top of the hill or feedback from the air to tell him where the shells are landing and if he needs to move to the left or right or change the elevation. In answer to the question, 'How effective has your work been?', the only honest answer was 'I don't really know.'

There were a number of early media analysis and evaluation techniques which attempted to answer or at least to get round this question. PR people tried measuring column inches and calculating the advertising equivalent value of the space – but it was realized early on that the technique couldn't cope either with an announcement of pivotal importance, or with negative news and adverse comment. Others tried stacking piles of basically positive coverage against basically negative coverage and seeing if one outweighed the other. But there was no way of assessing strength of comment or the editorial weight of the publication. For most of the past 50 years the media analysis business has been a non-starter.

Since the beginning of the 1980s, a number of things have happened to change all this. The first has been the encroachment of computer technology into the PR business. The second has been the sheer growth of the business itself. With growth, public relations has started attracting practitioners with classical management skills and training: managers who demand the same kind of information from their departments and consultancies that their colleagues expect of their finance and manufacturing departments. And with the availability of computer software enabling the rapid development of application-orientated systems, the industry has, to the surprise of some older PR practitioners, found itself able to respond.

In some organizations, this response has taken the form of a hand-crafted system designed by the PR team or an adviser, to meet the needs and wishes of that team specifically. In others, the response has been to acquire a system whereby the team processes media data itself using consultancy or departmental resources. A further group have chosen to use the services of an evaluation or media analysis bureau, who agree measurement criteria with the PR team and then carry out the bulk of the analysis externally in order to preserve the integrity of the measurement process. We'll be exploring all these options later in this book.

Media analysis is the analysis of editorial media coverage to ascertain underlying facts, opinions and trends. As we will be discovering in Chapter 3, there are numerous different truths which we can find from even a single newspaper cutting. For many of us, however, media analysis is of interest because the coverage is likely to have an effect on readers rather than because there is some intrinsic worth in determining the publications' editorial stance.

Public relations practitioners, and other people who are concerned about the relationship between their organization and the outside world, are among the foremost users of media analysis techniques. For them, media analysis can be used to determine the extent to which they have been successful in reaching, informing and persuading the people who constitute their target audiences. This is a process which will go far beyond crude equivalent cost measures.

WHY ANALYSE MEDIA COVERAGE?

The reasons given for analysing media coverage are numerous and varied.

In many instances, managers responsible for the media relations function simply feel the need to be more accountable and want to demonstrate the worth of their activities to their purse-string holders. In western Europe, being seen as accountable is demanded increasingly frequently – especially in recently privatized organizations, and in public bodies such as local authorities and other government funded institutions.

In companies, public relations managers usually need to make a case for improved (or maintained) budgets for the following year, and facts are needed to back up the arguments – facts presented in charts and graphs, and in language which will be understood by hard-nosed board members.

Another force driving public relations people in the direction of media analysis is the increasing popularity of quality management techniques. Many companies are actively seeking certification under international quality management standards in the International Standards Organization's ISO 9000 series and their local equivalents such as the British Standard's BS5750 in the UK. In these standards, the emphasis is on measurement against established benchmarks, and chief executives, seeing manufacturing, storage and distribution functions differentiating their departments through quality systems, are asking awkward questions of their public relations departments. Media analysis can provide some of the answers.

MEDIA ANALYSIS COSTS

There is a fundamental problem which the PR industry managers will have to face and overcome before it can make full use of media analysis techniques, and to no one's surprise it concerns money.

In the big growth years of public relations, PR fees rose to dizzy heights. In 1994 in the UK, a PR executive's charge-out fee to a client could vary between £50 per hour and £250 per hour depending on seniority and experience – rates comparable with lawyers and other professionals. If PR staff are to become involved in media analysis, the same kind of charges will apply to the analytical process.

Media analysis is a time-consuming business, and the biggest cost element is the cost of reading the coverage: analysing the results of a major campaign is going to take these busy and expensive people considerable time. A campaign generating 125 newspaper and magazine cuttings, 20 radio tapes and 5 television items will take an average reader approximately 10 hours to read, hear, view and record his or her judgements. Even at the lowest charge-out rate quoted above, the client is facing a potential charge of around £500.

Until the development of a computer-based expert system which can 'read' a newspaper article for sense and apply a set of evaluative criteria to the content and context, this assessment must be carried out by human beings. Until an even more sophisticated system is devised to analyse television coverage for factual content and semiotic significance, again, the analysis must continue to be carried out by human beings.

So the would-be users of media analysis must either be content to use strictly non-analytical techniques which will, in essence, measure coverage by the kilo, or reconcile themselves to paying for a professional analysis which will give the depth of analysis required. This in turn means budgeting for media analysis, and convincing holders of financial power to contribute for a service which has, in many instances, not been required in the past.

CAN PR PEOPLE EVALUATE THEIR WORK?

The question, 'Can you evaluate the effectiveness of your public relations programme?' used to be the question that PR people dreaded. Such a question could bring a PR business presentation to a halt in five seconds flat. In some organizations, it still can.

The question is a reasonable one. It must seem incomprehensible to an engineer, scientist or accountant, all of whom are used to concepts such as quality control, error calculation and audit, that an otherwise competent group of strategic thinkers can create a programme of activity with no checks and balances, no feedback loop.

This book is concerned with the media, but the question of measuring effectiveness of public relations goes far beyond the boundaries of an organization's relationship with the media. There is hardly any PR programme which comprises only media relations, and an answer to the evaluation question must encompass all the intertwined strands of a complex communications programme.

Figure 1.1 illustrates the highly simplified structure of the communications function of a fairly typical large corporation. At the top of the triangle are the corporate objectives of the organization. Supporting these and derived from them are the communications objectives comprising the delivery of agreed corporate, marketing and other messages to defined audiences such as customers, the local community, stockbrokers' analysts and others.

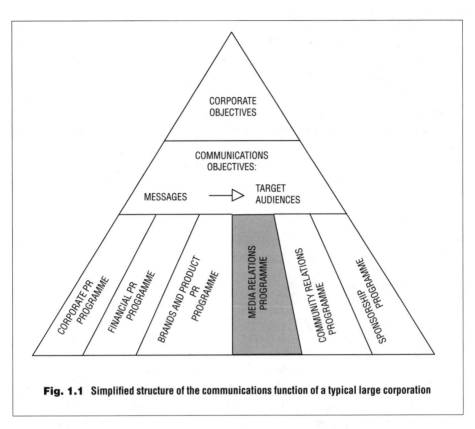

Fig. 1.1 Simplified structure of the communications function of a typical large corporation

In order to meet the communications objectives, the communications team, comprising advertising managers, public relations people and others create a range of communications programmes. It is clear that evaluation of the media relations programme only tackles part of the whole communications programme. The other, non-media strands of the communications programme also need to be evaluated – and each element of this diverse array of functions needs to be evaluated separately.

Most of these elements can be evaluated fairly easily. A direct mail shot can be evaluated for effectiveness within three weeks of posting by examining the responses. A sales seminar programme can be evaluated for numbers attending, and for sales resulting from the seminar. Movements in share price and the take-up of shares following a flotation can indicate the success or otherwise of a financial project. The effectiveness of a community relations programme – perhaps involving a local sponsorship or the announcement of an extension to a factory site – can be measured directly by tracking changes in audience opinion.

Media relations effectiveness, on the other hand, has always been the communications element which has been the most difficult to measure. It is difficult because it is usually operating across the territories of the direct corporate and marketing communications programmes. It is doubly difficult because the

7

players in the media relations game include journalists – who are supposedly not under anybody's control except their own. Newspapers, radio programmes and television programmes have their own communications agendas, and do not see themselves as convenient delivery mechanisms for our messages.

Evaluation mechanisms should be devised for all PR work, not just for the media relations elements of it. But the companies offering media analysis should be welcomed as the bearers of the last, missing piece in a jigsaw, not the bearers of an unwanted solution to a non-existent problem. To those who complain, 'Media evaluation is all very well, but what about evaluating all the other PR activities?' I would say, 'Do you complain to your greengrocer because he doesn't sell butter?'

ANALYSIS AND EVALUATION

The meaning of media analysis was given some attention in an earlier paragraph. The concept of media evaluation is a more difficult one to express.

It is tempting to think of media evaluation as the act of giving a monetary value to press coverage. Those who have attempted this in the past have usually done so by comparing the coverage with the equivalent advertising space cost. There are great difficulties with this as indicated above and as detailed in Chapter 15.

Evaluation is concerned with value, and in *Chambers Dictionary* the meaning of value is given as: 'worth: a fair equivalent: intrinsic worth or goodness'.

The actual monetary value of press coverage probably could be calculated, but let's consider for a minute what this would involve. Taken literally, it would require tracking all the readers of a publication in which a message had appeared, and determining how their behaviour had changed as a result of reading it. If the change in behaviour has had an intrinsic value to the organization, then this will need to be summed for all readers of all publications in which coverage had been obtained, together with all viewers and all listeners. The task is impracticable because it would involve more work than the work required to gain the coverage.

A much easier way of establishing a monetary value is to start from the opposite end of the problem, with a change in behaviour. This may have a real monetary value such as an increase in revenue or a change in capital value. Using market research techniques, it is possible to establish why this change of behaviour has occurred.

Let us take the example of a simple sales programme involving the promotion of a new washing machine. The sales promotion has resulted in sales of $1 000 000. If the research establishes that half the sales leads arose as a result of positive press coverage generated by the company's PR team, it is tempting to talk of the PR as being 'worth' $500 000. In fact, it is 'worth' rather less than this figure, because the product brochure, the sales team effort, the strength of the brand itself and the availability of good service back-up will all have helped to clinch the sale. The division of this 'value' figure between the various functions of marketing is a matter for negotiation rather than of absolute determination from basic principles. It's likely that a figure of between $100 000 and $200 000 will be reached.

Unlike the calculation of advertising value equivalents (AVEs), the evaluation procedure outlined above is valid, because it determines a real value of press relations activity to the organization. The problem is that it begs the question, 'So what?' Knowing that a given programme is worth $150 000 will not help the media relations manager to fine-tune future programmes. It will not help the manager to find out what went wrong, or which successful aspects could be enhanced in the future. And it cannot evaluate a containment programme devised to keep adverse coverage out of the media.

Media analysis, on the other hand, yields a rich harvest of data on which the interpretive manager can base future activities, and it is with the techniques of media analysis that most of future chapters will deal.

In conclusion, let us return to the dreaded question which opened this section of the chapter: 'Can you evaluate the effectiveness of your public relations programme?' Armed with media analysis techniques, the practitioner can nowadays answer:

'By all means. If you want media evaluation we can work with you and help to provide it.

'But we can do better than this. We can supply media analysis which can give you a constant stream of management information about our effectiveness in delivering your corporate and marketing messages to your target audiences.'

In Chapter 2, we explore the concepts of media profile and image, and start to examine the process by which an excellent media profile is established. We also examine what can happen when a media profile begins to deteriorate.

2 What is a Media Profile?

This chapter explains how an image of an organization can develop, and describes the media's role in contributing to the images of organizations in people's minds.

In April 1991, Gerald Ratner, the then Chairman of the well-known High Street jewellery chain, in the course of a speech at a conference at the UK's Institute of Directors made a jocular but arrogant remark about his company's products: he stated that one of the Ratner range of products – a sherry decanter, six glasses and a tray were able to be sold for a low price because they were 'total crap'.

Not many of the people listening to Mr Ratner's speech would have realized, at the time, the full extent of the damage this seemingly innocuous and amusing remark would have caused. Product sales dropped dramatically, the company's share price rapidly declined and some 18 months later Mr Ratner felt obliged to resign from the company which had been named after him. The Ratner image never recovered: by Christmas 1993, the group had decided to change the Ratner name to Signet.

I remember looking for an item of jewellery in Winchester just before the Christmas of 1992. I passed by the Ratner store. Even though I was in a better position than most to understand the process which had taken place and believed that there would be some desirable items in there, nothing would have persuaded me to go in. Ratner jokes still abound, and Gerald Ratner's name has become almost synonymous with the word which caused his downfall.

The casual remark was responsible for starting the process which culminated in plummeting sales figures. The accelerating decline was due to media coverage: the press and other media were there to report it. The broadsheet national press in the UK, which is a key medium for companies in the jewellery trade, used the word 'crap' in association with Ratner no fewer than 276 times between April 1991 and May 1994.

HOW IMAGES DEVELOP

How on earth did a casual remark like this one get Ratner into such a mess? The process which caused the above chain of events is at work on every organization's image – usually (and fortunately) at a rather slower pace. Every conversation, every sales call, every letter in which a company features affects the way in which that company is perceived. The image of a company which is present in our minds is being changed all the time – sometimes for the better, and sometimes for the worse.

When an organization has a media profile, the processes accelerate; the swings become more pronounced. A good set of results in the *Financial Times* will add 'successful company' to the image of a company in the mind of a stockbroker's analyst. A damaging oil spill in the North Sea will be reported widely in the national press and add the accusation 'polluter!' to the phrases we store in our minds next to the name of the tanker owner.

In their classic marketing book, *Positioning: the Battle for Your Mind*, Al Ries and Jack Trout (1986) describe that forbidding piece of real estate – the mind of a potential customer. There's not a great deal of room in there, and in the bit of territory labelled with a company's name (if it exists in there at all!) there is room for perhaps four or five words with which an organization will be associated.

Perhaps, at the moment, those words are words like 'hick outfit', 'old fashioned' and even 'untrustworthy'. Words which will go a long way towards preventing that customer from buying a product or service. It is partly the job of the PR professional to change those words to words like 'quality', 'fresh ideas' and 'leading edge'. By changing people's knowledge and opinions of an organization, you can also change that person's behaviour, and in doing that, you are well on your way to achieving your objectives. Sometimes, this requires a complete change of image.

WHAT IS AN IMAGE?

'Image' is a concept which many people feel they can relate to. But it's a concept with blurred edges and one which evades analysis. It's a term we don't hear communications professionals using very often these days, but one which is nevertheless worth exploring.

A useful image is one which consists of attributes which can be defined and measured. A successful corporate communications programme is one which delivers messages to the organization's target audiences in such a way that they enhance these attributes and thereby improve the image of the organization.

If a good image is what your organization is trying to project then it is a sound idea to write down the attributes you are trying to build in the minds of your target audiences. Only when you have made a few tough decisions about these attributes will your image come to life.

ACTUAL IMAGE AND DESIRED IMAGE

Organizations have two types of image and in most instances they are vastly dissimilar.

The first type consists of the *real images* – that is the images which target audiences and other groups actually hold. In other words, these images reflect what the company is really like, warts and all. An older person may have an image of a particular bank as a building with steep steps, long queues, unhelpful staff and nowhere to sit down: this image overlies any feelings he or she may have about the ideal place to keep money. A child may think of the local library as a boring place where he or she is not allowed to run around, and must keep quiet: it may well not be, in his or her mind, the place for finding things out and solving homework problems.

The second type of image consists of the visions – the *ideal images* which the company would like its audiences to have. The bank manager wants older people to think of the bank as the ideal place to invest, offering flexibility with stability. The County Council wants children to see the library as a knowledge centre in which it is easy to look things up and find things out.

It takes a good deal of honesty for an organization to accept these very different images for what they are.

The further apart they are, the more difficult is the task of bringing them together. Both categories can be measured. Companies' existing images can be measured using conventional opinion research, which we will be discussing in more detail in Chapter 19.

Visions, on the other hand, can be constructed by carefully interviewing managers, staff and audiences, often within the context of a communications audit as described in Chapter 8. It's essential to have clear information on both: only then will the corporate communications function of an organization have a clear sense of mission. Comparing the reality with the vision sets the communications agenda and goes part of the way towards writing the corporate and communications programme for the year ahead.

A perennial problem for PR professionals is that senior managers sometimes think they can buy image by the kilogram. They tell their PR professionals, 'Get me a good press' while other managers in the same organization are acting in such a way that they will ensure that they get a bad one. It's important for both the communications staff and other senior management to realize at the outset that the achievement of the vision is a task which all must share.

Changing a company's images usually means changing the company – and that takes a massive and sustained act of will requiring many people working very hard over a long period. To do this, consultation and cooperation are vital. A PR professional may start the process – drawing up an initial list of attributes – but he will need to share his ideas thoroughly and formally with his colleagues in other departments before he will start finding them appearing regularly in the media.

A PR professional alone can not 'own' an image of a company. He can write down on a piece of paper that his company should be a quality company, that it should be environmentally sound and that it should be a good employer. He can even tell these things to the press! But he will need the cooperation of his manufacturing director if he is to project the quality image with any force. He'll need the help of his packaging, transport and other managers if the environmental image is to be sustained. And it may be that the personnel director will need to be fired before the company is seen as a good employer. But, get these people on your side, and your vision becomes achievable.

IMAGE AND MEDIA PROFILE

We saw in the example at the beginning of this chapter how media coverage can change an organization's image. When a consistent and repeated group of views, opinions and facts keeps appearing in media coverage of an organization, that organization acquires a media profile.

Here's a selection of short extracts from UK press coverage about Gerald Ratner nearly three years after the infamous remark:

> ...Gerald Ratner survived for another 18 months after his fatal 'crap' remark despite widespread calls for his head. *Independent on Sunday*, 20 March 1994

> ...For readers from another planet Ratner infamously disparaged one of his own products, a sherry decanter set, as 'total crap'. *Independent on Sunday*, 13 February 1994

> ...Last night Mr Ratner, whose jocular use of the word 'crap' to describe one of his products in April 1991 was blamed for a dramatic decline in his business, would not comment. *Daily Mail*, 29 January 1994

> ...Chat-show personality Michael Parkinson has learned the peril of living near Gerald Ratner. One of the former jewellery king's trees has turned out to be, you might say, slightly imperfect. *Today*, 29 January 1994

> ...Gerald Ratner, who took his jewellery chain to dizzying heights only to return it to ignominy by describing its products as 'crap', is believed to be poised for a comeback running factory-shop outlets. *The Times*, 1 January 1994

These reports consistently communicate the 'poor quality' message associated with the Ratner name. The fact that the joke is still being repeated so long after the event demonstrates an underlying fact about media profile: it is a robust and long lived entity which is extremely difficult to change. The unwritten rule about jokes being unfunny on the second telling seems to have passed the press by.

Media relations people who have had to work at displacing negative perceptions of a person or an organization will confirm that negative media profiles are more robust and less easily displaced than positive ones. The mechanisms for improving profile are beyond the scope of this book, but it is relevant to record here that it can be a long and difficult process.

Even after a basic wrong has been righted, individual journalists need to be contacted, fact files need to be assembled and a constant stream of positive news needs to be issued in order to displace the negative perceptions in the journalists' minds. The journalist who thinks of a company as the outfit that sacked 50 people last March must be told that they are also the company which is opening up a new production line with excellent medium-term prospects. If not, that journalist will continue to think of the company as the one that's in trouble.

The process of adjusting media profile needs to be controlled carefully. And careful control implies a stream of accurate information which will enable the communications professional to track progress against benchmarks. Media analysis will provide that information stream.

The craft of media profile management doesn't only apply to companies with problems. It's necessary with organizations with a positive profile as well.

Take the case of the RAC, the UK based motoring organization. The RAC enjoys a generally positive profile by taking a strongly proactive stance on a number of issues connected with motoring and the motorist. Over the past few years these have ranged from environmental policies to vehicle crime. One of its most positive campaigns in recent years has been its ongoing campaign to regulate private wheel-clampers. Here is a selection of short extracts from the press during the campaign:

> New laws to tackle wheel-clamp bandits were being urgently considered by Home Office ministers last night.... The demand is backed by the AA and RAC, which have been deluged with complaints about cars being clamped in pub and hotel car parks, on waste ground and in shopping centres' *Today*, 20 June 1992

> The others are good practice guidelines and self-regulation of the wheel-clamping industry; clarification of the civil law; statutory regulation of the wheel-clamping industry; statutory licensing of wheel-clamp operators; and statutory licensing of land on which wheel-clamps may be used.... The RAC described the consultation paper as an 'overdue' first step in curbing excesses' *Financial Times*, 24 February 1993

> Edmund King, campaigns manager of the RAC, which estimates that private clamping firms have a turnover of up to £150 million a year, said: 'Licensing of land on which clamping is permitted appears at first sight to have some merit' *Guardian*, 24 February 1993

> She had been arrested after she arranged for her VW Golf to be lifted off private land in St Anne's, near Blackpool, then cut the wheel-clamp free herself.... The RAC even stepped in with an offer to pay Mrs Le Masson's legal costs' *Daily Mail*, 11 February 1994

These extracts paint a picture of an organization getting involved in the wheel-clamping issue at a level of deep corporate commitment. There is no doubt at all where the RAC stands on this issue, and it is clear that the organization has the backing of its board. These extracts, which are a very small selection of the coverage on the issue, convey the messages 'The RAC looks after the interests of the motorist' and 'The RAC does more for you than fix your car when it breaks down away from home'.

The RAC's most important target audiences are motorists and decision-makers. It is important for the RAC to build a positive media profile if it is to compete as one of the largest motoring organizations in the UK. The RAC understands the need for a positive media profile if it is to maintain positive images in motorists' minds. If the RAC had decided to condemn the wheel-clampers who operate on private land from the press office without high-level corporate and campaigning support, the coverage – and its effects – would have been limited.

Edmund King, Campaigns Manager of the RAC, has the specific task of communicating public policy issues to the media. He sees a dual purpose in raising the RAC media profile. The first is to show that the RAC fights to protect the interests of motorists; the second is to help the lobbying process to get present legislation changed. The extensive coverage of wheel-clamping helped the RAC to win support of MPs and put pressure on the Home Office to take action.

As part of its weaponry, the RAC uses media analysis techniques to guide and control its campaigns. The monthly analysis charts not only show volume of coverage, but, more importantly, it tracks the success in delivering particular messages to the motorist and the media impact of coverage which may influence Government. The dual objectives of RAC campaigning are well covered by media analysis. The analysis is also used as part of the process to track the corporate image of the RAC on the Group Quality scorecard.

COMPLEX PROGRAMMES

In the two cases described above, we have just looked at one issue. But at any one time, a large organization with a public profile may be dealing with anything up to 100 different subjects and issues on which it is likely to be reported. This poses problems for the communications director where monitoring and media analysis are concerned.

Communications departments can have large staff numbers, each with a portfolio of different projects to support. Some will be working on product-related programmes, others will be dealing with corporate and Government issues; others will be dealing with financial matters. The communications director will find it hard to keep a finger on the pulse of each issue, and without media analysis, it will be difficult to work out whether the vision is being attained.

Media analysis is at its most useful when it is applied across a large programme, evaluating message delivery and media profile across project boundaries. Using media analysis, it's possible to look for a customer care message across product and corporate programmes; to search out the 'success' message in the financial pages of the national press and in coverage of a detailed issue management campaign. Media analysis techniques can show whether the visions are being reached, and chart the organization's success in reaching them.

MEDIA PROFILE AND TIMESCALE

Charts or graphs showing a snapshot of an organization's profile – perhaps as a result of analysing coverage of the previous month – can be very useful in establishing benchmarks and giving an instantaneous indication of success or otherwise. Media analysis techniques can also chart an organization's profile over time.

In complex programmes, a company's media profile can improve or deteriorate rapidly, sometimes without the communications team becoming aware of the situation. Situations involving poor regional profile and problems with product returns may be at the bottom of the list of worries while senior members of the communications team are busy unravelling an industrial relations problem or issuing the annual results. The problem will soon acquire much higher priority when it is raised in the AGM however.

Media analysis can provide the communications team with trend analysis which can track the profile over time: issue by issue, message by message. As a profile begins to deteriorate, the team can put a strategy in place which will correct the downward trend. When the profile begins to improve, the details can be analysed to determine the reasons for the improvement.

The data once captured becomes a source of reference data of immense value. Theories can be tested against real historical data, and the effect of new strategies can be measured against the old.

COMPETITORS AS BENCHMARKS

Trend charts only provide one type of benchmark against which an organization can determine its progress – that is by comparison of one month's results with another. There are other, far more immediate benchmarks against which many organizations must also measure progress however – the profiles of their competitors.

Using media analysis, a company can establish that it has effectively delivered its key 'leadership', 'quality' and 'environment' messages. In a competitive marketplace however, where every paragraph in the trade press is fiercely contested, it may be that some companies' messages are being delivered more effectively than others. There's only room for one in the 'leader' slot in the minds of the people who represent key audiences and opinion-formers. If someone else is delivering the 'leadership' message more strongly than you are, your company is going to be out in the cold.

Analysing a competitor's coverage alongside your own is a valuable cure for the dangerous corporate disease of complacency. The front-line troops of an organization's salesforce are meeting competitors head to head in sales situations daily: it's the duty of the PR professional to take them on in the media, strategically outthinking them, shutting doors and answering arguments. Charts featuring two companies' volumes of coverage, visibility and message delivery will tell the PR professional very clearly who is winning the war in the media. We'll be dealing with competitive analyses and the use of benchmarks in much more detail in Chapter 11.

CAUSE OR EFFECT?

Before we conclude this chapter, I want to touch briefly on causality and the old question of the chicken and the egg. Which came first – the company's excellent product sales or the press coverage about the product? The Government's poor reputation, or critical reporting of Ministers' decisions?

Of course it is the primary role of the press and other media to report events and comment on issues. But all who read this book will be conscious of the media's other role in causing events and developing issues. The advocacy of the press has changed the course of elections, share issues and product launches, and has caused the rise – and downfall – of people, companies and governments.

If the media existed purely to report events and comment on issues, there would be no need for media analysis. As it is, media coverage (as has been shown in the opening paragraphs of this chapter) can change the course of an organization's future. That is one of the reasons why public relations has evolved as a business discipline and why, more recently, media analysis has been developed as one of its primary control mechanisms.

CONCLUSION: SOME MEASURES

In Chapter 2 we have looked at how images of an organization can develop, and the media's role in their development. The concepts of existing images and visions were considered, and the case for defining precisely the corporate attributes which make them up was argued.

Once we have determined the desired reputation and vision, we know what aspects of our organizations' media coverage we need to maximize and which to minimize. Media analysis will help us to measure our progress in achieving this.

So far we have talked about concepts rather than units of measurement. In Chapter 3 we introduce some of the measurements used in media analysis, and outline their purpose.

3 What Should be Measured?

What communicators have attempted to measure in the past, and why some existing techniques are flawed. What you want out of it – that is your organization's communications objectives – should dictate the methods you use. The relationship between communications objectives and corporate objectives is described.

In the preceding chapters, we explored the concept of media analysis. We also examined the idea of media profile and showed how media analysis can supply us with the information we need to improve it. In this chapter we will begin to look at what it is possible to measure in media coverage.

Everybody who watches television or who reads a magazine or newspaper is a media analyst of a kind. Even people in a bar discussing a football game they've seen on television, are busy analysing. They're more likely to be analysing the worth of the manager and the quality of the goals than the objectives of the sponsors whose names appear on the shirts. But they are nevertheless analysing the content of the programme they have been watching and will probably have come to certain conclusions as a result of their observations. They will – possibly – remember the name of the opposing team's shirt sponsor, but they will definitely know the result of the game.

Executives of the companies sponsoring the teams will have been analysing the programme from a very different point of view. Having watched the programme, the executive responsible for sponsorship will probably be able to tell you how many times the company logo was clearly in view during the game, and whether the advertising hoardings bearing her company's name were obscured by the marching band who came on at half time.

She will know roughly how many people watched the programme and she may also know how many opportunities there were for her target audiences to see the logo she is keen to promote. She will also – probably – remember the result.

SOME MEASURES

There are dozens of suggestions for what you can do with a pile of press cuttings and tapes of broadcast coverage. Here are a few of them:

- Weigh the coverage
- Count the press cuttings and tapes
- Count the number of words
- Count your organization's namechecks in the coverage
- Calculate the advertising value equivalents
- Calculate cost of getting the item published or broadcast
- Record whether the articles are positive or negative
- Record position on the page
- Record the impact of the headlines
- Judge the quality of writing/filming of the item
- Judge the newsworthiness of the item
- Judge relevance of media to the communications objective
- Judge the quality of the media
- Measure the impact of any photographs or illustrations
- Look for the presence of and count key words
- Establish how many people read/saw/heard the items
- Establish how many of target audience read/saw/heard them
- Look for the presence of key messages
- Find out how strongly key messages come across in the item
- Compare organization's coverage with a competitor's
- Find out how the coverage has changed readers' knowledge
- Find out how the coverage has changed readers' opinions
- Find out how the coverage has changed readers' behaviour

It is perfectly possible to measure all of the above in a collection of press cuttings and tapes, but after we have done it, will we honestly be any the wiser? It is a confusing list and it begs the questions 'Where on earth should we start?' and 'Is it worth it?' Isn't it best, perhaps, simply to read the coverage and hope that we'll be able to get a general impression? This last, is, of course, what most people who work with the media have been doing for decades.

In truth, the organizations we work for deserve better than that. And the measures we use should be driven by the reasons for carrying out the analysis in the first place. For instance:

- Publishers will be interested both in measuring the quality of writing, and in the number of people who read their publication.
- PR professionals will be interested in establishing whether the coverage contains key messages and how effectively they have been delivered.
- Sponsorship consultants will want to know how many namechecks their clients receive in a programme about an event, player or artist they have helped to fund.
- Marketing and sales managers will want to know how many people went out and bought their product as a result of reading, seeing or hearing the item.

● Chief executives will need to know how their organizations' reputations are being reflected in the media.

All the above are potential users of media analysis methods. One of the most important skills of the media analyst is in matching the specific requirements of the organization to the appropriate measures available. These requirements vary enormously from organization to organization: in six years of carrying out media analysis for a wide range of different clients, I've yet to meet one that wanted exactly the same analysis as another.

CONTENT ANALYSIS AND OBJECTIVES

Important assumptions have been made in the discussion of different measurement criteria below and in the pages which follow. Media content is usually measured by people who wish to change or improve some aspect of the media coverage using public relations, sponsorship, or other techniques. Choice of criteria is therefore approached from the perspective of those who won't be satisfied with measurement itself, but who will be keen to use the information to fine tune a communications programme – and reach the communications objectives they have set.

Media coverage can be analysed for some very complex and highly academic reasons. These include counting how many times certain phrases are used in order to work out who the author is. This book is not written for people in this business. Neither is it written for scholars who are trying to disprove the authenticity of Shakespeare or the Dead Sea scrolls, or for detectives trying to track down writers of poison pen letters. I'll be leaving these no doubt fascinating niches for others to explore.

The type of media analysis you carry out should be dictated by what you want to do with the information you gain from the analysis – and should be related to carefully defined corporate and communications objectives.

OBJECTIVES

Let's start by deciding what we understand by objectives, beginning with the fundamental corporate objectives found in the engine room of all well-managed companies and other types of organization. The other subsidiary objectives – such as communications objectives – are deduced and developed from these.

CORPORATE OBJECTIVES

An organization's declared corporate objectives are often embodied in a mission statement and can cover issues such as citizenship, employer profile, environ-

21

mental responsibility and such like. But it's a rare company whose publicly available mission statement reflects the totality of the wishes of its shareholders.

Many companies are driven by a simple profit motive. Sometimes this is extended into concepts such as exit route, acquisition of other companies and market leadership.

The objectives of a non-profit organization such as a political party or a charity will be different, and may be as varied as maximizing membership, winning votes, electing a new Prime Minister, stopping a species of bird from becoming extinct or getting a law changed.

Corporate objectives like all the above are good starting points for a public relations programme and equally good starting points for media analysis, but before rushing into detailed programme development and message delivery computation, it's necessary to deduce working communications objectives from these.

COMMUNICATIONS OBJECTIVES

Communications are deduced from an organization's corporate objectives and should contain a target audience(s) and should also contain or be designed to accommodate a message or messages. Here are some examples of communications objectives:

- To inform car owners living in New York State of new legislation concerning exhaust emissions;
- To tell people between the ages of 50 and 65 that Company X has a new high-return investment scheme;
- To position Company Y as a caring employer;
- To persuade people to join Charity Z.

All the above are highly specific objectives that are designed to be measurable. The first two are designed to inform people about something; the third is designed to enhance or change an employee's or a potential employee's opinion of a company. The fourth is designed to change people's behaviour – it is a stimulus to action.

One of the reasons why media analysis has been so slow in coming to the PR industry is that many of the objectives public relations people work to are poorly defined. 'Promoting company A as a flexible and dynamic organization' is a worthy enough aim, but it is altogether too general to be a useful working tool. It poses problems for media analysts and PR people alike because it is impossible to measure how successful the communicator has been in achieving it.

All the communications objectives listed above contain target audiences, either explicitly (the first three) or implicitly (the last). We will be discussing audiences in much greater detail in Chapter 4.

They also contain 'messages' – for example: 'Company Y is a caring company'.

Sometimes a communications objective can be extended to accommodate messages – for example: 'By joining Charity Z you will be helping to change the law to ban fox hunting'. There are a number of different types of messages, and we will be considering them in more detail in Chapter 5.

COMMUNICATIONS AND MEDIA ANALYSIS

Whatever your reason for analysing the media, you will benefit from going through the process of objective definition prior to the measurement process. It sounds obvious, but there are many measurables, and it is only when you are certain what information you want out of the exercise that the selection of appropriate measurement criteria becomes possible.

If you are in the communications business, the choice of which parameters to look at and measure is a relatively easy choice. A good start is made by looking for answers to the five questions posed below.

1. HOW MUCH COVERAGE DID WE RECEIVE?

First you need to find out how much coverage there was. Not just coverage of your company, but if you are operating in a competitive marketplace, how much your competitor received.

Coverage measurement is one of the most popular activities for PR people after a successful campaign, but it's difficult to do consistently and well. However, it remains one of the analyses which a PR department can, with the appropriate resources, do in-house without an outside supplier's help (see Chapter 7). Units of measurement fall into two groups – units such as column centimetres or column inches, and number of words. There are practical problems with column inch measures. With desk-top publishing now the norm for magazine production, word count within a column inch can vary enormously, not just from issue to issue of a particular publication, but from page to page within one issue!

Beware also the photocopier-reduced press cutting. My own company, Infopress Communications, was recently asked to analyse three years of retrospective coverage for a financial services provider who had all their press cuttings stored on microfiche. The extent of photo-reduction (and, incidentally, the legibility) varied between publications, and a true column inch measurement would not have been possible within a realistic timescale.

In many ways, simple word count, allowing a pro-rata figure for illustrations (see Chapter 17) and headlines, is a much more useful measure. Again, there are problems however, and complex layouts, particularly of some consumer publications, will give analysts a headache.

Volume measurement must be consistent if it is to be useful, and to be consistent it's necessary to apply rules of measurement. Ask two people to calculate the

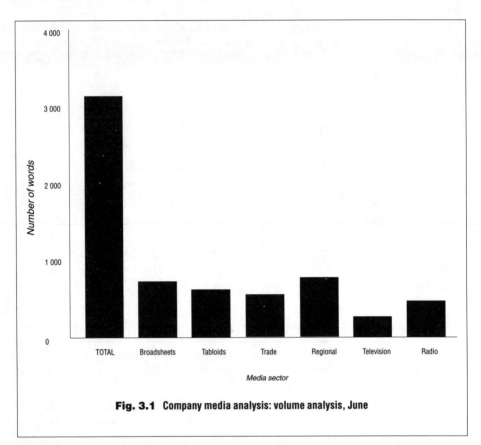

Fig. 3.1 Company media analysis: volume analysis, June

word count of a long and complex magazine article, and you could receive answers varying by up to 50 per cent. If you apply measurement rules, and both analysts use them, the consistency will improve, and deviations as low as 5 per cent will be more common.

A typical volume result analysis for a month is shown in Figure 3.1. The data is entered as a table of figures, and the chart is produced on a simple spreadsheet package which will run on a personal computer.

A more useful measure is the namecheck count – resulting in measures of product or corporate visibility within the target media. Counting namechecks can help the analyst to track the visibility of a product, brand or company and enable the PR professional to calculate which names are making the news. A namecheck count does not, however, tell you anything about whether the all-important messages are getting through, and if your communications objectives are being met. A typical namecheck chart for the same month is given in Figure 3.2.

2. DID OUR MESSAGES COME ACROSS?

Answering the question 'Did our messages come across?' is a good deal more

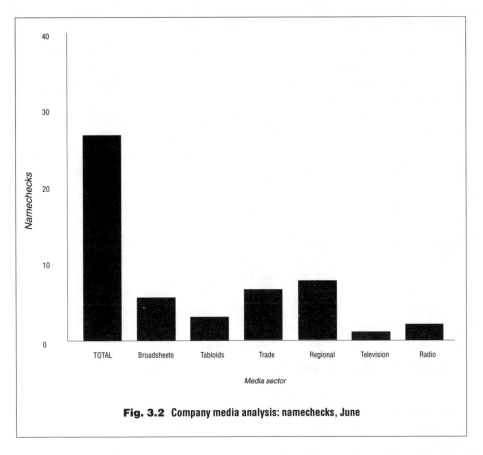

Fig. 3.2 Company media analysis: namechecks, June

difficult than calculating volume of coverage and visibility, and considerably more subjective.

Consider a company which imports fashion goods, which is trying to communicate the message 'Our clothes are sexy' to teenagers and young adults. An article in *Just Seventeen* describes a garment in factual terms, accompanied by a picture of a young girl wearing it. The text does not communicate the message, but for some people, the picture will have strong sexual connotations; for others it won't. Does the item taken as a whole communicate the message or not?

Analysing media coverage for messages is one of the most difficult aspects of media analysis, and requires its own rules. It also requires an independent viewpoint because there are connotative aspects. Public relations professionals who have been working on a promotional programme for months, and deliberately embedding visual indexes into media coverage will be more sensitive to these indexes in text and pictures than will casual readers. They should rule themselves out of this phase of the measurement process (see Chapter 7).

3. HOW STRONGLY DID OUR MESSAGES COME ACROSS?

As well as looking for presence of messages, the analyst should assess message strength. Grading message delivery or message strength scores on a range of +10 to –10 gives a depth of field to the analysis which you will not obtain by applying a 'yes/no' test.

Here are two extracts from reviews of forthcoming BBC television programmes in a British regional newspaper, the *Southampton Daily Echo*.

One is a review of a documentary on a mining industry strike called 'The men who kept the lights on'. The concluding sentence begins: 'This compelling programme...'

A second reviews the comedy series 'Seinfeld', and is not so complimentary: 'This award winning comedy returns for another series.... Despite being mildly amusing, this was far from being the next big thing to set the TV ablaze.'

The phrase 'compelling programme' has behaviour-changing potential, and strongly delivers the 'You must watch this' message. In the second, the yawn factor is in evidence and despite the words 'award winning' and 'amusing', readers aren't being persuaded to tune in. The first deserves a higher score than the second, though both are positive (just).

4. HOW MUCH IMPACT DID THEY HAVE?

There is a gulf between the first and main news item on the front page of a newspaper and the same but shortened item at the bottom of page 17, even though the item covers the same ground and carries the same message using the same words.

Most media analysis services differentiate between items having differing impacts, and some award different scores depending on whether the item is a feature or a news item, whether it has the company name or product name in the headline, and whereabouts in the article the key messages or product details are carried. This kind of analysis can be very useful in analysing a high impact programme of relatively short duration, or assessing the effect of a crisis.

It is tempting to become involved in too much detail however, and end up generating too much information which is in itself too complex to be immediately useful. For most programmes, I advocate analyses in which message strength and impact are combined in a single parameter – message delivery. The impact, after all, has a direct bearing on how strongly the messages are delivered, and this key fact is what communicators are most interested in finding out. A message delivery chart for a single month is shown in Figure 3.3.

5. DID WE REACH THE RIGHT PEOPLE?

When we discussed communications objectives above, we stressed that the objective should accommodate both messages and target audiences. Finding out

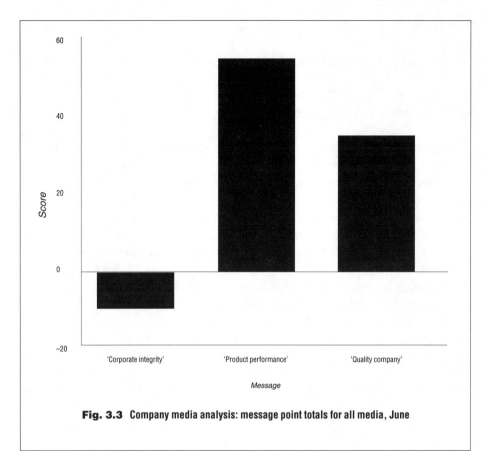

Fig. 3.3 Company media analysis: message point totals for all media, June

who the messages have reached is one of the main reasons for carrying out media analysis.

If you have achieved exposure in each of the main publications you are targeting, you will be in no doubt that you have reached the right people, but for a sustained programme, the 'being in no doubt' feeling is not good enough.

Media analysis (Figures 3.1 – 3.3) enables you to track your performance in each of the key media sectors. This will tell you what your profile is in each of the sectors which you are targeting, and this information will give an indication of which readers have read your messages.

A further level of sophistication is to calculate the number of 'impressions' you have obtained. This is calculated from the number of times one of your messages has appeared and the circulation statistics or readership/listenership/viewership of the medium concerned.

There are dangers in putting too much reliance on impressions unless your programme is targeting a very broad consumer audience.

Here's why. Let's remind ourselves of the examples of communications objectives given earlier:

- To inform car owners living in New York State of new legislation concerning exhaust emissions;
- To tell people between the ages of 50 and 65 that Company X has a new high-return investment scheme;
- To position Company Y as a caring employer;
- To persuade people to join Charity Z.

The first objective only concerns car owners and drivers in New York State. The second objective only concerns people in late middle age. The third objective only concerns existing and potential employees – possibly less than 100 people in all. It is only the programme driven by the final objective – for Charity Z – where the 'impressions' parameter becomes a truly useful figure.

The ultimate audience calculation is one in which the numbers of people in your target audience are calculated for each of the publications in which your messages have appeared. If it is possible to establish these figures for your target media, then it is going to be worth tracking it regularly.

It is sometimes achievable. If the audiences are broadly defined (for example by age, socioeconomic group, region), relevant statistics are often available for large circulation newspapers and television programmes which will enable the analyst to work out true audience figures. Unfortunately, however, readership analysis available from smaller circulation and more specialist publications are much more difficult to find and less consistent in quality when you do find them.

EFFECT ON TARGET AUDIENCE

At the risk of complicating the picture, there is another important range of measures which we have not discussed in detail above. These are the measures given at the end of the list on page 20, and which concern the changes in knowledge, opinion and behaviour among our target audiences. Changes which occurred because our targeted readers have read the newspaper, watched the TV programme or heard the radio broadcast. These measures are very useful to the PR professional because they represent the end results – the changes which the communicator is trying to effect.

Market research companies have been measuring changes in awareness, opinion and behaviour for many years, and studies of this type should be used in parallel with media analysis to get the full picture. We discuss the direct measurement of changes in awareness, opinion and behaviour in Chapter 19.

Opinion and behavioural changes should correlate with the measures of message strength, delivery, volume and impact. So why bother analysing media content which, after all, only represents a halfway house? It is necessary because opinion and awareness studies are unreliable in exposing the mechanisms by which these changes occurred, and are not usually used to differentiate between advertising, PR and other influences.

MEASURES AND MEANING

Before concluding this whistlestop tour of media analysis techniques, I want to make a very brief detour into semiotics – the science of symbolism and the meaning behind signs, text and images.

A few years ago, I gave several would-be analysts a press cutting to evaluate as a test. The item concerned a bank and chronicled a rather poor set of year-end figures in which the profits announced had slumped considerably since the previous year. I asked them to score the item for the message 'this bank is financially successful'. To my surprise, one applicant gave the item a mildly positive score. When I asked her about her reasons behind the score, she said, 'Anybody making any profit seems financially successful to me – you should see the size of my overdraft!'

Every word has more than one meaning. Its denotation indicates the literal, dictionary definition of the word. Its connotations, however, vary depending on the knowledge, opinion, attitude and values of the person reading or hearing it. There may be as many connotations of a press cutting or broadcast news item as there are human beings. Any analysis of the message content of media coverage must, therefore, be subjective, because there is no absolute way for the analyst to interpret it.

CONCLUSION

If you've read the paragraphs above, you will probably be coming to the conclusion that media analysis comprises numerous different methods and concepts – perhaps rather more than you had originally thought.

The public relations business would love to have a single, simple measure for media relations effectiveness that would tell the client company, 'Our reputation is excellent', 'This piece of work has been effective', or 'This project could have been handled better'. In a recent conference on the subject in London, many speakers referred to this elusive 'Holy Grail' of media analysis. They were disappointed to be told that this Holy Grail does not exist.

In the past, PR people have used a spurious measure called 'advertising value equivalents' or AVEs, in which editorial items are costed in terms of advertising space cost. We discuss these in Chapter 15. They are simple to calculate, they can be done quickly … but they don't tell anybody how much coverage you've achieved, whether it communicates the right messages and how much impact it has had.

There is no 'Holy Grail' of media analysis, but if the communicator is sure of the objectives behind his or her communications activities, developing or choosing suitable analytical techniques is a straightforward task. In the next chapter, we deal with the most important element in the communications process, the groups of people we are attempting to communicate with.

4   The Concept of Target Audience

All organizations have audiences or 'publics' ranging from customers and influencers to suppliers, staff and others who are of importance. Each of these groups will read, watch or listen to certain media; these media will together comprise an organization's target media.

There is an unpalatable truth about people which all competent PR professionals must realize at some stage in their careers: many groups of people the PR professional is keenly interested in addressing may not be especially keen to talk to the organization they represent. Conversely, the people who are constantly trying to reach an organization will not necessarily be on any priority list for high-level communication!

Take the case of a new stationery supply company in the locality. The supplier has no profile, has no contracts and offers a range of products which are remarkably similar to every other stationery supplier's products. Are the local firms interested in this new company? Not especially. They're getting their stationery from the local branch of Rymans and they haven't too much cause for complaint.

But there are some people who are very keen indeed to get to know the new firm. There is, for instance, a local newspaper, and its advertisement manager will be round to see the new firm like a shot. There are, for instance, 3000 unemployed in the town, and it will occur to quite a number of them that this new company may have a job opportunity for them.

The point is that the groups who are naturally attracted to an organization are very rarely the only groups that the company needs to target in order to be successful.

WHO DOES YOUR ORGANIZATION NEED TO TARGET?

It's not too difficult to write down a list of the categories of organizations who represent a company's target audiences. Ignoring unhelpful generalizations like 'potential customers' and 'influencers' most companies will derive a list similar to this one: the audiences of an imaginary medium sized, publicly quoted manufacturing company:

- Existing customers
  - board directors
  - technical staff
- Potential customers (vertical markets)
  - plastics industry
  - electronics industry
  - brown goods industry
- Potential customers (horizontal markets)
  - purchasing managers
  - heads of manufacturing
  - engineering design staff
- Shareholders
- Stockbrokers
- Analysts
- The company's bankers
- Staff
- Potential staff (graduates and key technical staff)
- The MPs in whose constituencies they have sites
- Technical consultants
- Management consultants
- The local community in five areas surrounding the sites
- Suppliers of key components

A good starting point. But the PR person will need to ensure that all these people get the company's corporate and/or sales messages. Making it happen is going to be tough.

STARTING MEDIA ANALYSIS: A STRATEGIC APPROACH

At the start of every financial year, many press relations people turn over a new strategic leaf. They:

1. Write down their objectives;
2. Agree (or define!) their target audiences, arriving at a list rather like the one above;
3. Deduce the target media from the target audiences;
4. Agree their messages (see next chapter); and
5. Put together a PR strategy comprising activities which will – hopefully – achieve the objectives.

All competent media analysis should be designed to answer the question, 'How successful have I been in delivering our messages to our target audiences?' But how often is it done?

At the end of the year, it is tempting to take a rather less strategic approach. Rather than revisiting all the communication objectives of a year ago, some PR people simply analyse all the coverage achieved, count the column inches and calculate how many people have had the opportunity of reading their material – even though the vast majority of people who have had that opportunity will not be among their target audiences. With true media analysis, the analytical process starts at the beginning of the year, rather than at the end. It begins when the list of media we know your audiences read, rather than a pile of your press cuttings, is drawn up.

EXAMPLE: A MANUFACTURING COMPANY

Let's take the example of the manufacturing company mentioned above.

The PR professional, depending on his or her priorities, may choose a target media list like the one shown in Table 4.1 when deciding on the company's media relations programme. Each media target group is associated in the table with a particular group of target audiences.

If Table 4.1 represents the company's media relations targets, the PR professional will need to monitor all these categories. Let's now go to the end of the year and look back.

Media	Audience
National broadsheet press	shareholders
	stockbrokers
	analysts
	staff
	banks
	customers (board level)
	management consultants
	technical consultants
National tabloid press	staff
	customers (technical staff)
Vertical market media	potential customers (all)
• plastics press	
• electronics press	
• brown goods press	
Purchasing and supply media	potential customers (all)
Manufacturing press	potential customers (all)
	analysts
	technical consultants
Regional press	staff
	local communities

Table 4.1 A target media list for a manufacturing company: a starting point

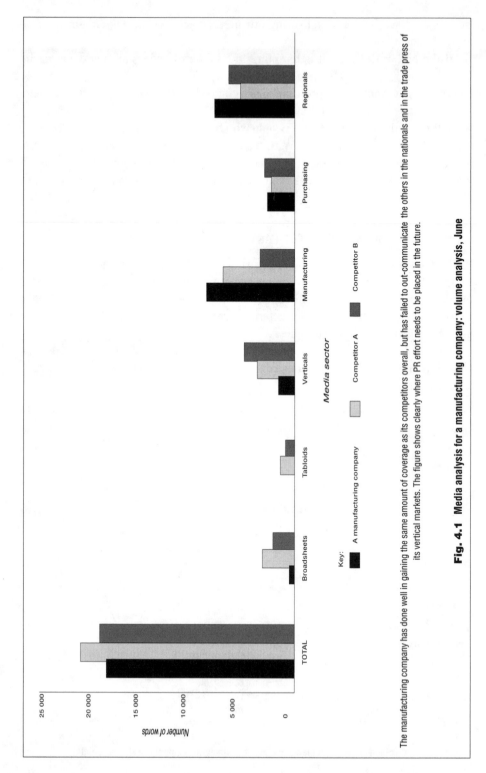

The manufacturing company has done well in gaining the same amount of coverage as its competitors overall, but has failed to out-communicate the others in the nationals and in the trade press of its vertical markets. The figure shows clearly where PR effort needs to be placed in the future.

Fig. 4.1 Media analysis for a manufacturing company: volume analysis, June

Our PR professional may have discovered that:

- The marketing department was unable to give him or her the list of target vertical markets until half-way through the year – so no vertically targeted material was distributed.
- Two key journalists – well-known to the company – had left *The Times* and the *Guardian* respectively, and it was found to be almost impossible to get anything published there.

The company, for two very good reasons, has been unable to gain a profile in two key sectors of the target media. A useful media analysis service will expose these two shortcomings (Figure 4.1). They've got great regional coverage and their profile in the manufacturing press is excellent. But there's something missing.

Media analysis which highlights the gaps as well as the successes of the programme will be a constant spur to fill those gaps. The PR team will be forced to think up new strategies or gain new contacts in the national press, and will probably show the analysis charts to colleagues in marketing to encourage them to find (or decide on!) the information they need.

CORPORATE AUDIENCES

Marketing textbooks may suggest that all target audiences exist in watertight boxes, and that they neither communicate with nor influence each other. Of course the very opposite is the case, and great care must be taken to ensure that messages are mutually consistent.

Telling a journalist on the *Financial Times* that your company has enough cash resources to fund a massive expansion into a new marketplace may be used in evidence against you in your next round of pay negotiations; an indiscreet comment in the diary column of a trade paper may be pounced on in an annual general meeting and turned into a major issue.

Nevertheless, corporate audiences often deserve their own PR programme and their own messages – especially when the company is publicly quoted. They include potential business partners, the company's bankers, the City and parliament. These groups need to be told different but consistent facts when we compare these to sales and marketing audiences, and there are many ways of reaching these without contacting the press. Nevertheless, media analysis is essential to ensure that these groups are learning correct and appropriate information about the firm via the media route.

MARKETING AUDIENCES

We need to bear two important categories of marketing audience in mind when we

35

decide to look at the publications which reach them.

The first is the vertical market audience, in which we divide the marketplace into its industry types such as banking, engineering or shipping.

The second is the horizontal market audience, in which an individual's job function is of greater importance. These include job functions such as 'fleet management', 'sales' and 'packaging'.

There are occasions where the two types of audience may overlap, one example being the computer or IT industry. A company might sell products such as switches to the (vertical) computer manufacturing industry, and at the same time sell replacement switches to (horizontal) IT departments large enough to have a repair department. It's going to be possible to reach both categories of customer via some titles in the computer trade press. As far as the media relations professional is concerned, vertical and horizontal sectoring is important because it allows him or her to address the trade press of each sector. And it is these trade press sectors which will be the most fruitful to examine when media analysis is carried out.

REGIONAL AUDIENCES

Regional audiences are relatively easy to reach – but it is easy to waste a huge amount of money doing it. Simple common sense helps us to decide which publications to monitor.

The media relations team must ask themselves why they need to address these audiences via regional media. If staff live in a specific locality, it is possible to reach these both by staff newsletters and by using publications essentially local to the towns where the company has sites. If the local community is sensitive to specific corporate developments such as factory extensions or smoke emissions, it is again possible to look at a very specific range of press, radio and regional television without going further afield.

In consumer oriented businesses however (for example banking, retailing, utilities) an organization may be keen to reach all local audiences throughout the country, with specific information regarding a local introduction of a product or service. In these instances, media monitoring will be a time-consuming and perhaps expensive business. With such information, it should, however, be possible to graph coverage and message delivery in each area against sales enquiries and conversions and get an excellent idea of which audiences are being penetrated and which are proving resistant.

One final note on the subject of competitive analysis in a regional context. Here, I am particularly concerned with regional utility companies such as water, electricity and gas suppliers. These companies need to monitor local newspapers, radio and television to gain an early indication of audience reaction and opinion leadership at a local level.

Clearly, if a comparison is to be drawn in media analysis between two organizations operating in different localities (for example a regional electricity company in the north and a regional electricity company in the south), the differences in population sizes in the areas concerned should ideally be taken into account when any comparison is drawn between volumes of coverage and message delivery effectiveness.

INTERNATIONAL AUDIENCES

International media analysis deserves a book of its own. I only have the space here to touch on some aspects. Language creates its own problem and is referred to on other pages, but another even more fundamental difficulty is concerned with different types of economy. In a strongly centralized economy such as that of the United Kingdom, the concepts of 'national newspaper' and 'regional newspaper' are quite different from each other. In the United Kingdom, a group of individuals such as AB business people can be reached relatively easily via the broadsheet national newspapers. In distributed economies such as the USA and Australia, there is no true national press to speak of, and many audiences must be reached via essentially regional and trade media.

For the media analyst, any sector-by-sector comparison between, say, the UK press and the US press must be carried out with great care to make sure that inappropriate comparisons are not drawn. Conversely, a US marketing manager may be deeply concerned by a lack of visibility of his company's UK subsidiary in the regional press in the North of England. If the subsidiary is enjoying good coverage in the UK national, trade and vertical market press, his fears may be largely unfounded.

DEDUCING YOUR TARGET MEDIA

Media analysis is going to be a strategically useful tool in controlling your PR programme. Your target media are therefore going to be the building blocks of your PR programme as well as the basis of the media analysis you will be carrying out. It therefore deserves a great deal of creative thought and judgement.

Small companies who generate only a small amount of coverage will be able to justify analysing all the press coverage generated about them. Larger companies who are featured in the press and on the broadcast media every day may be able to apply sampling techniques to the coverage and analyse a selection rather than all. Decide at an early stage which are the most important audiences, and make sure that the media sample you choose to analyse reflects this importance. We will be talking about media sampling in Chapter 6.

CIRCULATION AND READERSHIP DATA

For many years there have been a number of excellent directories available which give circulation details of publications, the names and addresses and other details.

These include publications such as *Benn's Directory*, the *Pims Directory* and the *Two-Ten directory* in the UK, and *Bacon's* and the *Ayer Directory* in the USA. Other directories, such as the *National Readership Survey*, are used by market research professionals and media analysis companies and provide much greater detail.

Most media analysis services integrate circulation and readership data of this kind into the charts and tables that they produce. It's interesting to see how many people have had an opportunity to see the coverage you have obtained – but the media relations professional should ask him or herself just what this information means. Take these two examples:

● There are a handful of people living in Southampton who read the *Portsmouth News*. But if you are attempting to reach people affected by your factory extension in Southampton, a positive article about it in the *Portsmouth News* won't help much.
● If you are trying to reach people approaching pensionable age with information about an investment product, an article praising it in the *Guardian* will help – but most of those who read this newspaper will be too young and therefore uninterested even if they see it.

The figures which count are the ones which tell you how many of your target audience you have reached with the article, or who have seen the programme.

CALCULATING AUDIENCE REACH

If all the readers of a publication are in your target audience, then the circulation of that publication should be taken into consideration when calculating how many of your audience you have reached. In most instances, however, only a fraction of readers will be people you are specifically targeting. It is sensible to build this fraction into any computation you are carrying out to calculate audience reach.

In consumer PR programmes, the fractions will be relatively large ones where the UK national press is concerned. According to the *National Readership Survey*, 717 000 (out of 1.29 million) readers of *The Times* in March 1994 were between the ages of 15 and 44; only 582 000 were age 45 or over. If you are targeting an age or a socioeconomic group using the national press, it is worth taking fractions like these into account.

Once we enter the specialist and business-to-business areas, the computation becomes much more difficult. Some relevant data can be gleaned from the appropriate trade magazines. It is usually possible to find out from the publication's advertisement department, for instance, how many of the publication's readers are at director level or above, how many belong to companies with more than 1000 employees, and how many belong to certain specific industry job classifications (for example design, manufacturing, sales and marketing). The trouble is, magazines publish different types of audience information and the quality and accuracy of the data they provide is, to put it kindly, variable in quality.

As to how many engineering designers read the *Huddersfield Examiner*, or how many university lecturers read the *Toronto Globe and Mail*, it's going to take a considerable amount of research to find out – and more to update.

CONCLUSION

An organization's target audiences are vital to its communications programmes (including the PR programme) and to any editorial media analysis which is carried out. Considerable care should be taken in deducing which are the publications and broadcast media which reach these audiences.

For most PR programmes, simple circulation or readership data aren't very helpful, and don't facilitate determination of how many of your target audience you have reached. If you can narrow your audience down into broad categories like socioeconomic group or age range, you can calculate reach for national newspapers or large-circulation consumer magazines. Deducing reach for regional newspapers and specialist publications poses many more problems, especially where the target audience is very precisely defined. Fortunately, we can extract useful data from our media analysis without this detail.

Of much more importance is deciding which messages you need to embed in your press releases, articles, background notes and briefings, and how we should detect their presence and calculate their strength in the resulting coverage. This is dealt with in Chapter 5.

5   The Concept of Message

Corporate and marketing messages are the things you want to say about your organi-
zation – but they don't always get said in the pages of the media! Various types of
messages are defined and their relative importance is spelt out.

I make no excuse for making a brief deviation from the subject of analysis and
evaluation in this chapter, and touching on some basic public relations.

Clearly defined messages are at the very heart of all successful communications exercises. Yet in talking to hundreds of companies about media analysis, I
frequently find companies and other organizations which have, at the outset, very
unclear ideas of what messages they are trying to transmit. It is surprising how
often media relations professionals still use the objectives of 'raising visibility' and
'improving their image' as the mainsprings of their programmes, with little or no
strategic infrastructure beyond them.

So in this chapter we will visit the area of message formulation, and we start
below with a definition of public relations.

THE TWO-WAY NATURE OF PR

The UK Institute of Public Relations defines public relations as follows:

> Public Relations practice is the planned and sustained effort to establish and maintain
> goodwill and mutual understanding between an organization and its publics.

There is currently some feeling, even among senior members of the Institute, that
the definition is a little too technical and remote, but few question the following
about the definition:

1. Public relations is essentially a two-way process.
2. Public relations is concerned with making things happen as a result of
   good communication, rather than simply putting an organization's point of
   view.

I'll be dealing in more detail with the first point and how media analysis can make public relations more of a two-way process, in Chapter 24, but I want to touch on both points briefly now.

ONE WAY TRAFFIC

As we saw in Chapter 3, most public relations professionals are driven by behavioural objectives rather than the altruistic desire to improve mutual understanding. They work to objectives such as 'improve sales figures', 'keep the share price from dropping', or 'prevent the XXX piece of legislation getting passed in the House of Commons'.

How many PR people are driven by an urgent need to improve mutual understanding? I suspect not many. How many take the word 'mutual' at its face value and make genuine efforts to represent the feelings and attitudes of these publics to their boards? Again, I suspect they are in the minority.

Many PR operations are one-way streets, where the PR professional's skill is used to promote the organization's corporate or marketing aims. If they find that there is opposition to or lack of interest in those aims, then it falls to the PR department to persuade those publics to take up a different position.

This chapter does not take an ethical stance on the issue of the PR one-way street. But I do wish to stress that if the job of the PR department includes reaching, informing and persuading target audiences as defined in the previous chapter, then detailed and accurate message development becomes of crucial importance.

DECIDING WHAT YOU WANT TO SAY

Nearly everyone in an organization has an opinion about what the PR department should be saying. It is for this reason that care must be taken to get the messages right.

EXAMPLE: AN INFORMAL SURVEY OF OPINION

Try this exercise in your organization. Pick six people, three from within the PR department (if there are three) and three from outside, spreading the sample between senior and junior staff. Ask them all to write down six corporate attributes which would most benefit the organization if reflected in its media coverage. Take care not to prompt them with examples.

You will be surprised by the diversity of opinions. Some will decide that financial stability is of prime importance; others will stress the need to be seen as responsive to customers' needs. Yet others will respond with their environmental hats firmly in place ... and so on. If you felt you had a clear idea what you should be saying before the exercise, you may feel that the ground is a little less firm when you have finished.

An interesting exercise for widening horizons – but I don't recommend straw polls as a method of deciding what the messages should be. The messages which underpin your PR programme should be dictated by the communications objectives you have agreed (see Chapter 3), the position you and your company wish to occupy, and the image you wish your organization to have.

As we learnt in Chapter 2, a good 'image' can be built by delivering positive images of your organization in the minds of your target audience. Messages are the quanta of information that change the image held in the minds of your target audiences: they're the ammunition of communications professionals. To become lodged in people's minds, messages must be delivered regularly and with force.

MESSAGES THAT CHANGE KNOWLEDGE

People need information, but the human mind is only capable of accepting a certain amount each day – and it doesn't stay there for long. To prove this, try and remember the stories you read in your newspaper this morning. If you are reading this chapter in the evening, the odds are you will be able to remember the outline of perhaps five or six stories only – and it's likely that at least two of these will be in the 'furry animal rescued' or 'defrocked bishop in gay sex drama' category. The vast majority of the stories will have entered your brain but won't have found anywhere to stay. They will have gone into your mind's garbage can.

Now try and remember the stories in yesterday's paper. You've remembered two, or one ... or perhaps none. I'm sure you now see what I mean.

To build a favourable image in somebody's mind, it's necessary to choose information which you know will interest them. Tell an engineering apprentice about the changes in employment law affecting university lecturers, and it will go into his mind's garbage can. Talk to a vendor of fruit and vegetables about a shortage of chips in the computer industry, and he'll forget it instantly. And talk to the average male about the latest Paris fashion and it will have zero impact.

If you need to change the knowledge which people hold in the precious space in their minds, you'll need to choose messages which will stick there.

EXAMPLE: A MANUFACTURER OF PLASTICS MOULDINGS (1)

Take the example of a small manufacturer of plastics mouldings who sells products mainly to the toys and electrical appliance industries.

The first time the PR professional tries to write down an ideal image, he or she might compile a list of attributes like this:

1. We are a quality company.
2. We manufacture excellent mouldings.

3. We are good employers.

4. We are flexible.

5. We are responsive.

6. We are technically competent.

7. We are good business partners.

8. We are concerned about the environment.

These attributes, and the image they build in the mind are all very worthy. But is this a powerful enough image to get there in the first place, and stick around? Will such an 'image' be strong enough and long-lived enough to make a real difference to the way people think about the company? I doubt it.

The PR professional should try taking each of the above attributes and asking him or herself how important it is, and eliminating the least important. He or she should then try 'mapping' each attribute on to the target audiences and then, if necessary, refining it. Then, the image will spring into existence:

1. We are the only UK manufacturer with the latest generation of Bosch moulding equipment.

2. We regularly win design awards.

3. We spend 10 per cent of our turnover on R&D.

4. Most of our output is manufactured from recycled plastics waste.

The image is beginning to take shape. The more specific you can make these attributes the better. Precise attributes mean that the image is a sharp one, and from a practical viewpoint, precision in message formulation also makes them relatively easy to deliver.

If you are running a PR programme to change people's knowledge of your organization, be ruthless with the messages you give them in your media relations work. Then, when you're analysing the results of your work later on, you'll be less likely to be disappointed with what you find.

MESSAGES THAT CHANGE OPINION

There's a world of difference between the kind of PR programme that tells its audiences 'IBM makes computers' to the kind of programme which says 'It's good to live in a town where IBM has an office'.

The first type of message is relatively easy to deliver; the second is a good deal more difficult. If you are embarking on a programme to deliver messages like these, then make sure you don't try to deliver too many (five or six should be the absolute maximum). The majority of people don't have many opinions. They will have correspondingly few about your organization and the things your organization stands for, so make sure they are the right ones.

It's also a good idea to make sure that your opinion messages are at least deliverable. Take as an example the message 'We are a caring company'. You can almost see the communications director rubbing his or her hands together and smiling beatifically, while fellow directors and staff nod in bored agreement. Now try telling a hard-bitten newspaper journalist that you're a caring company, or send him or her a press release about your care policy, and see how much of it is taken seriously. It's an uphill struggle, to say the least. Now wait for the time one of your staff maltreats a customer, or the time a senior citizen collapses in your waiting room. That's the time when your care policy will hit the headlines.

When you need to change the image of your organization, the odds are that you need to change people's opinions of it, and this means you should decide – in advance – just what opinions about the organization you want your target audiences to have.

EXAMPLE: A MANUFACTURER OF PLASTICS MOULDINGS (2)

Returning to the small plastics moulding company and the rather fuzzy range of attributes which our PR professional wanted to promote about them (page 43), let us again take the example of the company's most important audience: its customers. It wants to change the opinions of its customers (and potential customers) towards the company to something like these:

1. You never get surface blemishes with products they make for us.
2. They can cope with our last-minute design changes.
3. Their technical people always seem to know the answers to questions I ask.
4. I feel they're on my side of the table when we meet.
5. They know the environmental laws relating to the toy business back to front.

All the above are the kind of opinions which our PR professional wants his or her company's customers to have. So the messages which should fill the company's product releases and application stories should be designed to build these opinions in its customers' minds.

MESSAGES THAT CHANGE BEHAVIOUR

Even with simple messages like 'Stop smoking or you'll die', it's tough making behavioural changes.

You must tell people a number of different times to get your message across, and you have to tell them in a number of different ways. Every year, dozens of PR men employed by the UK's Royal Mail spend thousands of pounds telling people:

1. To write return addresses on their envelopes;
2. To pack parcels strongly when posting them;
3. To post early for Christmas.

These points make good sense, but I still don't do (1) or (3). And I try and avoid the problem of (2) by giving my flimsily wrapped parcels to the (disgracefully few) recipients in person.

Getting audiences to change their behaviour is one of the most difficult things PR people have to do. Voters who have voted Republican all their lives are going to need some very convincing arguments to persuade them to vote Democrat. Getting a smoker to stop smoking is an enormous challenge for organizations such as the UK's health lobby. And getting a customer to stop buying competitor's products and buy yours is one of the most difficult of all.

It's a great idea to write down the ideal behaviour patterns you want to encourage, and base your promotional messages on those.

EXAMPLE: A MANUFACTURER OF PLASTICS MOULDINGS (3)

Let's now complete our exercise on the mouldings company by seeing what behaviour we want to induce in another of the company's audiences. This time we'll use the example of potential employees. Each year, the company needs to employ seven to ten materials science HND graduates and train them as managers.

Our PR professional wants to fill the job vacancies, but doesn't want to create a massive over-demand situation. So his or her preferred behaviour pattern will be something like 'I want them to ...

- Write a letter to the company asking for a background leaflet and an application form;
- Visit the careers fair at one of the colleges;
- Visit the company's stand at the careers fair.'

All the attributes on the PR professional's original list are going to promote a vague feeling of 'this seems to be a good company', and, if they get through to the potential employee, may be enough to induce students to write the letter. But the third attribute (good employer) is the one which should be stressed in articles in plastics trade journals, in careers magazines and (if our PR professional can arrange it) in in-house publications of the preferred colleges.

The messages our PR professional might seek to promote will be:

1. New employees receive a removal allowance.
2. New employees receive superb induction training.
3. Most trainee managers spend time abroad in their first year.
4. From day one, junior managers help us to form company policy.

All the messages we have coaxed out of the example are precise and specific. The more precise we can be, the easier it is to deliver them. As we will see in later chapters, precision in message formulation means better quality information going back to the PR team from the people or systems doing the media analysis and evaluation.

MESSAGES AND NEWS-HOOKS

Before going on to the problem of getting messages agreed, I want to spend a little time differentiating between 'messages' and 'news-hooks'.

The media relations professional has two selling jobs to do – the first is to the journalist or editor of the medium concerned; the second is to the audience reading the item concerned. Sometimes the two get confused in the minds of companies and their advisers.

Some years ago, as part of a PR strategy for a computer company, I was asked to draft a press release for the computer trade press. The main messages the company wanted to promote about the new system were the substantial increases in performance resulting from a new design. After some time spent studying the specification, I found that the computer was the first of its kind to use a particular type of electronic chip of very high specification.

Having read the publications in the sector in some depth, I knew that this chip was long awaited, and I suggested to the client that we should build the product announcement around the fact that this new chip was present in the computer's construction. This was far from being one of the company's central messages and the client disagreed at first with the suggested balance of the story. We managed to talk him round to our point of view however, and the amount of coverage achieved was higher than even we had anticipated. Far from de-emphasizing the performance claims, the focus on the chip design enabled us to reinforce and justify them.

Tracking and evaluating the effectiveness of news-hooks as well as the messages they introduce, is possible using media analysis but I believe the most important function of media analysis techniques is to tell us to what extent the messages are getting through.

CHOOSING THE RIGHT MESSAGES

If we take virtually any organization and write down everything we want to say about it to all its audiences, the odds are we'll finish with a message list of 20 or 30.

To analyse all your media coverage for all these messages in part of a single, regular, integrated exercise is impossible and pointless. So which ones should we choose to base the PR programme on and which ones should we analyse for?

There are no hard or fast rules. A corporate image programme may contain a number of fundamental 'image' and 'opinion' messages as described above. Six of these may be too many, and three or four is probably ideal. A hard-hitting product programme could have up to six 'behaviour' related messages, but these will change frequently as products develop and will vary from product to product and from division to division.

When the programme is about issues such as exports to Iraq or is an issues-related promotional programme such as, say, Government campaigns about smoking or sexual health, the messages can be singular and stark (smoking can kill you!) or a more complex message with different facets:

1. Smoking can harm your family.
2. There are benefits to stopping smoking.
3. Help is available when you decide to quit.

Choosing the right message to transmit is as important as delivering it with force and conviction.

DETECTING THE MULTIPLE MESSAGE

When formulating your messages, ensure that you don't agree a message which contains two or more sub-messages. Messages such as '... is a flexible and dynamic company' can cause real problems for evaluators. They will not know how to evaluate a paragraph which portrays the company as flexible, yet not particularly dynamic.

Similar problems occur with messages containing causal statements like '... is market leader through its quality policies'.

If in doubt, always break the message into its component parts, and then re-examine the parts to make sure that all need to be included.

MESSAGE POINT READERSHIP

Once the messages and the target audiences are agreed, and the relevant data collected on volumes, visibility, circulation, readership and message delivery, it will be necessary to consider how the various data elements should be combined in the presentation of a media analysis report. Collecting accurate data is only part of the problem; the other part is in processing and presenting the data in such a way that it tells the communication team how effective it has been in achieving programme objectives.

Figures 3.1–3.3 shown in Chapter 3 are sufficient for many organizations, giving an indication of the effectiveness of the communication function. Often, however, organizations need to take the analysis a stage further and compute the impact the communication programme is having on the target audience.

Is there a unit of 'impact of message on target audience'? It's a question which will, I fear, keep people in the media analysis business busy for a number of years yet. But a multiple of two of the parameters we have talked about comes near. This multiple is called message point readership (MPR) and assumes message delivery scores ranging between +10 (very positive) and –10 (very negative) as described in Chapter 3. It's this:

message delivery × audience readership.

This is a parameter which can be graphed and charted in the same way as the others we have dealt with. But how often are we able to obtain all the data we need to gain a complete picture given the difficulty of obtaining accurate readership data (as opposed to circulation data – see Chapter 4)?

For programmes restricted to the UK national press and other media for which good readership infrastructure information is available, this parameter can be computed (Table 5.1) and charted (Figure 5.1). For broad-spectrum campaigns in which the consumer audience consists of all readers or a large proportion of them, the word 'publication readership' or even 'publication circulation' can be substituted for 'audience readership' and the parameter

message delivery × publication circulation

can be computed and will then, but only then, have great significance. Summing MPR figures for a campaign comprising hundreds of cuttings and broadcast items is likely to result in very large and unwieldy MPR totals. MPR totals are useful to an extent, but they are much more useful when related to the audience as a whole.

	Score	Readers 30–60	MPR	–MPR
Regional press	8	100 000	800 000	
	–2	50 000		–100 000
	7	200 000	1 400 000	
	9	12 000	108 000	
	–1	15 000		–15 000
TOTALS:			2 308 000	–115 000
National press	0	1 500 000	0	
	3	1 500 000	4 500 000	
	6	2 500 000	15 000 000	
	–1	1 650 000		–1 650 000
	–4	1 650 000		–6 600 000
TOTALS:			19 500 000	–8 250 000
Consumer magazines	7	1 000 000	7 000 000	
	3	500 000		1 500 000
	9	500 000	4 500 000	
	5	21 000	105 000	
	–2	1 000 000		–2 000 000
TOTALS:			11 605 000	–500 000
Regional press			2 308 000	–115 000
National press			19 500 000	–8 250 000
Consumer magazines			11 605 000	–500 000

Table 5.1 Message point readership for 'management strength' message in adults, aged 30–60, June

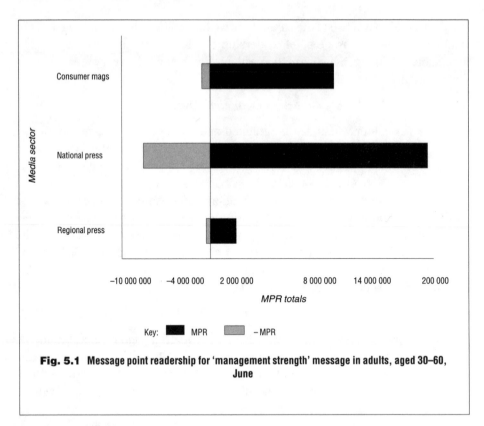

Fig. 5.1 Message point readership for 'management strength' message in adults, aged 30–60, June

MESSAGE PRESSURE

One further parameter deserves a mention which is derived from message point readership. Again, it depends on accurate and relevant data being available.

Where the TOTAL audience numbers are known, message pressure can be computed:

$$\frac{sum\ of\ (message\ delivery \times audience\ readership)}{size\ of\ audience}$$

In practical terms, message pressure is the strength of the media campaign to which an individual member of the target audience is, on average, being subjected.

Like MPR and other media analysis measures, this parameter has its limitations. Some members of the audience won't read the publications in which coverage has been gained and won't feel any pressure; others will be subjected to more than their fair share.

Again, this parameter can be adapted for certain types of consumer programme for which only circulation data is available. Here the MPR total should be divided by the relevant population figure:

$$\frac{\textit{sum of (message delivery} \times \textit{publication circulation)}}{\textit{population}}$$

Another uncertainty enters at this point, and it concerns the validity of population figures. In the UK, the Office of Population Censuses and Surveys will provide a useful breakdown of population by postcode but the accuracy of the information drifts as the date of the latest population census recedes.

Message pressure figures are much more useful than MPR totals, partly because they can be regarded as absolute measures of performance. Typically, a very successful consumer campaign will over a period of a month result in message pressures between 1 and 10. Message pressure scores above this are very hard to obtain because people only read, listen and view so much and media are reluctant to devote more than a small proportion of their editorial space available to any one issue. Message pressures can also be charted (Figure 5.2).

AGREEING THE MESSAGES AND THE CONCEPT OF MESSAGES

At the beginning of this chapter, I stressed the importance of persuading other company executives to share and contribute messages prior to a repositioning or image-building programme. This is especially important when drawing up corporate messages.

Before sharing the detail of the programme with colleagues in other disciplines, however, there is another job to be done, and that is to persuade them to take up

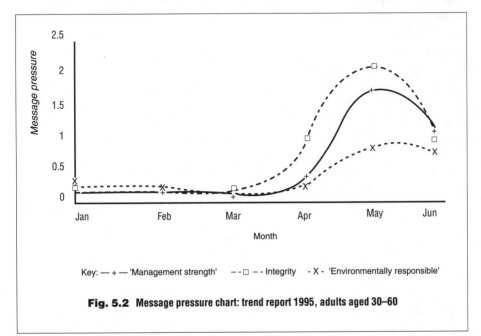

Fig. 5.2 Message pressure chart: trend report 1995, adults aged 30–60

the idea of messages at all. There is still a distressingly large number of senior managers who regard the job of the PR professional as simply putting an acceptable public veneer on an organization's activities. There's an even larger number of PR practitioners prepared to go along with this philosophy.

Go as high in the organization as possible at every stage of the process. The concept of corporate image should always start and end with the board or its equivalent, because the board is – or should be – the driving force of the organization, and will in many instances contain key spokespeople for external communications.

This isn't intended as a book on internal communications. However, here are some ideas on getting approval and support for the drafting or redrafting of the organization's messages.

First, present – or persuade the most senior person to whom you have easy access to present – a short paper to the board on the nature of the exercise you are starting. It should start by outlining the organization's existing image, backed by external research if possible. Then it should present a number of alternatives for the future, perhaps borrowing ideas and statements made by board members with which the image or position could be updated. Finally, suggest a mechanism through which the new image – containing the messages you are about to develop – can emerge. This could take the form of a small steering committee (or an agenda item on an existing group) taking a cross-section through different strands of management.

Finally, when you have a consensus on what the messages should be, share these and the philosophy behind them with your board, and get their backing for what you are doing. Share them with some of your key audiences using qualitative research like focus groups or one-to-one, in-depth interviews, making sure in the process that the messages you are intending to unleash on the unsuspecting world make sound business sense.

Every minute spent in getting approval and checking with others inside and outside the organization will be worth hours and even days later in the programme. If done properly, the work you put in early on will not only make the media coverage easier to analyse and evaluate – it will make the entire PR programme easier to manage.

And when you know who your audiences are, and have agreed what you want to say to them, you are ready to embark on the practical side of the analysis problem and start capturing the press coverage which you – and others – are generating.

6 Collecting and Sampling

Once you have decided to analyse your media profile, you need to decide how you should collect material published about your organization. Which should be discarded, if any? Are you collecting all you need?

When you have agreed your target media and your messages, all you have to do is gather the press coverage you obtain and analyse it ... or is it quite that simple?

For some organizations, it may well be that simple, but others will have to apply sampling techniques to make sure that:

- They are getting all (and only) the information they require as feedback for the organization's PR or communications programme;
- They are not paying more for their media analysis than they are for all their other promotional or corporate communications activities put together – a problem encountered often among very large and visible organizations.

Which category your organization belongs to will become clear later on, but in the meantime, consider a strange phenomenon which has been happening in homes, agencies and other organizations all over the world for centuries.... People have been gathering press cuttings about themselves for almost as long as newspapers have been published. But in most companies, the cuttings have been carefully clipped from the newspaper or magazine, categorized into scrap-books and folders and, well ... ignored!

Why do we have this compulsion to keep press cuttings? Many groups – families, companies, actors and politicians are examples – keep a press cuttings book or file. They represent something very personal, like the obituary of a dear friend or relation or a life-time hero or heroine. They can be a record of an achievement, or a justification of one's opinions. For others, the press cuttings book can be a source of research or the sum of knowledge on a particular subject in which one takes a special interest. But, whatever the reason for collecting them, in most organizations, press cuttings entering the cuttings book never see the light of day again. To all intents and purposes, the cuttings are dead once they're pasted in the book. They needn't be.

101 USES OF A DEAD PRESS CUTTING

PR people collect press cuttings, transcripts and broadcast footage because they want some kind of feedback on the results they've obtained from their media relations activities, but many feel that they don't really have time to examine the coverage in detail because they have so many other jobs to do. The cuttings book in the cupboard in the corner has been an embarrassment.

Some companies (they are in the minority) put their press cuttings to much more positive use, such as the following:

- Create a 'news digest' to circulate among senior managers and directors.
- Circulate positive reviews of products to the salesforce – sometimes for use in sales presentations.
- Obtain reprints of product reviews and articles for use as direct mail and enquiry response material.
- Use as rapid feedback mechanism on the company or organization – writing letters to the editor in response to critical comment.
- Create a press cuttings library, accurately indexed and categorized, so that issues and areas of special interest can be researched quickly and efficiently.
- Re-run broadcast footage at company meetings and in sales presentations.

All these are useful, positive activities which can help the media relations professionals in their work and help generate a positive attitude among work colleagues. But they don't analyse the coverage for facts and meaning, and they won't create that vital return element in the feedback loop which will help managers to improve the quality of the organization's communications programme.

If you mean to do this, you will need to start a few steps further back, and decide what type of media coverage you need to collect.

PRESS CUTTING AGENCIES

If you are a small company which has targeted the UK national broadsheet press to communicate your chosen messages, you may not need to employ the services of a press cuttings agency: you'll probably know when an article appears and can purchase the relevant issues as needed.

If you are targeting the regional audiences or a number of busy vertical market sectors however, it is unlikely that you can capture all the material you will need, and this in turn means that you will need professional help. Press cuttings agencies – companies which will look out for your key words in the press and send you the cuttings on a regular basis – exist throughout the USA, Europe, and most other developed countries, but the quality of the service is enormously variable.

These organizations usually charge a monthly fee and a price per cutting retrieved on the basis of your brief.

Press cuttings agencies tend to use people rather than computers to find the articles you want. These can be part-time workers, students earning extra money, or professionals who spend the hours of 9.00 a.m. to 5.00 p.m. looking for press mentions. One day soon, computer scanning techniques will be used to do this tedious job, but right now, we rely on people, and just as people vary in efficiency, so does the service they provide.

BRIEFING A PRESS CUTTINGS AGENCY

It's fashionable for PR people to criticize press cuttings agencies. In fact, many do a superb job, and a large number of the so called errors they commit are the fault of the people who brief them – the PR people themselves. Consideration of the following points will help you develop an accurate brief:

Media sectors

Make sure you know in advance what media sectors you want your agencies to monitor. Some agencies will not monitor the consumer press; others will not monitor the trade press. In larger agencies (such as Romeike & Curtice in the UK) you may need to pay a separate fee for individual media categories.

Reading lists

In some smaller agencies you may specify a detailed reading list and only pay for the coverage it finds which is on that list. If you are in any doubt at all, ask for its reading list: if your target media aren't on its list, you'll need to look elsewhere.

Subject area and keywords

Be very careful to tell the agency exactly what you want it to look for. Do you want it to look for all cuttings relating to 'smoking' or just those items which mention cigarettes? Or just cuttings which mention the anti-smoking organization ASH? Or only those which mention Benson and Hedges? The volumes will vary enormously and the cost is likely to vary accordingly: there are well over 1000 press cuttings mentioning the word 'smoking' every month in the UK press alone.

Timing

If you have a media analysis schedule, you must ensure that you get all the coverage you need in time. Ask your agency what kind of a delay you can expect.

Notice period

Clarify with your agency what period of notice you need to give before terminating or changing your instructions.

Competitors

If you intend to carry out a competitor or benchmark analysis, be sure to brief the agency on the companies or brands you want cuttings for. Give special thought to companies which have high visibility outside your own area of interest: if you are only interested in PC operating systems, it might be best to ask your agency to look for the acronym 'PS/2' rather than 'IBM'. If you are in the handset manufacturing business, choose 'telephone handsets' rather than BT or British Telecom.

Once you have written the brief, ask your press cuttings agency what it thinks of it, and if it feels there is anything missing. If, after receiving cuttings for a month (or not, as the case may be!) you are unsure what the agency's cuttings policy is, call them and query it.

Change instructions if necessary – change agencies only if you are sure that serious and consistent errors are being made. You have spent considerable time and effort deciding on your target media and messages: collecting the cuttings you need for media analysis is much more difficult for a press cuttings agency than it seems to you.

ON-LINE DATABASES

Press cuttings agencies are still one of the most popular ways of obtaining press cuttings, but they have a serious drawback – they are unable to retrieve press cuttings retrospectively. To do this we may be able to find what we need by making use of on-line databases.

Here is an example of a search carried out in the UK national press and selected regional press on the subject 'cola' – and the steps that some UK stores had been taking to establish their own cola brands. I was especially interested to see how much coverage two of the leading supermarket groups, Sainsbury and Tesco, had obtained on the cola issue and how the new entry into the marketplace – Richard Branson's Virgin Company – had fared at the hands of the UK broadsheets and tabloids.

The database I used was the FT-Profile database, which is owned by the Financial Times Group. It contains the full text of all the UK broadsheet press, and some of the tabloid press, going back over a number of years.

In the search I carried out, I was looking for all references to cola. I then wanted to examine this material for references to Sainsbury, Tesco and Virgin. I restricted the search initially to a single year of coverage: 1 November 1993 to 25 November 1994, the latter being the date of my search.

In FT-Profile, it is possible to narrow down a search area to your precise requirements: this is how I carried out my search, using Profile's menu-driven Infoplus interface:

EXAMPLE: AN ONLINE SEARCH

After logging on to FT-Profile and responding to requests for identity and giving my password, I was asked to choose between items in this menu:

1. News
2. Companies
3. Industries
4. Markets
5. Supergroup
6. Files

As I wanted to remind myself of the media sectors available, I decided to choose option 6 which allowed me to go through all the files and electronically flag up the newspapers I was interested in.

For my first search I flagged up all the UK broadsheets:

European
Financial Times
Guardian
Independent
Independent on Sunday
Observer
Telegraph
Sunday Telegraph
The Times
Sunday Times

Keying a return takes me to the second stage of the search specification – time range. The default is a single retrospective year to the date of the search. I selected this default. (It is possible to specify a different year, a month, a week or even a single day.)

I was then invited to write down my search parameters, so I keyed in the phrase:

COLA + SAINSBURY

The source informed me that it had found 109 items – items which mentioned both the word 'cola' and the word 'Sainsbury'. I then modified the search, asking the source to search for

COLA + TESCO (68 items)

and

COLA + VIRGIN (67 items).

I could have downloaded all of these items into my computer for analysis at this point had I so desired.

I then examined another part of the database – the tabloid section. Unfortunately, of the UK tabloids only the *Daily Mail*, the *Mail on Sunday*, and

Today appear in full text on FT-Profile.* The equivalent search in these tabloids yielded 24 items (COLA + SAINSBURY), 21 items (COLA + TESCO) and 21 items (COLA + VIRGIN). The marketing and retail sectors of the database, incorporating titles like *Campaign* and *Supermarketing* contain more references: they could also have been combed for relevant published items if required.

This search would have allowed me to carry out a detailed analysis of the cola brand issue, but it may not cover all the media sectors you may be interested in, and it's worth remembering that databases like FT-Profile do not yet contain illustrations.

The Infoplus/FT-Profile combination does however enable the user to store his or her own search parameters such as a selection of publications (which can be a media analysis media category like 'broadsheets'), and a detailed key-word specification so that the same data doesn't have to be rekeyed every time. This cuts down the expense of the search and ensures repeatability if exactly the same search needs to be carried out each month.

If I had wanted, I could then have asked Profile to give me the full text of all the items in the search. I have not done so here simply in the interests of conserving space.

Using on-line databases is not cheap. The cost of the search above was a few pounds, and to have retrieved the full text of all the items would have been much more. But to have taken out a press cutting service for a year, and tracked the two companies mentioned would have been thousands of pounds.

On-line databases, however, have two serious drawbacks for the media evaluator apart from the cost.

First, they only hold a small proportion of the total press. These are useful proportions in the USA and UK media (though not necessarily in convenient media categories for the analyst) but frankly rather patchy in Europe and elsewhere in the world. But the use of on-line media databases is becoming more widespread as more material goes on-line.

The second problem is that the popular databases – at the moment – only store text, not illustrations. We discuss illustrations in Chapter 17, where it will become apparent that illustrations contribute significantly to volume, impact and message delivery. Our search did not tell us anything about the illustrative material which accompanied some of the material we had identified. It could be some years before the digital superhighway brings us on-line media coverage in significant amounts.

*Since this search was carried out, titles in the Mirror Group have been added to FT-Profile.

CD-ROM

While talking about on-line databases it's also worth mentioning CD-ROM. If you are going to be examining the same media time and time again, it's worth invest-ing in a CD-ROM of the text of the publication concerned, and many are currently available.

Like the on-line solution, however, CD-ROM also brings a unique set of dis-advantages. The most annoying is that unlike an on-line service it doesn't update itself: your data is only as recent as the last information recorded on the disk. You need to top up the data with an on-line search in a database like FT-Profile – or its competitors Dialog, Compuserve or Nexis.

OBTAINING BROADCAST COVERAGE

If you are targeting the broadcast media, it's worth registering your name with a monitoring company such as Tellex Monitors in the UK and Europe. They will call you in the event that they pick up a mention of your organization's name, or an issue in which you are interested, on the radio or television.

Broadcast coverage presents organizations with something of a dilemma as it's possible to keep your programme for posterity either as a transcript or as a tape. If you are taking your media analysis seriously as most readers of this book will be, then you should analyse the coverage – particularly television coverage – as a taped record. Sometimes, there is information in visual surroundings and body language which a transcript of a conversation, an interview or a news item can't supply. In radio coverage, there can be an implication in tone of voice, and more information for the listener in background sounds and music.

Imagine an interview with a bank's finance director taking place in a casino, with roulette wheels spinning in the background as the speaker talks of the need for greater financial stability and good housekeeping. An extreme example, but one which illustrates just how much non-verbal information enters our brain via the small screen.

OBTAINING OVERSEAS COVERAGE

Obtaining coverage from your target media overseas, and evaluating it, can be expensive. All the rules we have outlined in the last three chapters still apply, but the international dimension adds complexity, as has been indicated in Chapter 4.

Two pieces of further advice apply, however. If you are targeting three or four vertical market areas in Europe, it doesn't follow that you must take out a press cutting service for the whole of Europe: it's likely that you would do better to buy the key vertical market journals in each relevant country.

If you are only targeting one vertical market in Germany, and if you need an improved corporate profile just in France, keep your measurement exercise to those sectors in the countries concerned. Don't set yourselves impossible targets by monitoring all sectors of the press across the European continent: it will cost your department a fortune, and you will find the results very depressing!

CRITICAL MASS

Commonly, at some stage in the development of an organization – usually after it has developed a strong international profile – its media profile reaches critical mass. In other words the organization is so large, visible, important or interesting that the key media will continue to write about the company, together with its products, services and shortcomings, even if the flow of press material comes to a stop. Most companies are well below critical mass, however, and it is essential to keep the interest of the media alive by issuing a constant stream of material.

The point was illustrated to me very graphically in February 1974 when I was working in the Press Office of the British Labour Party during the first of the two General Elections of that year. Every time a press release was written, or a speech made available, these would be whisked away by motorcycle messengers from the national press, television and news agencies. Every word was avidly consumed: there was no question of selling each story, and no problem whatsoever about gaining coverage. I was brought down to earth some months later when I joined my present employer, Infopress, then a PR consultancy with six staff and a number of small clients, for whom getting coverage in the national media was sometimes a considerable challenge. It was much later, when the company's client list had expanded considerably, that I experienced the critical mass effect once more.

Companies and organizations above critical mass sometimes attract huge volumes of coverage, the vast majority of which is written about them rather than generated by their press officers. It becomes expensive and difficult to manage the media analysis process in a short timescale for all the media coverage available, and it may be decided to apply sampling techniques.

SOME SAMPLING TECHNIQUES

Sampling techniques only really become applicable when there is so much coverage that the evaluator can extract the volume, visibility and message delivery data from a representative proportion of the coverage obtained. Here is a selection of techniques which can be applied.

Numerical sampling

Numerical sampling is relevant where there is duplication of stories within the media categories. In this technique, a half or a third of the coverage is analysed, and the items to be analysed are selected randomly. This is especially useful for utilities addressing a very widely distributed regional programme, in which many of the published items are covering the same story in a similar way.

Time sampling

In this technique, applicable to corporate programmes in which seasonal changes are thoroughly understood, an organization may choose to dip into the coverage across all media categories, and examine the coverage for a single month every quarter or half-year. This should not be used until at least two years of full or numerically sampled data has been gathered.

Sector sampling

Some companies prefer to stop the regular analysis of some of their target media sectors because they have established that the organization's performance within them closely follows one or more of the other sectors. In the UK, organizations sometimes stop analysing regional media, for instance, because they know that their performance in the regional press will shadow their performance in the national press. Sometimes, sector sampling can be implemented because the profile in one or more of the sectors is static, or responds to well-understood PR stimuli.

Regional sampling

Regional sampling is sometimes used as a measurement technique for very large campaigns, in which it is necessary to look at a particular region and compare it with another which is exposed to different stimuli, or a control area in which there is no activity.

CONCLUSION

We've discussed how we can collect the press clippings and broadcast coverage both at home and abroad, and we have examined some ways of sampling the data you have collected using some sampling techniques.

The next decision we need to take is the decision about who we put in charge of the analysis itself.

7 Who Should Evaluate?

The most important decision you need to make is who should be doing the analysis. This chapter explores the pros and cons of doing the analysis within your own organization, and outlines the relative benefits of performing the analysis in-house and by an external system or service. The danger of biasing the evaluation by involving PR staff in the analysis is underlined.

Imagine a court of law where a man accused of a felony appears in court, and on turning to examine the jury finds that it contains the man who accused him of the felony, his old headmaster (who never had a good word for him), and three members of the board of the company who sacked him from his last job.

'Sorry, chum', says the poor man's defence lawyer, 'but that's the way it's done in this court'.

It's a nonsense of course.

Imagine a market research exercise where a researcher is testing a new confectionery bar and only invites the people who work on the production line which makes it, and whose livelihoods depend on it, on to the tasting panel.

'There seems to be great enthusiasm for this product,' he tells his client.

Again, a completely wasted exercise – the panel was hopelessly biased.

Imagine a situation in which a public relations consultant or press officer is invited to be judge and jury on the effectiveness of her own work.

Stupid idea? Well in hundreds of companies, the very same team who have been entrusted with the task of being guardian of the company's reputation are given the additional task of finding out if that job has been done effectively or not. Hands up all those who can even imagine a PR consultant putting his or her hand on his or her heart and saying, 'I failed!'

The trouble is that in many organizations, the PR person is the only person close enough to the media to be able to make an intelligent evaluation, and as a result, holds the job. But as PR becomes a more and more important promotional and communications tool, our corporate paymasters are going to demand much more thorough analytical procedures.

WHY ARE YOU EVALUATING?

As indicated in the opening chapter, there are many different reasons for analysing a company's profile in the media, and evaluating an individual's or a team's contribution to it. If one of the reasons you are doing the analysis is to audit the success or otherwise of your in-house PR team or consultancy, you should take particular care to ensure that neither the PR team, nor the people responsible for employing them, are actively involved in the generation of the data.

If you are concerned with mapping the media environment in which you are operating, and are only secondarily interested in the performance of your PR team, then the argument for keeping the measurement process away from the media relations professionals is a little less compelling.

THE DIY OPTION

The do-it-yourself option has both advantages and drawbacks. And there is an important line to be drawn between specifying and managing the evaluation process, and carrying out the measurements which form the evaluation itself.

It must be said that the in-house professional who lives and breathes the target media and the machinery of the press relations function will undoubtedly be the person who is in the best position to understand the issues behind the figures. He or she will undoubtedly have an intuitive feel for the reasons why certain messages are being delivered successfully, and why the delivery of others is failing.

Contrast this position with the busy PR consultant who spends only a third or a quarter of his or her time on the company's account – and who needs good scores to be sure of retaining the account next year. Contrast this also with the position of the busy research executive who has been given the job of measuring and interpreting the facts behind the figures – and who may well have dozens of other clients. The in-house PR professional has a sound case in staking a claim to a portion of evaluation territory. But the communications director or public affairs director, if one exists, has a stronger one.

The communications director has responsibility for the PR team, including in-house professionals and any external retained consultancies, and is in a good position to take a responsible and unbiased view. He or she may also be responsible for buying other kinds of market research and will be experienced in interpreting the results – and acting on them. It is the communications director who should take personal charge of specifying and managing the media evaluation system to be employed.

But the communications director will not wish to become involved in the detailed analysis of individual press cuttings and audio and video tapes. And the communications professionals in his or her department will probably have been recruited for their creative and administrative skills and detailed sector knowledge and experience: the process of measuring media profile, representing a considerable investment in time and expertise, is unlikely to present the ultimate career challenge.

Before deciding on whether to embark on an in-house media analysis and evaluation service therefore, the communications director should ask him or herself the following questions:

1. Is our main requirement to evaluate the performance of the PR team?
2. Or, is our main requirement to monitor the organization's media profile?
3. Do I have the internal resources to carry out a tedious yet intellectually challenging task to a sufficiently high degree of accuracy?
4. Can I commit the same level of staffing to this task on a regular basis (even when the annual results are about to be announced, for instance).

THE INTERNAL SYSTEM

If the answer to the second and third questions is yes, then the communications director may consider setting up an internal measurement and evaluation system.

This will require a considerable degree of organization. The following job-list gives an idea of the task which lies ahead:

- Brief a press cutting and broadcast monitoring service on the organization, its competitors and issues.
- Calculate the anticipated volume of coverage per week or per month.
- Find an analyst (ideally with a back-up) who is able to measure volumes and namechecks in a methodical and reliable fashion.
- Develop or purchase a system for analysing the data and presenting the results in an understandable way.
- Agree the issues, messages, target audiences and target media, and develop a consistent sampling routine which will give repeatable results from one month to the next.
- Establish a regular routine for reviewing all these parameters.
- Find a further analyst, who may or may not be the same one that was mentioned before, who can interpret the press coverage from an industry or issue perspective, and score the coverage accurately and consistently.
- Maintain a carefully catalogued library of press cuttings, transcripts, tapes and other published material.

THE EXTERNAL SERVICE

Even though the communications director is carrying out a full profile monitoring exercise and has the resources to get the work done in his or her department, the external service may still be the chosen method.

There are a number of reasons why he or she may wish to opt out. Perhaps the main reason is that the in-house evaluator may be just too close to his or her subject to make a rational judgement about an individual piece of coverage.

Imagine that you're the press officer for a big supermarket chain and your department has spent six months trying to get the food editor of the *New York Times* to do a corporate profile. Eventually, the journalist agrees and after a further two months of matching diaries, arranging photographs and putting briefing notes together, the interview takes place, it goes well, the piece appears, and the exercise is felt to have been a success.

You would be a brave evaluator if you had given the piece less than the possible maximum. An independent evaluator, on the other hand, won't be saddled with the hopes and troubles of the PR department while carrying out his or her work. You'll simply be told what the article says about the company and how much impact it makes. And his or her opinion will undoubtedly be fairer than yours.

Take the opposite case of an article which is written by a wine writer who has not had the benefit of an interview with a representative of your company. She writes in ignorance, and the article she writes is about Californian red wines, a subject on which you and your company are the world's leading authorities. She mentions your company, yet the quotes are three years old, she mis-spells your president's name, and she criticizes a product which was discontinued last year. Your award-winning Cabernet Sauvignon does not even rate a mention.

The article could induce apoplexy in a sales manager, it could cause a PR executive to be fired, and it could even (in some companies it most certainly will) lose the publication a good deal of advertising revenue. But what effect will it have on your reputation, and on your customers' buying habits? The employees and senior managers involved in the corporate gnashing of teeth are not the ideal people to decide. An independent evaluator, on the other hand, has every reason to give it to you straight, and has no reason to respond emotively.

THE CONCEPT OF OUTSOURCING

The other fundamental reason why external evaluators are an appealing option to senior PR management is that they will have the systems established to cope with the job. Why re-invent the wheel? Why employ extra staff when by buying a service someone else will have that worry?

There has been a development in the computer industry since the mid 1980s in which client companies, unable to cope with rapidly changing technologies and unable to predict the cost of future systems, have turned to facilities management companies to run their systems for them. Many companies are going to media analysis bureaux for the same reasons: the technologies and systems of media analysis are improving all the time and it is unlikely that a corporate press office, however big, can justify a continuing investment in research and development which will keep it abreast of the field.

ROLES OF THE IN-HOUSE TEAM

There are all kinds of reasons why out-of-house analysis and evaluation is a good policy. But there are still a number of vital roles for the people working on the inside.

The brief

The communications director or a colleague working closely with the communications director will need to develop the evaluator brief (see example below). Only he or she can decide what needs to be measured – because the communications director decides the objectives of the communications programme, of which media relations forms such a vital part.

The cuttings and tapes

The press cuttings and tapes about you in the target media need to be gathered either by the in-house PR team or by an agency and scanned as soon as they arrive by the PR team. Some will need to be copied to other executives; others will need responses in the form of a phone call to a PR consultancy or a letter to the editor. Only then should they be processed for analysis and evaluation.

Sampling

If you are analysing only a proportion of the media you appear in (see Chapter 6), you will need to sample the cuttings accordingly. This should be a clerical job, rather than a professional job. If you need to read the item to decide whether to evaluate it or not, then it should be done outside.

Reviewing

The world does not stay still. Messages change as issues arise and target audiences and media will change as new markets emerge. The communications director should keep a watching brief on the evaluation parameters and formally review them annually at least.

Using the results

It sounds obvious, but in just the same way that many press cuttings remain unused, evaluation data remains unused as well in some instances. Evaluation data is great for fine-tuning the PR programme (see Chapter 20), for waging internal battles (see Chapter 24), and for arguing your corner when the annual budgeting exercise comes round (see Chapter 23).

EXAMPLE OF AN EVALUATOR BRIEF

In this example, an evaluator's media analysis brief is illustrated (Table 7.1) for Impco, a fictitious importer of apples from the little-known island of Goodland

Example media analysis for Impco Limited

Impco is an importer of Goodland apples (Gapples). We need to evaluate the press coverage which we and some of our competitors obtain so that we can determine whether basic messages about our brand are getting across to our target audiences.

A further reason for the exercise is that we are reviewing our PR arrangements at the end of the year with a view to employing the services of a PR consultancy. We wish to establish the nature and extent of any image problems we may have with the media.

Our product: Gapples
Our competitors: Cox's Orange Pippins
                   Golden Delicious

Messages (consumers and purchasing executives)

1. Gapples are available June – December
2. Gapples are sweeter than European apples
3. Gapples are firm

Messages (wholesalers, retailers, distributors)

4. Gapples stay fresh longer than European apples
5. Gapples are attractively packaged
6. Impco will be promoting Gapples with a media advertising campaign throughout the summer

Target audiences

1. Consumers (mainly B-C2 women)
2. Purchasing executives in large grocery retail stores
3. Wholesalers and distributors

Target media

1. Regional press – food writers
2. National press – food writers
3. Grocery and retail press
4. Food trade press

Expected volumes:

Gapples: 25 cuttings per month
Others: 100 cuttings per month in total

Report

The company will need monthly reports on an ongoing basis throughout the year, within three weeks of the end of the month of publication.

Evelyn Adams
Communications Director

Table 7.1 Example of a media analysis brief

located in the middle of the Atlantic Ocean.

This is the document on which the external evaluator will be able to base his or her judgements about press and media coverage. The example shows that the more specific you can be about the programme you are managing, the more specific the evaluator can be about the programme's success. The example also shows how the parameters of a moderately complex programme can be written down in a relatively brief document.

CONCLUSION TO PART I

In Chapters 1–7 we have outlined some of the purposes of media analysis and examined some techniques used by media analysts. In Chapter 7 we examined the role of the evaluator and put forward some suggestions about who should carry out the analysis itself.

In Part II we apply some of the principles we have developed in Part I. Most of this section is devoted to the application of media analysis to particular PR functions. But before we become too deeply involved in applications, we again visit territory which will be familiar ground to many PR communication professionals – the communications audit.

Part II
Media Analysis in Action

8 The Communications Audit

Many organizations find it difficult to reach a point where they can analyse their media purposefully, simply because there is no corporate consensus on what the messages are and who the main target audiences should be. This chapter introduces the concept of a communications audit as a method of establishing the parameters needed.

Ask a PR professional to outline (a) the target audiences and (b) the messages to be communicated to them, and you will receive some very varied and very revealing answers.

Sometimes, PR professionals clearly don't know the answer to either question when they should do – but as the PR business continues to become more and more professional, this situation is encountered less often.

Much more often, professionals exhibit symptoms of anguish and frustration when asked questions like this – because the organization which employs them doesn't have a well-defined and visible sense of direction, and the measurement parameters we need are therefore impossible to determine.

Organizations like this would benefit from a communications audit.

New companies and new organizations rarely need one. Because a group of people with shared views has come together to decide on a course of action, the sense of mission is strong, and the way ahead, however rocky, is clear. Older companies, however, especially those in which there is a mature infrastructure, and those which have undergone fundamental organic change, or which have been through a takeover or a merger since formation, often do.

The need for a communications audit, of course, goes far beyond the need to determine a few parameters for media analysis. The communications audit is a prerequisite tool to help an organization to:

1.   Determine (or redetermine) communication objectives;
2.   Review target audiences;
3.   Review the content of information transmitted;
4.   Review methods of communication used.

In other words, the communications audit gives the organization an opportunity to take a step back and view itself objectively as a communicator and an information provider. The audit answers the questions, 'Is communication working for us?', 'Are we making the best use of the avenues open to us?' and 'Are we making the best use of the information we own?'

WHO NEEDS AN AUDIT?

There are a number of reasons why an organization might need a communications audit.

In older companies there is quite often no mission statement at all, or if there is, it is hopelessly out of date and has fallen into disuse. The problem for the PR professional becomes more acute if there is a need to work with people who have a strongly held, but poorly articulated sense of mission which is at variance with that of their colleagues.

New people coming into a mature company at a senior level can act as catalysts for change. But if they are poorly integrated with the organization, they can skew the image of that organization, thereby confusing audiences and introducing self-doubt among the old guard internally – even at board level.

Here are some of the symptoms of an organization which is in need of a communications audit:

1. Advertising and PR saying divergent or even conflicting things about the company or products.
2. Chief executives 'caught out' in media interviews by saying the opposite of press statements issued by their own media relations departments.
3. Media information differing markedly in style and content from information exhibited in an organization's reception area or appearing in product literature.
4. A policy of 'no comment' when questions about industry issues arise, displaying lack of confidence by spokespeople.
5. Poor public response to crises and adverse coverage.
6. Different divisions interpreting parent company attribution in divergent ways, or not referring to them at all – in press statements, interviews and literature.
7. Stylistically different literature and sharply divergent PR policies between different divisions, subsidiaries and product groupings.
8. No mission statement available, corporate messages unclear, no 'boilerplate statements' or 'motherhood clauses' in use in company literature.
9. Press calls always referred to the chief executive, and requests by suppliers to announce contracts linked to the company always turned down.

10. To the question 'Does your organization need a communications audit?', a representative of such an organization will usually answer 'No'!

Some of the above differences and inconsistencies will be found in all companies, often for very good reasons, but when many of them appear, it is a sign that all is not well with the communications function.

It's hardly surprising that when our media analyst asks about messages and audiences, such an organization will give a muddled, inaccurate or non-existent response.

WHO CARRIES OUT COMMUNICATIONS AUDITS?

There are organizations which undergo communications audits regularly as a matter of principle, and there are PR consultancies and advertising agencies who like to start off every new client relationship with a communications audit of their new client as a way of understanding the company, its people and the issues which affect it.

There are also organizations which resent audits as unwarranted intrusions, and there are PR consultancies who regard any other firm carrying one out to *their* client as a severe business threat.

I prefer to regard communications audits as a means of identifying core communication objectives and strategy parameters. As such, they can be implemented by a wide range of different people. Many are carried out by PR consultants or communication consultants, but there are just as strong arguments for asking a skilled in-house manager to carry out the work.

THE CONSULTANCY OPTION

A PR consultant will usually be delighted to carry out a communications audit, but before hiring the consultancy it is a good idea to ensure that it has performed such an exercise before, asking for a reference or two.

It is also a good idea to lay down some definite ground rules before you start: for instance, if an audit is likely to result in a large-scale PR programme to be implemented by a PR consultancy, ensure that the consultant isn't simply given the authority to write out a large company cheque payable to their firm. Divide the work up so that there is a competitive pitch *after* the audit, in which companies other than the auditing company are given a chance to put forward their ideas for the agreed programme.

THE IN-HOUSE OPTION

The arguments against the in-house auditor are analogous to those for not carrying out media analysis in-house: the in-house auditor may come to the job with his or her own array of built-in prejudices, company political leanings and marked cards.

A recently joined but experienced employee coming in at senior level, relatively unsullied by organization politics and with good communication skills, may be an excellent in-house choice.

WHICH COMES FIRST, AUDIT OR ANALYSIS?

Oddly enough, media analysis may be a good start-point for a communications audit, even though an audit may be essential before the company can get the best out of an ongoing media analysis programme.

A simple 'open analysis' will give the auditor, especially one coming from outside the organization, an idea of which questions to ask and which areas of policy to probe. Analysis against simple core criteria such as 'success', 'quality of products and services', 'trustworthiness', and so on will reveal aspects of the organization's profile and relate them to events and incidents which may not arise by putting open questions to senior management and staff. But the auditor will need to delve into the company's communication infrastructure in far greater depth if he or she is to decide the messages which need to be imparted via the media over an extended period.

TYPES OF COMMUNICATIONS AUDIT

Traditionally, communications audits have been divided into two categories – internal audits and external audits.

In the internal audit, the auditor reviews reporting structure, informal gateways, decision-making methodology, information technology (including the telephone system and answering procedure), internal literature, memos, location and existence of notice boards, frequency of meetings and methods of running meetings, and aspects of corporate culture.

The result of the internal audit is a report which may suggest a new mission statement and recommend who should be told what and how they should be told. The internal audit may establish the existence of useless and damaging information blockages which do nothing but demotivate staff and preserve the status quo; it can sometimes establish that apparently serious structural problems can be solved by establishing a dialogue between people who don't currently talk to each other very much.

The external audit looks outwards towards an organization's audiences from an internal perspective, and inwards towards the organization from the outside.

It usually contains a visibility, opinion and perception survey (see Chapter 19 for more details) but sometimes the organization can dispense with this aspect, thereby saving costs, if there has been a recent, thorough and publicly available sector survey in which the 'outside-looking-in' questions have been answered.

The external audit examines methods of reaching, influencing and persuading the audiences which have been identified. This will involve reviewing press and media relations activities (corporate and marketing related) investor relations, Government relations, advertising, external literature, direct marketing, and customer relations.

Superficially, the two types of audit are quite different and can safely be kept in separate compartments. But in practice, it is rare that one can be carried out without the other. The symptoms listed earlier on page 74 are symptoms of poor internal communications and lack of management confidence rather than an inability to communicate effectively with the outside world. So, however pressing the need to revitalize links with the outside, it's worth a check on internal communications effectiveness first of all, and our prime concern here will be with internal perspective rather than the external one.

PRINCIPLES OF COMMUNICATIONS AUDITS

Seymour Hamilton has written an excellent book on communications audits, and this one is not intended to replace it. It is worthwhile, however, outlining some of the basic audit techniques which can help generate the information which the media analyst and the professional communicator needs to do their jobs more effectively.

THE AUDIT OBJECTIVES

At the risk of stating the obvious, the auditor should start off by agreeing the audit objectives. These should be written down by the auditor and signed off by the client organization prior to any interviews or surveys.

The objectives may be as wide as 'Review current internal (or external) communication activity' or 'Formulate a new mission statement for the company'. They may be as specific as 'Review the relationship between the organization and the women's press and suggest methods by which it may be improved.'

The objectives, once formulated, need to be agreed at a high level within the organization, ideally by the chief executive or full board. And once the scope and depth of the audit have been agreed, all those within the organization who will be interviewed or otherwise affected need to be told formally what is going on by a senior spokesperson with the appropriate authority. That way, nobody will be affronted or shocked by the questions, and the expectations of the results will not be raised to too high a level.

SOME TECHNIQUES

There are no 'absolute' ways of carrying out a communications audit. It is best to adapt the techniques which are available to the objectives which have been agreed and the type of work being carried out.

In-depth interviews

The in-depth interview is a good way of determining and clarifying senior management aspirations. In particular it can capture the personal view of a senior member of an organization on where the organization should be heading, on the relative importance to the organization of different audiences and on how they see the role of different communication techniques.

They can also be used to establish the likely response to suggested changes in communication strategy. A chief executive or board director will sometimes say something in a one-to-one interview that he or she would not say in a group, for fear of being challenged by a colleague with opposing views. The auditor must, therefore, under these circumstances reassure the interviewee that any confidences will be respected.

To make the best use of management time and to ensure consistency of results, the auditor will often use a combination of open and closed questions to tease out elusive information on contentious issues – issues on which the experienced interviewee may be inclined to bluff or prevaricate. Open questions might include questions such as: 'What do you think the most important markets will be for XXX's products and services in five years time?' This might be supplemented by a forced choice question in which the interviewee has to decide where he or she feels his or her company belongs on a scale of 1–10 with ' system provider' at one end and 'consultancy' at the other.

It is the inconsistencies between one set of answers and the other which may provide the most useful and interesting areas to explore. The executive may be inadvertently (or perhaps even deliberately) concealing a concern or problem for which the communications audit can provide a solution.

The in-depth interview may also be used on a small sample of a broader audience elsewhere in the organization. It may not be possible – for cost and time reasons – to interview all the members of the design department, for instance, but it will be possible to interview one or two of the design team provided they are chosen to be representative of the department as a whole. Again, fears of contradiction in a group situation will inhibit an individual from saying the things likely to emerge in a confidential interview.

Focus groups

A focus group of six or eight people representing different departments and different levels of seniority is both a good way of finding a consensus on a particular question and in detecting dangerous fault lines in the organizational structure.

It is especially useful for exploring the internal perspective on a new strategy such as the introduction of robots, or a decision to apply for an ISO 9000 certificate. But the auditor or the moderator chosen to run the session will need to work hard to encourage the more junior and more retiring members of the group to participate fully.

A focus group of this type is not the ideal vehicle for solving important strategic issues such as which market to attack, but vital strengths are sometimes revealed in remarks like 'We stayed on late to run those figures through again – we hate it when customers phone with a complaint.'

Focus groups can throw up problems as well. Inter-departmental conflicts – undetected in the more structured and analytical phases of the audit – may emerge in a focus group. I worked in one company where a deep mutual distrust between Marketing and Public Relations lay undetected, and therefore unsolved, by senior management for years.

Resentments also sometimes emerge – like 'We didn't know it was happening until we saw it in the press – why didn't they tell us?' A respondent, especially a junior one, is unlikely to say this in an interview, and there will be no room on a survey form. But there may be nods of assent if others are saying the same thing.

Questionnaires and telephone surveys

When a large workforce is involved, or where a local community or marketplace or press sector needs to be interviewed, a self-completion survey form can be invaluable. It is a way of asking specific questions of hundreds or even thousands of people without confronting them physically on a one-to-one or group basis.

As with all survey methods however, there are drawbacks. People who fill in survey forms are sometimes the people who have the most 'establishment' views; often it's the people who don't fill in the forms who the auditor most needs to reach.

In an internal survey, company discipline can be used to ensure that all the questionnaires are returned, but with external audiences, no such means can be used. It is good practice to employ telephone opinion survey techniques on a carefully chosen sample of the audience to back up a self completion questionnaire. Sometimes, it's better to use the telephone survey alone, even if the budget will permit only a small sample.

Network analysis

The above techniques are useful for capturing opinions and for working out the formal channels of communication within an organization and between the organization and the outside world. Network analysis identifies the caucuses, the short cuts and the unofficial cliques and hierarchies.

In network analysis the auditor asks selected individuals to keep a detailed record over a working day on every communication they have with others – inside or outside the organization. Telephone calls (incoming and outgoing), letters, memos, faxes and e-mail is recorded and at the end of the day the auditor will have a detailed record of the actual communication activity around the organization.

Network analysis can shed an important light on audiences. While a sales representative may have said in the interview or on a self-completion form that he or she has direct contact with his or her customers, network analysis may show that most of this contact is through an intermediary such as a management consultant, an architect or a systems integrator. These audiences will need special attention in the new PR programme being constructed, and the media analyst will probably want to add *RIBA Journal* or *MCA Journal* to the reading list as a result of the findings.

Literature survey

The literature survey can encompass as much or as little of the organization's output as is required to meet the objectives of the audit.

An auditor will probably want to survey all the printed brochures, leaflets and externally or internally distributed newsletters together with news releases, media briefing material and information packs. Sometimes this aspect of the audit will need to encompass letters, proposals, quotations and outgoing faxes.

A brochure will sometimes be found to stress the key messages of three years ago, when the brochure was last designed, rather than the messages appropriate for today – and might be actively harming a company's chances of winning contracts as a result. If it's saying the opposite of the messages being stressed through the press office, the brochure will confuse the potential customer and create obstacles to prevent the sale taking place.

A press office often throws up its own communication problems. Deciding grand corporate messages is all very well, but has anybody actually told the press officer about them? If not, the content of press releases issued will reveal whether tricks are being missed.

The principle of reinforcement

All the above techniques have advantages, and all have drawbacks. By themselves they are of limited value. Used together, they can paint a clear picture of what communication is going on around the organization and how communication can be improved.

If network analysis reveals that intermediaries are of critical importance, and the interviews with senior managers reveal that 'We should do more with our business partners', this is a strong indication that better communication with these intermediaries should be put in place.

Reinforcement coming from external surveys is of particular value. If a sector survey or an opinion survey reveals that the customers need more contact with senior management, and managers reveal in interviews that they need more direct contact with their customers, it's clear that the whole customer interface needs to be rethought. Once the new relationship is in place, the PR function will need to promote the message that customers get director-level access and support.

Sometimes an external survey will reveal a completely unexpected need, or a hitherto unsuspected problem. Key decision-makers may reveal that they just don't understand the latest technology or are ignoring new legislation – putting them at risk of legal action: these are opportunities for a supplier organization to take the lead in educating them through their public relations function. This aspect of the audit will almost certainly have been reinforced in interviews with the salesforce or information department. The messages associated with any new aspects of the public relations programme will need to be tracked.

The external survey may reveal a corporate failing – for instance that the subject organization is thought of as boring and pedestrian when the company thought it was innovative and intriguing! Telling an organization an unpalatable fact is fraught with difficulties – and danger for the auditor – but it needs to be dealt with when it arises. If the problem has not been revealed in the internal aspects of the audit, it can be examined from a different perspective by revisiting key internal groups with one-to-one interviews or focus groups and exploring the issue specifically.

Any aspect of the communications audit which can only be 'seen' from one survey technique must be examined closely before it is incorporated into the final report and before measures to deal with it are drawn up.

USING SECTOR RESEARCH

External surveys are expensive – mainly because it is essential that they are carried out by external market research professionals. To get a good feel for a big consumer marketplace, it's often essential to carry out hundreds of telephone interviews.

It's a big relief therefore when a trade association carries out a sector survey which answers many of the questions we wanted to ask. There is no point in reinventing the wheel. I have recently carried out a communications audit for a prominent firm of chartered surveyors in which the need for the external phase was eliminated due to the existence of two recent industry surveys which told us all we needed to know.

If it is going to be of use, the sector survey must cover two vital areas of opinion. The first answers questions of the type: 'What do you need/look for/admire in suppliers of X?' The second will ask the respondents to rank suppliers in order of preference on particular issues or aspects of product excellence or service.

The auditor will need to look at the answers to both types of question. The first will tell the auditor what audiences are looking for and perhaps not receiving. The second will reveal how the client organization ranks against the opposition. The relative position can be monitored using media analysis, using the same companies in the media analysis as featured in the sector research.

THE AUDIT REPORT

No PR professional would dream of issuing a news release without first clearing it with the executive responsible in the client or employer organization. And the auditor shouldn't spring a final report full of recommendations and surprises on an unsuspecting organization.

The presentation of interim findings to the commissioning executive can be regarded as part of the reinforcement process we described earlier. An audit report which contains strategic suggestions, and which has the support of the managers who commissioned it, is likely to be put into action. A report which contains fundamental changes and which cause hackles to rise through inappropriate choice of wording is likely to be left on the boardroom table.

The report of the communications audit will be full of ideas, and be dense with information on audiences and on the messages which must be delivered to them if the organization is to realize its – perhaps newly defined – corporate mission.

The audit will have aligned the media relations department with the decision-making machinery of the organization. It will have made the board acutely aware of the importance of better communications in general, and of the role of the media in particular, in relation to the organization's various activities. It is now up to the media analyst to deliver regular high-quality information which will uphold the reputation of media relations as a controllable, effective communications medium which deserves high status.

Imagine starting media analysis built around the parameters of a communications audit – an audit in which messages have been debated in interviews and focus groups, audiences decided in tough meetings with marketing professionals and hard-nosed sales people operating very much at the 'coalface'. Contrast this with media analysis initiated by a PR professional who starts by plucking messages out of the air, deciding audiences on a whim. In the first instance, the media analysis will be doing a worthwhile job, and each report will be read avidly by all concerned with the management of communications within the organization; in the second, the reports will have little impact outside the PR department and will be accorded much less importance by the organization as a whole.

Having decided on the media analysis parameters, we now turn to implementation. In Chapter 9 we look at some case studies in which companies have tackled the core problems of media analysis in very different ways.

9   Deciding Your Analysis Technique

In this chapter we revisit the 'Who should do it?' debate by quoting some real examples of successful analyses. The arguments for choosing a particular route are outlined and justified. One case study deals with an in-house media analysis system; another three deal with analyses carried out by external consultancies. Finally, we give an example of a communications audit in which media analysis played a prime role, and which brought benefits to the company concerned.

In Chapter 7 we reviewed some of the ways of carrying out media analysis once the measurement parameters had been established. In this chapter we examine some of these options in more detail, considering each option from the viewpoint of the organizations using them.

These real-life case studies are divided into three groups. First, we consider a successful in-house solution in which the system was designed and the process implemented entirely by the communication team itself without recourse to external help. In the second and third examples two companies using the services of a media analysis bureau are described: two of these use the bureau only; the other uses the bureau to make judgements about message delivery, then puts the data through its own systems for further analysis. In our final case study, we cross the Atlantic for an example of how media analysis can be used as a part of a successful communications audit.

All of these examples are successful applications in which the organization is obtaining genuine benefits from the system it has established. No judgements are made here about which systems work best – readers are invited to make up their own minds. As in Chapter 7, the reason for conducting the media analysis in the first place should dictate how the analysis is carried out. Some readers will inevitably find themselves attracted to solutions at the DIY end of the spectrum, while others will find the bureau options more attractive.

THE IN-HOUSE SYSTEM EXAMPLE: BR TELECOMMUNICATIONS LIMITED

British Rail Telecommunications Limited – known as BRT to people in the rail and telecommunications businesses – started gathering media coverage of its own and its potential competitors' coverage in 1990. The main competitors were BT and Mercury Communications, both of whom generated a large amount of coverage. BRT soon realized that media analysis would be necessary if it was to make the best use of the information available.

In the 1980s – before the deregulation of the rail industry and rail privatization were tabled by the British Government – telecommunications was represented by a division rather than a separate company within British Rail. Even though British Rail's telecommunications network was the second largest in Britain (second only to British Telecom's) the network was rarely talked about in the press. By 1990 however, the decision had already been taken to create a new company, operating within British Rail, to manage the network and even before its birth, journalists had begun to wonder about its future: BRT had begun to develop a media profile.

BRT's founding Managing Director, Peter Borer, was faced with the prospect of having to compete with BT and Mercury (the so called 'duopoly') for telecommunications business in the railways. And the concept of a new independent telecommunications operator, based on BRT and competing with the duopoly, was being discussed in the Department of Transport, at British Rail, in various boardrooms, and of course in the media.

Peter Borer recruited a PR professional, Amanda Kay, to look after BRT's public relations – including the company's interface with the press. She was faced with a difficult task. Her assets included the strong links Peter Borer had already forged with the press, and the high level of interest that journalists were already expressing in the fledgling company. Her liabilities included the fact that she had very little to tell the media while detailed and highly sensitive negotiations were going on with Government, other telecommunications companies and colleagues elsewhere in British Rail.

Amanda had arrived during a period of limbo – after deregulation and privatization had been decided, but before the exact structure and role of BRT had been agreed. So any plans to re-engineer the company's increasingly visible media profile had to be put on hold. While the uncertainty continued, there were of course no funds for the kind of wide-ranging PR programme which her potential competitors were able to deploy. Every press release, every interview and every answer to journalists' queries had to be carefully directed to convey a positive, optimistic but otherwise neutral profile.

These constraints did not, meanwhile, apply to BRT's competitors. So BRT started collecting media coverage of other telecommunications operators at an early stage and needed to establish how BRT's profile compared. Whatever was decided on the shape of BRT's future, Amanda and her team would need to be ready to move in the right direction – fast. Amanda decided that the media analysis would be carried out in-house, and asked placement students studying for business and marketing degrees to help her in the compilation of the reports.

Sampling In-house, with the aid of press cuttings agency Romeike & Curtice. R&C's brief was to collect all items in the national press containing the words 'BRT', 'BT', 'Mercury', or 'duopoly'. The nationals were also scanned for other companies and developments generally in the telecommunications industry.

Companies analysed BRT, BT, Mercury plus other start-up companies, such as Energis and Ionica who were targeting the deregulated telecommunications industry.

Media categories National press, telecommunications trade press, rail industry journals.

Messages BRT did not carry out a message analysis, partly because they were not ready at the time to create a strong visible profile and partly because funds were not available to carry this out independently.

Analysis Volume of coverage (number of cuttings) and BNA (beneficial/neutral/adverse).

Report format Bimonthly report contained various tables and charts (see Table 9.1 and Figures 9.1–9.3) giving volume and BNA analysis. There was a written analytical commentary distributed to the PR team, PR consultancy and BRT Board.

The report was divided into three parts. Section 1 contained an executive summary and comments on the various positive and negative stories and how they affected the profiles of the companies they related to;

Week periods beginning	BRT positive	BRT negative	BT positive	BT negative	MCL positive	MCL negative	Energis positive	Energis negative	General	TOTAL
May 1–7	1	0	0	0	1	0	2	0	7	11
8–14	0	0	0	3	0	0	1	0	10	14
15–21	0	0	0	4	0	0	0	0	6	10
22–30	2	0	0	0	1	0	9	0	5	17
June 1–7	0	0	3	0	0	0	4	0	1	8
8–14	0	0	2	7	0	0	1	0	5	15
15–21	0	0	0	2	0	0	1	0	4	7
22–30	0	0	2	0	11	0	1	0	12	26
TOTAL	3	0	7	16	13	0	19	0	50	108

Key:
BRT British Rail Telecommunications Limited; BT British Telecom; MCL Mercury

Table 9.1 Report of media coverage for BRT and its competition (May–June)

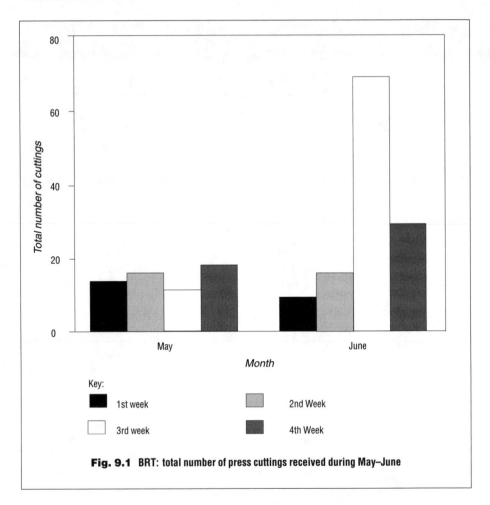

Fig. 9.1 BRT: total number of press cuttings received during May–June

Section 2 dealt with data collection; the final section was an appendix dealing with general comments on the industry.

Why this route? BRT's media analysis was intended to keep a communications team informed and in constant readiness, rather than as a control mechanism for a strongly proactive programme. The company adopted a lighter analytical approach, and with adequate in-house resources, Amanda felt it made sense to keep the operation in-house. Volumes of coverage were high, and use of external analysis would have been costly in the circumstances.

The BRT Press Report enabled the company to keep abreast of developments in the telecommunications industry, and at the same time keep management

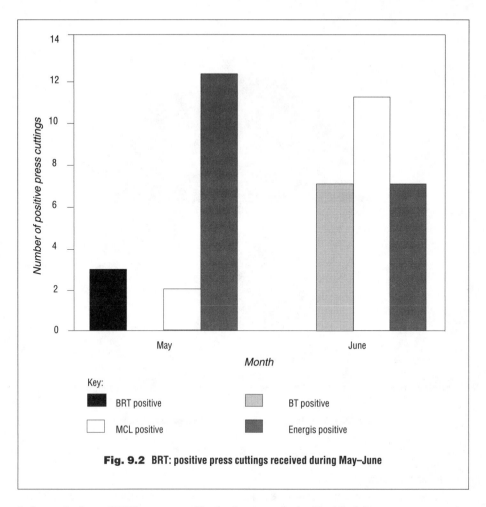

Fig. 9.2 BRT: positive press cuttings received during May–June

informed about BRT's own profile during a period of behind-the-scenes negotiation – a period when BRT needed to be reactive rather than proactive.

The reports were circulated within the company and also provided a stimulus to action in regular meetings with BRT's PR consultancy.

The future of BRT is now under less intense scrutiny than before, and its role within the telecommunications industry is much clearer to all concerned. The provision of media analysis was undoubtedly a factor which helped the company keep its media profile in a sharp perspective and helped BRT to achieve an improved profile.

EXTERNAL SUPPLIER EXAMPLE: ANGLIAN WATER

Anglian Water is one of the largest of the UK's new water companies, responsible for providing water and sewerage services to a large tract of England including parts of the Midlands, the Eastern and North Eastern home counties and the

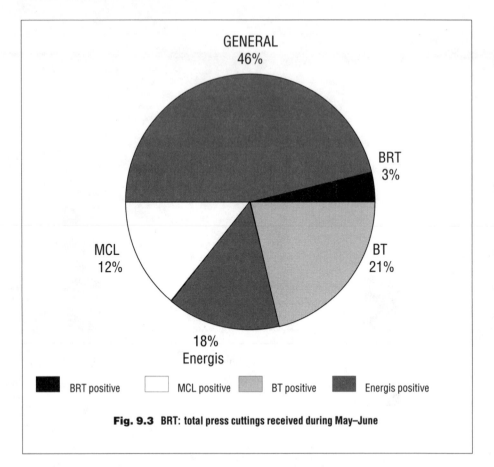

Fig. 9.3 BRT: total press cuttings received during May–June

whole of East Anglia.

The water company has a number of other interests including process industry products and services, which it sells to other process-based companies including other water companies both in the UK and across the world.

Although Anglian Water does not need to compete with other water companies in its own region, it does compete for investors' funds. However, an even more important driving force for the corporate relations team, headed by Jerry Dodd (replaced in 1994 on Jerry's retirement by Claire Mascall), was the need to communicate with customers and the local community – the people of Eastern England.

In 1992, Anglian Water's Chief Press Officer John McAngus decided he needed a rather better way of gauging the company's profile than poring over more than a hundred press cuttings which the company was receiving each week: he simply didn't have time to do this as thoroughly as he'd have liked. After attending a briefing about media analysis given by the author, he identified the parameters he needed to control and later in the same year the media analysis programme, using the IMPACT service, was started.

Sampling   Press cuttings are supplied by the International Press Cuttings Bureau, transcripts from radio and television by Tellex Monitors. Anglian Water produces a daily collage of water industry coverage and any other media-related material likely to be of interest to the board, key managers and members of the communications team. This, together with other relevant coverage, is sent to the IMPACT team for sorting. Only cuttings in the relevant media categories are selected for analysis: out-of-area local newspapers, non-target trade press and others not on the list of agreed media targets are removed; the others are sent to the evaluators for analysis.

Companies analysed   At the time of writing coverage is analysed without a comparison with another water company. As the company does not 'compete' with other water companies for provision of its main services, the need for competitive analysis was felt to be of less importance: adding another water company to the analysis would have added significantly to the cost. The idea of teaming up with one or more water companies to produce a comparative study is under consideration.

Media categories   National press, regional and local press, water trade press, local radio and regional television, process industry press.

Messages   The messages were as follows:
- Leading water company
- Excellent products and services
- Fair and accurate prices
- Invests heavily in Anglian region
- Friendly, personal service
- Well-managed company.

Analysis   Volume of coverage, namechecks and delivery of key messages, in each media sector, each quarter. The quarterly charts are in the form of a trend analysis so that the team can determine whether volumes and message delivery are improving or worsening. Figures 9.4 and 9.5 are snapshot charts showing volumes and message delivery in June 1993. Occasionally, a special analysis is carried out. For instance, when the water industry's 'K' price factors* were announced, two messages were added and a special report produced which

---

* 'K' factors are price multiples announced by the UK water regulator OFWAT which control the amount by which the water companies are allowed to raise their prices.

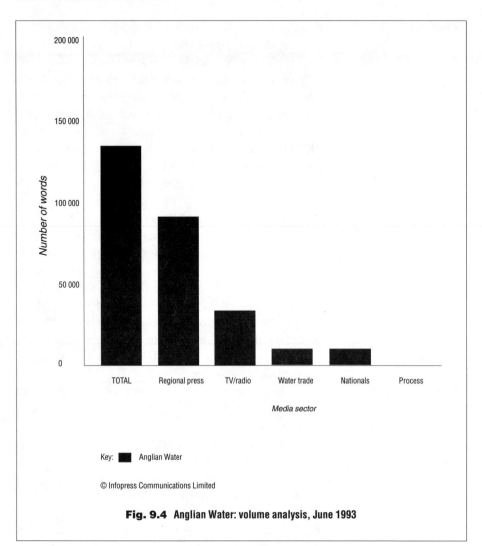

Fig. 9.4 Anglian Water: volume analysis, June 1993

looked at the announcement from a project rather than a monthly perspective.

Report format
Quarterly, three-monthly trend reports indicating volume of coverage, namechecks, and message delivery. The charts are accompanied by an analytical commentary. The company also receives six- and twelve-monthly trend reports giving an indication of performance over a longer period.

Why this route?
John McAngus felt he wanted reports which were easily understandable, but which were aligned precisely with the work actually carried out by his department. He was attracted to the idea of using independent evaluators –

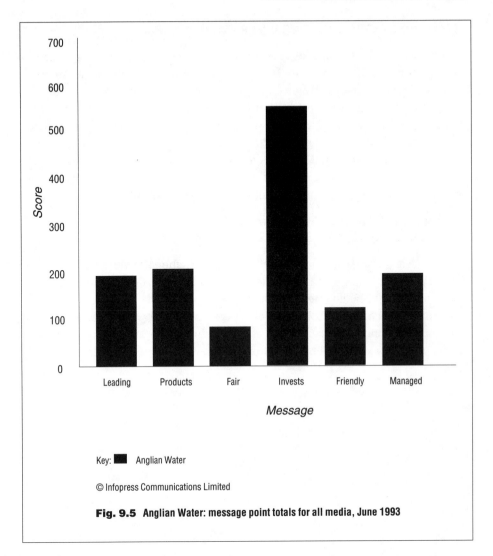

Key: ▮ Anglian Water

© Infopress Communications Limited

Fig. 9.5 Anglian Water: message point totals for all media, June 1993

one of the main factors which persuaded him to take this route. 'I need honest assessments of our media relations performance,' he said. 'When there's good news, I want to hear about it of course. And if there's bad news, I might as well have it on the chin!'

From the outset, John McAngus was very clear about the messages he needed to communicate and measure. The quarterly IMPACT reports give the board a regular measure of the communication team's success (or otherwise), and each of the charts helps him to set the communications agenda for the next few months.

DETERMINING THE CAUSES OF A GOOD PROFILE: AMEX TRS

In this case study we turn away from water and telecommunications to international travel and finance. In 1991, the communications team at American Express Travel Services (Amex TRS) wished to demonstrate to its senior UK management the value and effectiveness of the PR work which was being carried out. The public relations work was carried out by a team comprising an in-house public affairs department and their PR consultancy Hill and Knowlton.

The client wanted to find answers to two questions – questions which sound straightforward, but which required the expertise of CARMA, a media analysis bureau and consultancy, to answer fully and reliably. The questions were:

1. What kind of public profile does Amex TRS enjoy?
2. To what extent is the company's PR programme responsible for this profile?

CARMA analyses have been carried out on international coverage of Amex TRS for the past four years. Here are some of the results recorded, in the UK national press, for the year January to December 1993.

Figure 9.6 records the volume of coverage during the year, showing peaks in July and November. The CARMA analysis shows the amount of favourable, unfavourable and neutral coverage that comprise the whole. It is clear from the

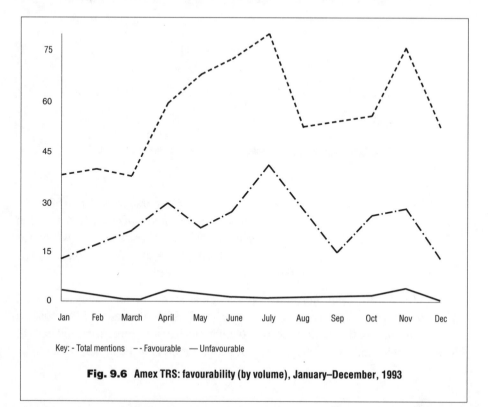

Fig. 9.6 Amex TRS: favourability (by volume), January–December, 1993

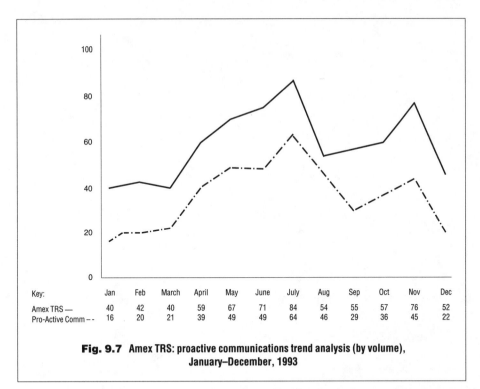

Key:	Jan	Feb	March	April	May	June	July	Aug	Sep	Oct	Nov	Dec
Amex TRS —	40	42	40	59	67	71	84	54	55	57	76	52
Pro-Active Comm – -	16	20	21	39	49	49	64	46	29	36	45	22

Fig. 9.7 Amex TRS: proactive communications trend analysis (by volume), January–December, 1993

chart that while the small amount of unfavourable coverage and the large volume of neutral coverage are reasonably stable, the volumes of favourable coverage vary considerably. There's noticeably more favourable than unfavourable coverage, and it is the favourable coverage which is creating the visibility peaks in the chart.

Figure 9.7 takes the analysis a step further by comparing the level of proactive public relations activity to the volume of favourable coverage obtained: the chart gives a clear answer to the second of the two questions posed: the level of activities (number of projects in the month) relate clearly to the volume of coverage obtained and a causal relationship between the two can be deduced. CARMA analysts looked for eight key messages (called 'leading arguments' in Figure 9.8) in the Amex TRS coverage, recording the volume of coverage in which the messages appeared and also recording the volume of coverage in which the opposite and contrary messages appeared. In all except the last message, Amex TRS is in the positive zone, indicating that strongly proactive message delivery had been obtained. This was a particularly useful chart for the communications team because while the simple BNA analysis of Figure 9.6 tells how much of the coverage is 'good' or 'bad', Figure 9.8 indicates to PR management where future effort should be directed.

Other charts – not included with this case study – include analysis and ranking of the most important journalists to the client during the year, analysis by industry

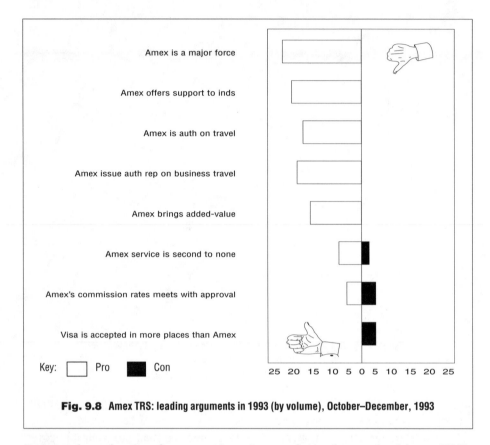

Fig. 9.8 Amex TRS: leading arguments in 1993 (by volume), October–December, 1993

issue, a chart showing the proportion of space devoted to each of Amex TRS's major competitors and a chart showing the number of impressions (the number of people exposed to the coverage).

Jane Drew is the company's Public Affairs Manager for Europe. She said at a recent conference on media analysis: 'We find the CARMA analysis useful because PR was not taken as seriously as marketing and finance. CARMA enables us to discuss communications in management terms and prove our value to the organization.'

EXTERNAL SUPPLIER EXAMPLE: ICL

ICL is a success story. Seen simply as a computer manufacturer in 1980, the company has, over the past decade transformed itself into a versatile systems and services provider with a strong European footing. As the marketplace has changed and the technology has continued to evolve at a great pace, many other British IT firms have gradually fallen by the wayside. ICL has done better than just survive – it has thrived.

ICL's ability to cope with change has probably helped to ensure both its survival and its current state of health. Originally confining itself to the mainframe computer marketplace, ICL welcomed the microprocessor revolution with open arms, and found itself better able than most to cope with the seismic changes which transformed the industry in the early 1980s.

On the corporate side, ICL has undergone a brief merger with STC. Since then, ICL shares have been sold to Fujitsu of Japan and Northern Telecom of Canada – but the company has retained its own identity and product range. On the product side, the company entered the then buoyant mid-range systems marketplace in the early 1980s, and subsequently started manufacturing PCs – all within the space of a few years. And with others merely talking about 'open systems', ICL has become an adaptable and successful systems integrator, supplying systems using the best of its own technology and that of other suppliers.

ICL has been a key supplier to central and local government for some years. The company also has a strong track record in the retail technology sector.

Media relations is an important weapon in ICL's promotional armoury. On reading a case study about media analysis in 1993, the marketing development manager Robert Goodsell approached the IMPACT team with a view to tracking corporate visibility and six key messages relative to a number of other computer suppliers.

Here are some of ICL's media analysis parameters:

Sampling	Sampling policy agreed with IMPACT but implemented by ICL. Media selected are sent to the IMPACT team on a weekly basis.
Companies analysed	ICL plus seven other companies – the world's other main computer manufacturers and computer service providers.
Media categories	UK national press, international press, selected computer trade press, selected vertical market press.
Messages	ICL's messages include a carefully chosen selection of corporate and product messages. For the purposes of this chapter, we focus on just one of these: 'ICL is a systems integrator'.
Analysis	IMPACT independent evaluators analyse the coverage for volume, namechecks, and key messages as described in the Anglian Water case study above. But the IMPACT team also compute 'message density' data (explained below) from the evaluators' scores.
Report format	Volume, namecheck charts, message charts broken down by media category plus an analytical commentary. ICL also receives a table of message density data (ICL data only) which it analyses using its own process improvement system.

The reports received are circulated within the press office and public relations team and the implications are discussed in planning meetings – not just in the UK head office but in the company's subsidiary businesses in Europe and the USA as well. But ICL also takes the IMPACT analysis several steps further.

First of all, one individual within ICL has recently been appointed the 'guardian' of each message, and this has resulted in a significant improvement in message delivery.

Second, IMPACT also generates a table of 'message density' data for the company, and ICL uses this to improve the processes within the press office. Message density is determined by taking the score totals for each message and dividing it by the number of published items received for ICL during the month. The result-

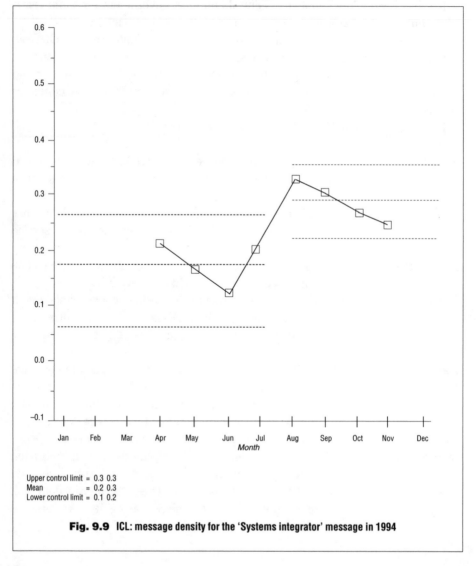

Upper control limit = 0.3 0.3
Mean = 0.2 0.3
Lower control limit = 0.1 0.2

Fig. 9.9 ICL: message density for the 'Systems integrator' message in 1994

ing message density varies for each message and for each media category depending on how successful the company has been in delivering the message in the media category concerned.

The ICL public relations team uses the IMPACT data as part of a process control mechanism. This is done by entering the message density data into a computer-based process improvement system, and the figures are charted month by month (Figure 9.9). That way, PR staff are less likely to over-react to particularly good (or particularly poor) results for a particular month: they seek instead a gradual improvement towards consistently high scores. The target message density scores have been suggested by Infopress, and are based on empirical data taken from outstandingly successful campaigns undertaken by similar companies in the past.

The ICL team use the IMPACT data – both the standard reports and their derivatives – as part of a true control mechanism, as discussed in more detail in Chapter 20.

MEDIA ANALYSIS AND THE COMMUNICATIONS AUDIT: BCBS

Fundamental changes to the healthcare industry – on both sides of the Atlantic – have swept the industry to prominence over the past few years. The UK has seen the formation of NHS Trusts and controversy over the future of the National Health Service; in the USA the Clintons' focus on healthcare during the 1992 election campaign contributed to this global upheaval.

In the USA the responsibility for healthcare insurance has shifted towards the individual, and as companies lay off workers to rehire them as freelancers and consultants, the question 'Who pays for health insurance?' has arisen as an important issue.

These factors have made healthcare very newsworthy, and in the USA they also changed the environment in which health insurance firm Blue Cross Blue Shield (BCBS) had been operating. By 1993, competition was everywhere and an insurance provider's image with the public had become much more important than a few years previously.

Hillary Clinton's new health plan and the emergence of a new competitor convinced BCBS that it was operating in hitherto uncharted territory and it called upon the services of US media analysis firm Delahaye. BCBS had become a 'healthcare company' instead of an 'insurance company' and Delahaye was asked to ascertain new strategies for communicating this concept to the company's various target audiences.

Delahaye decided to carry out a communications audit (see Chapter 8). The company needed answers to eight key questions before it could offer its client the advice it needed:

- Which audiences receive BCBS's messages?
- What are they seeing?
- What's important to them?
- How do they make their decisions?
- What do they think of BCBS?
- Where do they get their information?
- What does BCBS want them to think?
- What is needed to get them there?

Delahaye's audit strategy included an 'open' media analysis of press articles about BCBS and its new competitor, and a parallel telephone survey of selected audiences (see Chapter 19).

The media analysis was carried out first, covering 100 press articles about the two companies. The analysis was carried out by a single individual who was chosen as representative of the people currently in the market for health insurance. The articles were analysed for tone, message content and corporate visibility.

The telephone research started with decision-makers in a wide range of small to medium-sized businesses – people primarily responsible for choosing health insurance. A second round of telephone research then tackled the subscribers themselves: data was gathered from 250 anonymous conversations.

The audit found answers to all the questions. The media analysis identified the key issues, what people were talking about and what they were reading. Crucially, this stage of the audit revealed that BCBS's audiences were reading financial news about the company, but weren't learning much about actual benefit plans. In this, the competitor was proving much more successful.

The telephone survey identified an audience wish list – a list of benefits which audiences felt were of most importance. The audiences wanted a health insurance company that was easy to deal with, offering low premiums and the ability for the client to choose its own doctor. Neither the corporate clients nor the subscribers were too concerned about how innovative their health insurance company was, nor how much the company itself 'cared for the customer'. The details of BCBS's improved communications programme were beginning to emerge.

BCBS emerged from the survey as 'excellent', 'reliable' and 'accessible'. But there were negatives too. The company was seen by some as 'poor', 'cumbersome' and 'expensive'. The competitor was seen as 'innovative', 'flexible' and 'proactive'. More business decision-makers responded negatively to the BCBS name than positively.

BCBS's primary audiences received most of their opinion-forming data from magazines and newspapers and from mailshots and brochures. But they highlighted the role of a key secondary audience: insurance agents.

Delahaye's recommendations included refocusing the communications strategy on new messages and some new ways of delivering them. The new messages included the fact that BCBS was 'an easy company to do business with' and mutually consistent PR and advertising strategies were recommended. A sharper customer and product focus was suggested.

Four months after the research, the changes implemented had already begun to pay off. New subscribers had already been gained as a result of the company's new promotional efforts. But some of the most important changes were structural – three new board members with strong marketing backgrounds were already appointed and the telephone system had been replaced to help make the company – quite literally – easier to do business with.

CONCLUSION

The companies we examined above all carried out media analysis for different reasons. BRT had a watching brief and was using the analysis to interpret and comprehend developments in the rapidly changing telecommunications industry. Anglian Water needed an honest assessment of media relations performance which could be reviewed regularly to provide a stimulus for future activity. ICL had taken the media analysis data a stage further and had designed a management system around the information provided by media analysis with a view to improving message delivery and making message delivery performance more consistent. Amex TRS needed to communicate to internal audiences that the PR effort had resulted in a positive and helpful profile for the company.

These companies were seeking to deliver a variety of messages including corporate messages such as Anglian Water's 'Leading water company' message and product-related messages such as ICL's 'Systems integrator' message. They represent very different types of media relations activity.

In the next few chapters, the various types of media relations activity are described in order to see where media analysis can help. We start with corporate PR in Chapter 10.

10   Corporate Profile and the Media

After a quick reminder of the basics (messages, target audiences and target media) we develop the idea of identifying media analysis parameters from a corporate mission or vision statement. The mission statement of a leading company is analysed and an analytical strategy for this company is developed.

Twenty years ago, corporate public relations was regarded as an activity which was remote from the humdrum world of sales, marketing and community relations. Nowadays, most practitioners are involved in corporate PR: public relations people accept that everybody who speaks for the company is responsible, to an extent, for the way an organization is perceived.

To find the reason for this shift in attitude, we need venture no further than the success of large international corporations such as IBM, Glaxo and BT. They're in very different businesses, but, in common, the company name and all it stands for are managed very carefully. Sponsorships are chosen with great care, and company spokespeople are trained to treat issues in ways which will position the company in a unique as well as a broadly positive light. Financial statements and announcements of results are packed with messages about the company's activities and future plans. The opportunities presented by financial milestones are used as vehicles of delivery of key messages and help to hone the corporate profile. Corporate statements and press releases contain 'boiler plate statements' or 'motherhood clauses' in which the company's business is laid out before the reader in the precise way in which the company's corporate communicators want the company to be seen.

The days of simply achieving 'a good press' are disappearing from the public relations world as companies strive for uniqueness. The company profile is seen as a secure base on which to build product and brand reputations, and in a world which has seen three major recessions in the last 25 years, corporate stability and success are seen as a real weapon in the battle for sales and market share.

BACK TO BASICS

In Chapters 3, 4 and 5 we examined the idea of communications objectives and saw how these could be resolved into the audiences we need to address and the messages we need to deliver to them.

In Chapter 5 three broad categories of messages were aimed at – knowledge messages, opinion messages, and behavioural messages. All three categories can be deployed by PR practitioners operating within the corporate communications environment. Companies sometimes need to transmit messages like:

1. 'We export 60 per cent of our products to the Far East' (knowledge).
2. 'We do our best to keep our workforce on – even when times are tough' (opinion).
3. 'Don't sell our shares!' (behaviour).

There is a world of difference between these three messages and there is an equally wide gulf between the people intended to receive them.

The first message is designed to tell people that the company is a key exporter. It could be a useful fact to embed in the minds of MPs, of potential customers, business partners or suppliers. If the company is lobbying government or the EU for changes in environment laws, this is the kind of fact a company's PR manager will need to make sure the local MP, MEP and others are aware of.

The second, opinion message in the example is primarily directed towards potential employees, but a positive attitude towards the company's employment policy may be very useful when negotiating planning permission for a new factory site. Conversely, if a Labour councillor has just been publicly criticizing a company for laying off 200 of his constituents, he or she is going to find it hard to maintain an even-handed position when he or she makes a decision about the factory in the planning committee.

The third, behavioural message is directed squarely at shareholders. There are many ways of reaching a company's shareholders, but positive messages about keeping shares need to be transmitted via the press – both to complement direct communications, and to counteract contrary messages emanating from other sources.

ELEMENTS IN AN ANALYTICAL STRATEGY

As we have seen, communications objectives, messages and target audiences all represent pieces in the PR jigsaw which the communications director or PR manager needs to assemble. But who decides the priorities in a corporate PR programme? In many instances the messages are contradictory; the interests of the audiences are mutually opposed.

The carefully ranked priorities in a corporate communications programme need to be agreed at the highest level. Otherwise, in times of stress, different spokespeople become trapped into answering the same questions differently and perceptions of the integrity of the organization's position begin to break down. As suggested in Chapter 8, a useful starting point is to examine (or create) a mission or vision statement for the organization.

MISSION AND VISION STATEMENTS

Mission and vision statements are often the target of sneering employees, the press and others who deride the wording at best as lofty and conceptual, at worst as unnecessarily wordy and unreal.

In the UK, one national newspaper recently ran a competition designed to find the most fatuous, meaningless and insulting mission statement. Detractors of mission statements find these statements easy meat, but they have the twin virtues of embodying, in a short paragraph or two, what the company actually wants to happen and can be used by others to whip the organization into line when they stray. Here are a few examples.

A US manufacturer of ice cream, Ben and Jerry's has a product mission, a social mission and an economic mission. Its 'social mission' is to improve the quality of life of local, national and international communities. Its 'economic mission' is to make profits and create rewards for company employees.

Nurdin & Peacock, the UK cash and carry store firm, recently responded to a contraction in the UK independent retail sector by diversifying into Trade and Business Clubs. They say their mission is 'to become the UK's leading membership-based distributor of discounted consumer goods through large, low-cost sheds'.

The third example is a vision statement, and it comes from IBM, the computer company. I reproduce it here from an article written by Jack Schofield in the *Guardian*, in April 1994.

We will first examine the vision statement itself, then deduce from this the kind of messages which the company should be promoting if the PR programme is to be active in helping the company to achieve it. Next, we will deduce which target audiences are implied, and which media categories should be addressed if these are to be reached.

The mission statement and vision statement live very close to the soul of an organization – if they don't, they should do. The relationship between the vision, and the reality in the heat of a busy press office, however, is often a tenuous one and the following paragraphs should be viewed purely as an example of how the formulation of an analytical strategy can begin. It is proposed without the benefit of a detailed conversation with IBM.

EXAMPLE: IBM

According to Louis V. Gerstner Jnr, Chief Executive of IBM, IBM's vision is:

> to be the world's most successful and important information technology company. Successful in helping our customers apply technology to solve their problems. Successful in introducing this extraordinary technology to new customers. Important, because we will continue to be the basic resource of much of what is invented in this [i.e. information technology] industry.

The intended direction of this vision statement is apparent. The IBM statement, offered to a group of US analysts in 1994, was backed up by six 'strategic imperatives' indicating that IBM would achieve this and other corporate objectives by:

1. exploiting our technology far better than in the past,
2. increasing our share of the client/server market,
3. becoming a leader in the emerging network-centric world
4. re-engineering the way we deliver value to customers
5. rapidly expanding our position in key emerging geographic markets,
6. leveraging our size and scale to achieve cost and market advantages.

These words, written in the impenetrable patois of management and technological jargon that only commentators on the computer industry can really appreciate, nevertheless yield a number of pointers to what some of the corporate messages should be.

The vision statement deserves close scrutiny and a thorough analysis before deciding what IBM corporate messages should be promoted – and looked for in media coverage later.

Let's examine the vision statement phrase by phrase. The phrase:

> to be the world's most successful and important information technology company

would tempt many PR people to promote IBM as a 'successful company' and as 'an important company in the IT industry'. It could be that IBM does want to be seen as a successful and important company for the benefit of its stockholders, but that is not what the vision states. IBM wants actually to *be* a successful and important company and is very specific about the nature of this success.

It is the second phrase of the vision statement,

> Successful in helping our customers apply technology to solve their problems.

which tells us what the first three of the messages should be. They are a general industry message and two corporate messages:

Suggested IBM messages

1. Business problems can be solved using information technology.
2. IBM is expert in the application of information technology, and
3. IBM helps its customers to solve their problems.

If IBM really believes that it will achieve its 'success' goal through helping customers apply technology to solve problems, then it must tell its customers that it is a provider of this help, and that it has the expertise to be able to offer this help. Simply promoting IBM as 'successful' and 'important' may achieve other corporate objectives, but won't help the company achieve its mission!

The third phrase fills in the picture further:

Successful in introducing this extraordinary technology to new customers.

This phrase approaches the borderline between corporate communications and marketing communications and has strong sales significance.

Successful delivery of our second message will go part of the way towards achieving this part of the vision. To achieve it fully, we will need to assemble an array of product and brand benefits, and embed them in a series of product messages directed specifically at the 'new customers' to which the vision statement refers. There are indications in 'strategic imperative' 5 that some of these new customers are in 'emerging geographic markets'. A more in-depth discussion of the product and marketing area is provided in Chapter 11.

The final phrase in the vision statement is:

Important, because we will continue to be the basic resource of much of what is invented in this industry.

This phrase means that IBM needs to continue to invent new information technology, and to fund new information technology invention. Again it is tempting to read into the vision statement a desire by IBM to be seen as an inventive company. But again, the statement tells us that IBM wants to *be* the basic resource behind invention in the IT industry rather than simply being seen corporately as an inventor.

Extracting corporate messages from this part of the vision statement needs a further layer of interpretation of how the vision can be achieved – ideally in direct consultation with the visionaries within the company. To continue as an inventive force, IBM needs to retain existing engineers and scientists who have been responsible for earlier inventions, and perhaps attract new ones. It needs to make profits to continue to make R&D funds available, and it needs the technical and financial resources, and the culture which makes invention a natural corporate function. Once in place, the technical resources need to be promoted and the cultural environment needs encouragement (internally) and promotion (externally). Existing employees and suppliers also need to be told that the future of the IT industry depends, at least partly, on them.

Corporate communications can help achieve these secondary 'invention' goals. To achieve them, IBM must promote itself as a good employer, both internally and externally, to key technical groups. Achievement of the profit goal can be helped through sales programmes (see Chapter 11) and internal communications programmes. And the resources and culture can be promoted as part of the external corporate communications programme. Here are the final, very specific messages which we can deduce from Mr Gerstner's vision:

Suggested IBM messages (continued)

4. IBM is an excellent employer.
5. IBM has the technical resources for inventors of IT products, systems and components.
6. IBM has the financial resources to fund future IT products, systems and components.
7. There is a strong invention culture within IBM's laboratories and plant.
8. The future of the IT industry will depend on your inventiveness (that is, that of IBM employees and suppliers).

Selecting messages for a corporate communications programme needs interpretive and consultative skills – and the liberal use of a red pen. On close inspection, many obvious messages like 'successful company' and 'quality products' do not contribute anything towards achieving the company's corporate objectives and should be eliminated from the analytical process. And it's only after careful consideration that some of the most important messages become apparent.

So here is the complete list of messages which we have deduced from the IBM vision:

Suggested IBM messages

1. Business problems can be solved using information technology. ('IT')
2. IBM is expert in the application of information technology. ('expert')
3. IBM helps its customers to solve their problems. ('solution')
4. IBM is an excellent employer. ('employer')
5. IBM has the technical resources for inventors of IT products, systems and components. ('technical resources')
6. IBM has the financial resources to fund future IT products, systems and components. ('financial resources')
7. There is a strong invention culture within IBM's laboratories and plant. ('culture')
8. The future of the IT industry will depend on your inventiveness. ('inventiveness')

What can we derive from the vision statement about IBM's audiences and the media they read? The following is a list of people the messages would need to be directed towards if the objectives underlying the vision statement are to be met:

1. People in business – senior management
2. People in business – line managers
3. Management consultants and IT consultants

4. Existing customers
5. Potential and existing employees
6. Key technical people, scientists, engineers and systems people within IBM and in other companies
7. Key opinion formers within the IT industry
8. Stockholders

Not all the messages are relevant to all the audience categories, as Table 10.1 illustrates.

Key audiences	Key messages							
	IT	Expert	Solution	Employer	Technical resources	Financial resources	Culture	Inventiveness
Senior management	X	X	X	–	X	X	X	–
Line managers	–	X	X	–	X	–	X	–
Consultants	–	X	X	–	X	X	X	–
Customers	X	–	X	–	–	–	–	–
Employees	–	–	X	X	–	–	X	–
Key technical	–	–	X	X	X	X	X	X
Opinion formers	X	X	X	–	X	X	X	–
Stockholders	X	X	X	–	X	X	–	–

Table 10.1 Relevance of IBM's key messages to its key organizations

Research – and some common sense – is available to guide us on the preferred reading matter of each of the above audiences:

Senior management Broadsheet national newspapers, vertical market press, selected television and radio programmes, international business journals.

Line managers Broadsheet and tabloid national newspapers, vertical market press, selected television and radio programmes, regional newspapers, management journals.

Consultants Broadsheet national newspapers, vertical market press, selected television and radio programmes, computer media, management journals.

Customers IBM's own customer newsletters, vertical market press, computer media, broadsheet and tabloid national newspapers, selected television and radio programmes.

Employees IBM's own staff newspapers, computer media, regional newspapers, broadsheet and tabloid national newspapers, selected television and radio programmes.

Key technical Scientific and heavy technical journals, computer media, broadsheet and tabloid national newspapers, selected television and radio programmes.

107

Opinion formers	Broadsheet national newspapers, selected television and radio programmes, computer media, international business journals.
Stockholders	IBM's annual report, financial press, stockbrokers' circulars, broadsheet and tabloid national newspapers, selected television and radio programmes, international business journals.

To reach its goal as stated in its vision statement, IBM should be proactively seeking to deliver its key messages via the folowing ten media categories:

- National broadsheet press
- National tabloid press
- Selected radio and television programmes
- Vertical market press
- Regional press
- International business journals
- Management magazines
- Computer media
- Scientific and heavy technical journals
- Financial press

If IBM is going to use media relations techniques to move closer to its vision, it is these media categories which the company should analyse for volume of coverage, corporate visibility, and for delivery of the key messages identified.

As will have been noted, there is also a strong case to be made for analysing the company's own publications together with stockbrokers' circulars to ensure that the messages are present in strength there.

To carry it out will be a straightforward task using conventional techniques. If the analysis establishes that the messages are not getting through in some of the media categories, it means that the audiences aren't receiving them, at least by the routes we have identified.

This in turn may mean that the corporate goals as stated in the vision are saying just that – a vision on the horizon, and a too-distant reality. It will be interesting to observe how close IBM gets to its vision as the end of the millenium approaches.

CONCLUSION

Early in the IBM case study, we stressed that part of the company's vision was dependent on sales, and promoting strong brand, marketing and product messages to the company's potential customers. There is only a slim and ill-defined dividing line between corporate and sales PR activity, but we will nevertheless have to cross that line as we explore the sales and marketing area in Chapter 11.

11 Analysing Coverage of Products, Services and Brands

The role of media analysis is especially important in promoting products, services and brands. Here we introduce the concept of competitive analysis, and the idea of comparing one company's profile with another. The idea of one company out-communicating another is outlined.

I was discussing a media analysis assignment recently with the public affairs director of a UK bank. We had agreed the messages he wanted to communicate, and he was very specific about the target audiences he was trying to reach with those messages.

The target audience was teenagers and young adults, and he was keen to present his bank's offerings to this group as attractively as possible. I recommended that he should analyse the coverage he was generating alongside some other, similar coverage, perhaps from another bank or building society. He was horrified at the idea. 'No, if I compare our products with anything, it will be with a big name brand like Coca-Cola or Nike. Banks are inherently boring to young people, and I don't see the point of any comparison with them!'

The banker's comment raised some very fundamental questions about media analysis. What is the point of comparing your coverage with someone else's? And if you're going to compare, should you compare because you want to find out how the opposition's PR programme is going – or because you need a realistic benchmark against which you can measure your own organization's progress?

Let's deal with the first question first. There is always a point in carrying out a comparative analysis, even for organizations offering a unique product or service, but there are more pressing reasons for comparison if you are operating in a fiercely competitive marketplace.

A regional water authority or electricity company can expect to gain a great deal of media coverage in its area of operation. There are compelling reasons for analysing this as a basic control mechanism forming part of the PR process. There are also reasons for comparisons with other utilities: utilities have shareholders, and these investors are found outside the borders of the companies' areas of operation: the utility shares the national press with other utilities, and investors will be exposed to other companies' messages therein.

A motor manufacturer, on the other hand, shares all its target media with its competitors. Renault's PR team will be very much aware that its audiences are receiving Fiat's messages at the same time as they are reading Renault's own. If Fiat is generating more positive messages in the media about excellence of product, reliability and style than Renault is, then the Renault team will need to redress the balance – fast.

That brings us to our second question. Comparative media analysis can yield valuable information about competitors, and can also provide a benchmark against which an organization can judge success in communicating messages: a banker can indeed collect valuable information by comparing his or her coverage with a cola company or a trainer manufacturer. But this chapter is mainly about products, services and brands in the media and concentrates primarily on the problem exemplified by the automotive manufacturer fighting for positive coverage in crowded media sectors.

THE BRAND VISIBILITY CONUNDRUM

I'd like to return briefly to the question we raised in Chapter 2: does a brand create its own media profile or does the media profile create the brand? The answer will depend on the perspective of the person answering. The marketing professional will view the media as an influencer; the consumer will regard the media as a source of information. It's a question that not many TV viewers or newspaper readers will even consider. As far as most beer drinkers are concerned, for instance, an article about beer mentioning Budweiser is unlikely to send them straight to the nearest bar to drink some. It will, however, add to or subtract from the collection of words which the readers hold in their mind next to the word Budweiser: this in turn may affect their beer buying habits at some stage.

Images of big brands are created, promoted and maintained with great care. And press relations is an essential tool for their launch, promotion and upkeep. Brands launched by direct mail and advertising only will eventually develop a media profile of a kind, but it will be a twisted, stunted and uncontrolled profile which at best will be useless, at worst harmful to the brand's future. Leaving journalists to write their own coverage of a product without offering information on the product invites that journalist to make ill-informed judgements and comments.

Press relations is therefore an essential element in any company's brand management strategy and just as the marketeer wouldn't dream of forgetting to track the success of a multi-million pound advertising campaign, it makes sense to keep tabs on the success of the PR programme as well.

The trouble is, many marketeers are too easily satisfied. A beneficial/neutral/ adverse (BNA) analysis – a technique commonly used by brand managers – will tell the marketeer if there is a severe problem with the brand profile but it will do little else. Successful brands tend to have a far sharper character and a far deeper infrastructure than the good/don't-care/bad consumer opinion which this type of analysis reflects. Avis's famous and successful 'We try harder' campaign of some years ago would have been much less successful if Avis had simply told us 'We're better'. And analysing media coverage of Volvo cars to see if the good coverage outweighs the bad won't tell us if the 'You're safer in a Volvo!' message is coming through, or if the company has been successful in combating the 'boring' image.

COMPETITORS AND MESSAGES

There is every reason therefore to track a brand's media profile against a template of characteristics and virtues which together are the brand image. But how can we use this type of analysis to track media relations success relative to competitors?

Let's say a company called Promofiz launches a new health drink called Get-up-and-go. Promofiz is building a brand profile for Get-up-and-go which comprises the following elements:

Get-up-and-go gives you essential vitamins and nutrients.
Get-up-and-go is low in calories.
Get-up-and-go is used by leading athletes.

There is an existing health drink – Zoom – on the market, of course, and while Zoom is positioned rather differently, there is a considerable overlap in the target markets for the two products. The manufacturer of Zoom is trying to tell potential consumers that:

Zoom gives you essential vitamins and nutrients.
Zoom is good value for money.
Zoom is delicious.

It's clear what Promofiz must do. The company needs to analyse coverage of both brands, and look for all five of the messages we have listed above (the first in each group is shared). In analysing the coverage, the evaluator should therefore analyse all the coverage for:

1. XXX gives you essential vitamins and nutrients ('vitamins').
2. XXX is low in calories. ('calories')
3. XXX is used by leading athletes. ('athletes')
4. XXX is good value for money. ('value')
5. XXX is delicious. ('taste')

where XXX can be either brand. The words in brackets are the short forms of the messages. Figure 11.1 is a volume analysis chart comparing coverage of Get-up

111

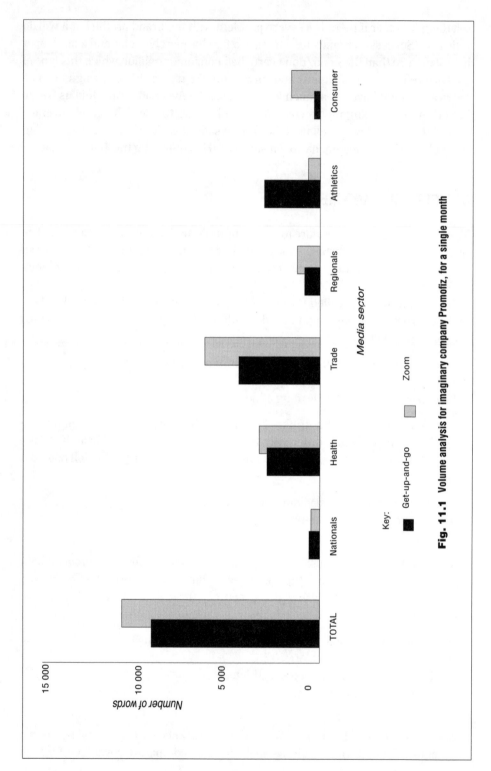

Fig. 11.1 Volume analysis for imaginary company Promofiz, for a single month

and-go with its competitor Zoom in various media sectors. The chart contains mixed news for Promofiz. While the new brand is holding its own in the national press and the health sectors, it is behind Zoom in the key consumer and trade press. Get-up-and-go has, however, succeeded in dominating coverage in the athletics press, which is important in the delivery of its 'athletes' message.

Figure 11.2, illustrating the message delivery chart for all media sectors, again offers a mixed picture to Promofiz. Delivery of all messages is positive, and it is clear from the chart that Get-up-and-go is out-communicating the more established brand in the 'athletes' and 'vitamins' messages – but it is behind Zoom in the others. On one of the Get-up-and-go key messages – 'calories' – however, the competing brand is in the lead, and Get-up-and-go is making little headway against Zoom on Zoom's own messages of 'taste' and 'value'.

The analysis will yield two important pieces of information.

1. It will tell Promofiz how Get-up-and-go's own brand elements are standing up in the media profile, and whether the manufacturers of Zoom are managing to encroach on Get-up-and-go's declared territory (messages 1–3).
2. It will inform Promofiz how Get-up-and-go is coping with the value and taste messages, Zoom's declared territory. The real battleground of course will be on the vitamins and nutrients message, shared by both brands, and should be monitored closely.

COMPETITORS' MEDIA STRATEGIES

A competitor's whole marketing strategy might well be different from your own, and this may require a different analytical approach for the evaluator.

When Clive Sinclair announced his popular and successful range of home computers in the early 1980s, the initial advertising and PR effort was through the consumer press. A competitor analysing the computer press and national broadsheets alone would have been lulled into a false sense of security by the results. It's paramount to gain a good understanding of the competitor's marketing strategy before deciding on the parameters of any comparative media analysis.

ANALYSIS BY SOURCE

Analysis of the media coverage by media category and message delivery can give the marketeer valuable information both on which messages are getting across and to whom, and on how the competition is performing. It will not determine how PR success (or otherwise) was achieved.

This can be done by source analysis – examining coverage for PR technique employed, or where the coverage arose from in the first place. It involves tracking all the different ways coverage was achieved – whether via a press release, an

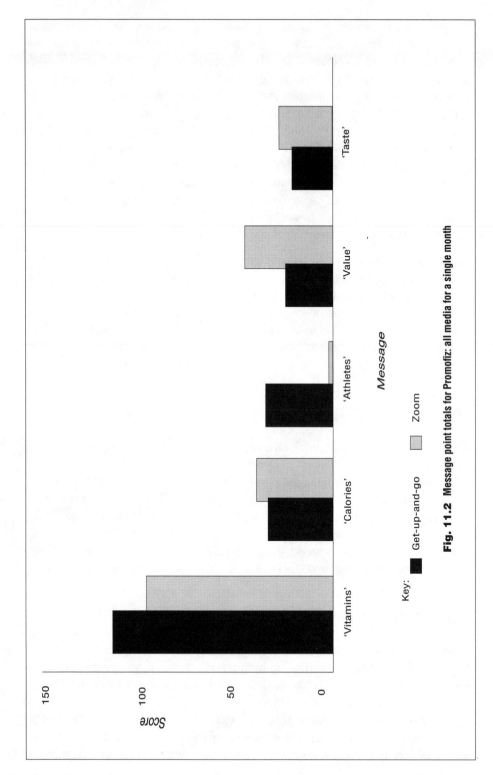

Fig. 11.2 Message point totals for Promofiz: all media for a single month

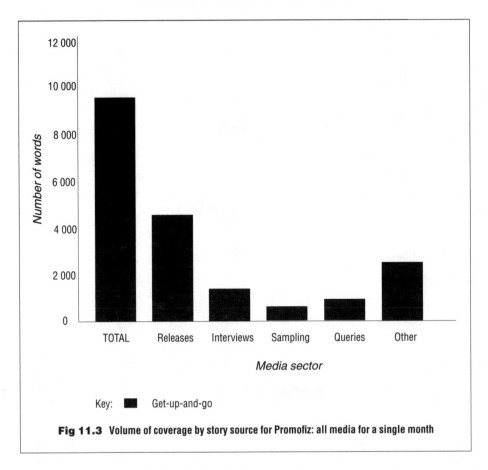

Fig 11.3 Volume of coverage by story source for Promofiz: all media for a single month

interview, an answer to a journalist's telephone call or the company's response to a feature opportunity. Using source analysis, the public relations team can learn to maximize message delivery effectiveness, stepping up efforts on the type of projects which deliver the messages and reach the audiences, placing less emphasis on those which don't.

The PR team isn't usually in the position of knowing how competitors' messages were deployed. Without resorting to industrial espionage, it's going to be impossible for them to find out. But the techniques which work for your company can be determined with ease.

As well as tracking by media category, analyse all the coverage by source. This will mean tracking the source – an action by the PR team. Don't expect an evaluation agency to do it for you because they won't know the answers.

Figures 11.3 and 11.4 show how Promofiz might analyse its own coverage to maximize its message delivery potential. Figure 11.3 shows a breakdown of the coverage of Get-up-and-go in terms of how the story originated. No comparison with the competition is available, unfortunately, because only the competing brand's press office would have been able to supply it. It is clear that about half of

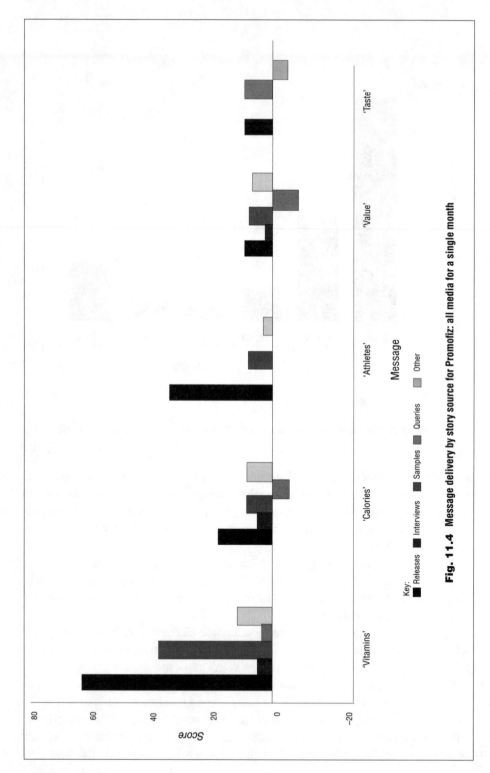

Fig. 11.4 Message delivery by story source for Promofiz: all media for a single month

the coverage has emanated from news releases, with the rest divided between other methods of communication. The relatively high proportion of 'other' coverage is worrying: presumably the press office don't know how the coverage originated.

Figure 11.4 illustrates how it is possible to determine how the various press relations activities have contributed to successful delivery of the messages. News releases have, in the main, been successful. The two interviews given by a brand spokesperson, however, have done virtually nothing of value in promoting the brand. Queries from journalists have actually resulted in negative coverage on three of the messages. If this pattern is regularly repeated, the brand's PR manager will need media training for his or her spokespeople, and some emergency measures will be required for press officers dealing with journalists' queries.

ANALYSIS BY ARTICLE TYPE

We may not be able to determine what percentage of the competitors' message-laden coverage came from press releases, but we will be able to tell what part of the publication they appeared in, or which TV programme they were featured in. Careful analysis of article type can help the PR team to make important decisions affecting the whole press relations strategy which should be adopted if message delivery is to be maximized. Figures 11.5 and 11.6 demonstrate message analysis carried out by article type rather than by media sector or article source. It is apparent that while the new Promofiz brand has done well in grabbing the news headlines, the message content was thin – and more importantly, Get-up-and-go coverage in round-up articles has been poor (Figure 11.5). In contrast, Zoom's coverage has been evenly spread across different article types giving a more even profile. Zoom has failed to achieve (or decided to ignore) delivery of the 'athletes' message (Figure 11.6).

The company (and not necessarily the PR manager) must decide why Promofiz's new product is getting negative scores for 'value' and 'taste' in round-up articles. What can be done to reverse the trend?

POLICING THE BRAND IMAGE

It is the job of the PR team to police the image of their company's products and brands in the media. Media coverage should be regarded as a densely wooded Northern border, through which hordes of enemies may pour at any moment. This boundary needs expert surveillance and intelligence.

Analysing media coverage of a prominent household-name consumer brand against the competition can be time-consuming and expensive, but the information which such an analysis can yield will quickly demonstrate where extra troops are needed and where ammunition is running low.

117

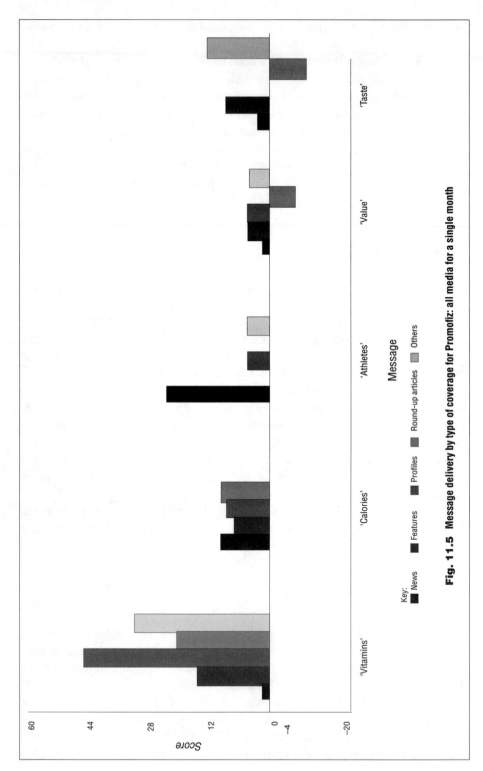

Fig. 11.5 Message delivery by type of coverage for Promofiz: all media for a single month

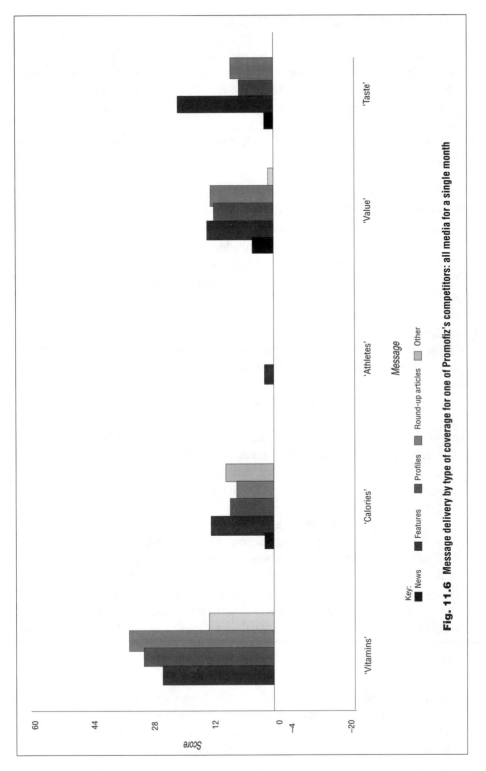

Fig. 11.6 Message delivery by type of coverage for one of Promofiz's competitors: all media for a single month

THE BUSINESS-TO-BUSINESS ARENA

Many of the measurement techniques used in the promotion of consumer brands can also be employed in the business-to-business arena. Here, the manufacturer may not have a big-name brand to promote and protect, but he or she still has a valuable opportunity to use the trade and vertical market press to promote products.

While the national distributor of a cola company is thinking up ways of using the press to hone and refine a single carefully integrated brand image, the manufacturer of a lubrication pump will be planning the next product launch. Like the company responsible for the distribution and promotion of the big brand, the pump manufacturer probably has a collection of generic messages (for example, 'our pumps are reliable'), but the most important messages to get across will be those which are associated with a particular product in an evolving marketplace.

The pump manufacturer won't often achieve coverage of his or her products in the pages of the national press and there will be few opportunities for radio and television coverage, but the company can expect product announcements, reviews, application stories and features in the trade press. There will also be opportunities to penetrate customers' trade (vertical market) press. But while cuttings associated with the big brands will probably be measurable in hundreds per week, the pump manufacturer may be fortunate to amass 10 cuttings per month.

Here the measurement process can get more complex with the range of messages encompassing product messages ('Pump XXX has been approved for use in the food industry'), generic messages ('Type X pumps are reliable'), and even corporate messages ('We are a successful company'). Again, competitive products should be monitored, and once more, some intelligent guesswork may need to be employed to make sure that you are outcommunicating the competition rather than the reverse.

Over-complex media monitoring and analysis should be avoided in circumstances where volumes of coverage are very low: a single article may well be a good result for an article about pumps in a vertical magazine such as an offshore oil title. It is likely that a programme generating only a few cuttings per month merits only a three-monthly analysis of coverage – otherwise the charts can look very spiky with individual articles and news items making the difference between success and failure. Many trade journals are monthly or quarterly, and a component supplier simply won't penetrate every vertical title in the target sector every time it is published.

If it's felt that there really must be a monthly report even where the volume of coverage is small, I would advise charts showing three-month rolling averages rather than the actual coverage in a month. Overreaction to charts showing very optimistic or very pessimistic results is easy and so a three-month average helps to smooth the data – and ruffled feathers as well!

Calculating target audience readership in the business-to-business sector can range from the impossible to a nightmare. A pump manufacturer will be rightly keen to promote pumps to the chemicals industry, the process industry, the gas industry and the food industry – but just try and calculate the numbers of readers with authority to buy and specify pumps from data supplied by the publishers of the trade publications in each of these industries. The analyst is better advised to analyse message delivery and volumes, and leave it at that. A comparison with sales and enquiry figures will give better quality data than poring over piles of advertising data.

CONCLUSION

In the last two chapters the specific problems of measuring message content generated in the course of corporate and marketing orientated PR programmes was discussed. In the next chapter we look at coverage in which there may be no specific message content at all.

Think of the last arts or sporting event you read about in the newspaper. Perhaps it was sponsored by an insurance firm or a tobacco company. Did the article tell you anything about the sponsoring company? Probably not. Did you find yourself wanting one of the brand of cigarette mentioned in the hoardings glimpsed in the photograph accompanying the article? Unlikely. So why do people sponsor anything – and how on earth can we use media analysis to tell us if it is all worth it? I'll try and supply some of the answers in the next chapter.

12 Media Analysis and Sponsorship

Sponsorship poses very different problems to the media analyst than the problems of corporate and marketing communications. This chapter introduces the idea of 'lifestyle values', with an example from a sports sponsorship.

The sponsorship of sports and arts events is usually associated with active promotion in the media. In the case of sports, this often results in huge volumes of coverage in newspapers, television and radio.

Sponsorship coverage poses problems for media analysts, however, and this chapter is intended to help those involved in sponsorship who wish to interpret the significance of the results they have achieved – or hope to achieve. Media analysis can also be used to help the would-be sponsor to select a suitable sponsorship project.

WHY SPONSOR?

The range of sponsorship options is enormous, and companies sponsor charities, campaigns, people, events and programmes for all kinds of different reasons.

Sometimes a company simply wants its name to be better known: the company's executives know that a certain event will be reported fully in the media, and it wants a share of that coverage. On other occasions a company wants to 'buy' a prestigious event or support a high-profile campaign because it wants to be associated with the values and the ideas that it represents. Occasionally, a company will use an event simply as a vehicle for corporate entertainment.

In some circumstances, a sponsored event can be considerably more focused. For instance, a supplier sponsoring an industry conference, as well as having its name featured prominently on the programme, may well be invited to erect a small exhibition stand in the foyer of the conference and can expect to generate sales leads as a side benefit.

These days, sponsorship opportunities are appearing with increasing frequency on television. The weather forecast is, increasingly, 'brought to us' by an electricity supplier; popular television series are sponsored by drinks companies. So-called 'infomercials' on the cable and satellite shopping channels take the idea a step further with the company's sales message becoming the main substance of the programme.

SPONSORSHIP BY OBJECTIVES

This book is not intended as a textbook on sponsorship. But it is worth examining the reasons for setting out on a sponsorship programme in the first place. Here, first, are some bad ones.

At the time of writing the 'Chairman's whim' syndrome is still rife. Although the sponsorship team may be able to give a cogent set of reasons for a particular sponsorship, the real reason for sponsorship is sometimes because senior executives are involved in the sport, the art form – or indeed the individual – at a personal level. It's no accident that golf tournaments are rarely short of prime sponsors, and chairpeople's children on the fringes of sporting stardom are seldom seen with begging bowls.

A decision to develop sponsorship to 'get the name around' is usually misguided. A namecheck by itself does little for an organization without some mechanism in place to tell the visitor, reader, listener or viewer what the company does apart from sponsor the event in question. If household-name status is suddenly required, it's usually because there has been a radical change of management style, and the lack of visibility is usually because conventional PR has been neglected: sponsorship is rarely a complete solution.

A much better reason to sponsor is to reinforce, improve or correct a public perception of a company or organization. To take two extreme examples, if a company is seen as a stuffy, conservative group, it may choose to sponsor an event such as a hang-gliding championship or an all-in wrestling contest; a waste management company heading for the stockmarket and worrying about its credibility might consider sponsoring an exhibition of an impressionist painter's work or a concert tour. The decision to sponsor something or someone may have been taken to correct a problem – a problem which has been highlighted, perhaps, in a media analysis report.

MESSAGE DELIVERY BY SPONSORSHIP

By dissecting an example of each of the sponsorship types we have touched on above, it will be clear that the analytical guidelines concerning messages, which we have outlined in the preceding chapters, do not really apply.

In the summer of 1994, the Irish company Waterford Crystal sponsored the

Women's World Hockey Cup for the eighth time. In a typical 700-word article in the *Observer* on 10 July, there is a single reference to the sponsor in the opening paragraph:

> The best prepared and fittest England women's hockey squad to leave our shores arrive in Dublin today for the eighth Waterford Crystal Women's World Cup, which starts on Wednesday in the new stadium at Belfield – but they will have a tough struggle to get amongst the medals.

In the same issue, a 500-word article appeared about the English Schools athletics championship, sponsored by TSB, a UK bank. Again the sponsor merits a single, first-paragraph mention:

> For most of the youngsters here, the TSB English schools championships are the closest they will ever get to sampling the Olympic atmosphere.

The *Observer* may well be on TSB's and Waterford Crystal's lists of target media, but is this coverage putting a particular message across about either company? It is hard to imagine any messages that items like these are communicating to us – directly – about either company. They say nothing – directly – about either company's success, the excellence of their products and services or the extent to which they are responsible citizens or good employers.

The media coverage associated with sponsorship of sporting events is successful for the sponsor only because of the peculiar working of the human brain. When we go into a shop to buy a gift for a friend we may start thinking 'Aren't those the folk who sponsored the hockey?' And because TSB helped to fund the English Schools championships, we might just be inclined towards the bank next time we have a row with NatWest over a bounced cheque.

In Chapter 3 we mentioned semiotics, and in particular the difference between the 'denotation' (absolute, dictionary meaning of a word or phrase) and 'connotation' (the subjective meaning implied by a word or phrase, filtered through the reader's knowledge, prejudices and opinions). If sponsorship media coverage is good news for the sponsor it's usually because of these associations and connotations. The media coverage of sponsored events works because it grabs the attention of a part of our brain where we don't usually store information about the company, and because we change our knowledge and opinions of that company as a result.

EXAMPLE: FOSTER'S LAGER AND RUGBY LEAGUE

To see how associative messages are delivered in practice a recent example from the brewing industry is given here.

Foster's Brewing Group owns the UK brewer Courage, and Foster's lager is brewed by Courage in the UK. In 1991, Courage and Foster's sponsored the Rugby League World Club Challenge and promoted the Foster's brand alongside the event. As a result, a good deal of the coverage of the event was associated with the Foster's name, and this ranged from national press (both tabloids and broadsheets) and specialist sporting press. There was coverage in the specialist licensed trade press as well but this was not analysed in this exercise. There was also some television coverage of the Cup in the UK and in Australia.

I asked a group of 40 undergraduates from Portsmouth University's Marketing and Strategic Management Department to examine the coverage. Nearly all the coverage they examined was of the type highlighted in the hockey and athletics examples above: that is, a single mention of the Foster's name in association with the event.

There were no brewing messages in the coverage. Similarly, there were no corporate messages coming through in the copy either. The fact that Courage chose to link the Rugby Championship specifically with the Foster's brand name prevented Courage from having any association with the event at all: not many people outside the brewing industry, I suspect, even know of Courage's links with Foster's. The sponsorship team at Courage told me that they were attempting to communicate three associative messages in the coverage. They were:

Foster's is associated with enjoyment.
Foster's is associated with relaxation.
Foster's is international.

Each student was asked to examine one item of coverage, and score the item for each associative message with +10 representing the maximum score, and −10 representing the minimum (worst) score, zero being neutral.

Analysis by the students indicated that the coverage was highly successful. The average scores per item awarded by the students were as follows:

'Enjoyment'   7.2
'Relaxation'   2.5
'International'   5.3

In a discussion between the students after they had completed the exercise, they indicated that the style of the coverage and the subject matter itself communicated a feeling of enjoyment which was the reason for the particularly high 'enjoyment' score.

The 'relaxation' message caused a few problems for the students and there was a huge range of scores. Some of the students thought of Rugby League as a sport that you played; others thought of it as purely a spectator sport. The 'players' tended to give a minus score for relaxation, while the 'spectators' thought of a relaxing Saturday afternoon watching from the terraces – and scored their item positively. The spectators were in the majority, and the overall score average was still strongly positive.

The fact that Foster's is an international brand was not spelt out in many of the items the students examined. However, the strongly international nature of the event became associated with the brand as a result of the coverage, and this was communicated to the students – hence their high score of 5.3.

As a side exercise, I also asked the students to score the coverage for one further associative message. This was the message 'Foster's is a patron of the arts' – definitely not one of the Foster's messages! The students' scores varied between a neutral zero and large minus scores, giving an overall average of –2.8. In this sponsorship, Foster's weren't trying to become associated with arts patronage, or lay claim to any intellectual high ground. The score is unsurprising.

It's important to note that the communications programme surrounding a major sponsorship such as a Cup competition or an arts event can be highly complex involving advertising, printed material, posters, programmes and other devices and methods. Media relations is likely to form only a small part of the overall programme, and judging success on the basis of media analysis alone is risky.

However the Portsmouth exercise shows how the choice of a sponsorship event can, through media relations, change the way an organization can be perceived. Many of the messages entering our minds about companies are these associative messages – which in turn help to produce the connotations we associate with an organization or brand. How the transmission of these messages benefits the brand can be measured by direct communication with audiences, and takes the sponsorship into the realms of market research.

CHOOSING AN EVENT TO SPONSOR

One of the big decisions a potential sponsor has to decide before reaching for his or her cheque book is to decide at what level to get involved.

Every large corporation is bombarded daily with sponsorship 'opportunities' ranging from the sponsorship of the Football Association Cup costing millions of pounds to the sponsorship of an annual programme to help support a rookie Formula 3 racing driver – costing £5 000.

Media analysis can help to guide organizations towards the right decision. Looked at from the perspective of media analysis, backing an event is relatively expensive but safe; backing people can be lower cost but much more risky.

An event with a track record going back several years will have generated coverage in the media, and there will be a rich history of the event to explore for potential message delivery potential. Most event managers keep a cuttings file. Promotion based on AVEs ('This coverage was worth £3 million') should be ignored. But it is worth carrying out an analysis for the associative messages important to your company.

An individual competitor or artist on the other hand will create news only through an innate talent or strength. A competitor may succeed beyond his or her (or the sponsor's) wildest dreams; he or she may be overtaken by those with more talent, may succumb to injury; may fail a drugs test. In competitive sport and in the arts and other fields there can of course be no guarantee of success.

How can a sponsor capitalize on a sponsorship of a not-so-successful individual through the media? The competitor's own regional press may mention the local hero's sponsor occasionally, but a person who comes seventh doesn't usually make much of an impression in the national media unless that person was expected to do better: under these circumstances the sponsor becomes associated with, well ... failure. Support for a potential winner who may rapidly become an also-ran should be regarded as patronage rather than sponsorship, and if they are to be granted support, there should be other, better, reasons than any media coverage that that person may be expected to generate.

A MEDIA ANALYSIS POLICY FOR SPONSORSHIP COVERAGE

Coverage of sponsorship coverage is well worth analysing, but the analyst must take care to distinguish sponsorship coverage from the rest of the coverage.

Analyse any bundle of newspaper cuttings dealing with a large corporation, and some coverage will be the results of direct product and corporate PR. If the PR has been effective, the cuttings will be rich in marketing and corporate messages. The balance of the coverage may contain cuttings dealing with the company's sponsorship and patronage activities – which probably won't.

It's worth dealing with these sponsorship items separately. The objectives of the sponsorship programme will complement rather than replicate the objectives of the PR programme, and it is worth finding out what these are and agreeing with the sponsor the associative messages which the company is attempting to communicate.

The other aspects of the media analysis are as indicated in previous chapters. The question: 'Who are we trying to reach?', is of paramount importance. Analysis will reveal whether the event or person is going to be written about in media likely to reach the groups you are targeting. If not, the sponsorship will not generate media coverage of any value. If the sponsorship generates associative messages which are inappropriate for your mission, then again, the media relations benefits will be negligible.

CONCLUSION

Media analysis has clear roles in helping to select a sponsorship which is appropriate for an organization, and in analysing the sponsorship's success – from the sponsor's own viewpoint.

The converse is also true. Charities, event managers, and contestants can analyse media coverage of events and programmes and use media analysis to demonstrate effectiveness in communicating valuable and marketable lifestyle attributes. Hard evidence of success can reassure both potential and existing clients, and give existing client contacts the ammunition to fight for more funds next year.

Sponsorships, like other forms of communication, can go wrong, generating poor, adverse or even aggressively hostile coverage. How can media analysis help an organization interpret poor coverage, and how can the analysis get the company back on the road to a better media profile? We will be addressing that question in Chapter 13.

13 Analysing Adverse Coverage

The media analyst is frequently told 'Ah, but I spend most of my time keeping bad news out of the press. How do you measure **that***?' Chapter 13 answers this question in detail and looks at the whole area of negative messages – touching* en passant *on strategies for announcing poor financial results and redundancies.*

A large percentage of PR professionals spend the first few years of their careers without any experience of adverse media coverage. These people are the ones who work with small companies or clients with small budgets, and who deal mainly with their own trade press.

This kind of PR has its own problems. The national press and the big consumer titles rarely take any notice of news releases – but when they do it's because they've carried a new product notice or appointment release. And it's congratulations and champagne time when it happens. These people know about adverse news. They might even have learnt about how to deal with it at college or university. But, like death, it's something that tends only to happen to others.

And as with life, all good things tend to come to an end. An ex-employee denouncing working conditions, a product coming bottom of a *Which?* league table, or 50 redundancies after a poor trading year, can change all that. As the weeks go by, the press cutting envelopes start filling up with cuttings from publications with unfamiliar titles, the headlines are more raucous, and the press office needs to start operating in a different way – quickly. This is also a time for congratulation in a way, because it means the PR professional has been introduced to the other side of the PR business. Handled correctly, bad news and the adverse coverage which accompanies it can provide the learning experience which will help the press office to counteract or even avoid a poor media profile in the future.

PR people working in large, quoted companies have a very different story to tell. The press office is geared up to handle a potentially difficult interview from a journalist who has an angle on a faulty product, who has talked to the disgruntled ex-employee, or who wants to interpret a relatively harmless results release in a novel and potentially damaging way. Talk to those who work in this environment about media analysis and many will say 'I spend much of my time keeping bad news out of the press. How does your fancy system analyse THAT?'

In football, it's the strikers who seem to cover themselves in glory to the annoyance of defenders and midfielders, and the same happens in media relations. The people who are placing two-page features in *Woman's Realm* will attract notice while the professional who spends two days keeping a two-line quotation out of *The Economist* will be passed over – the share of the glory or the PR industry's awards may be little for these professionals, but, fortunately, media analysis can provide answers to their measurement problems.

COMPLETELY BAD COVERAGE RARELY OCCURS

The problem with those measurement systems which only divide coverage into good, bad and indifferent is that this type of analysis is only telling half the story the client needs to hear. The underlying truth is that completely bad and completely good coverage rarely occur: adverse coverage very often contains good news; a piece of superficially excellent coverage often contains a badly worded or inaccurate paragraph or phrase or omits an important fact.

Consider this extract from a news item which could have appeared in any western tabloid newspaper at any time over the past ten years:

International oil giant Petroco declared sharply reduced profits yesterday.

Now ask yourself whether this piece of news conveys the message 'Petroco is an international company'. The answer must be yes, and if this message is on the company's PR shopping list, then this news will undoubtedly contribute positively to the delivery of this message. But an adverse message is also there, and one of the skills of the PR professional is keeping the balance of these messages tipped in the organization's favour.

ANTICIPATING ADVERSE COVERAGE

Coverage containing adverse messages can occur for a number of different reasons. Sometimes the coverage occurs because there is a straightforward piece of adverse news to announce, such as layoffs, a poor set of results, a factory closure, the withdrawal of a faulty or illegal product, or the departure of a key director. The list of potential sources of adverse news is vast and they have an important common ground: they are expected. Adverse news that is not expected also occurs – but we will be dealing with that in Chapter 14.

Any PR professional will realize that an event such as 1000 redundancies cannot be kept out of the press. If one of an organization's messages is 'We're a good employer', then the 'employer' element of the profile is going to suffer when the news hits the press. Here are some questions which the PR professional should answer – before the news breaks – to ensure that the news can be analysed afterwards and lessons learnt:

1. What negative messages could the news generate? If you are not monitoring the press for the 'successful company' or 'financial stability' messages, the poor figures announcement may leave the other message scores unaffected and give a false picture.
2. Who will be affected by these messages? Your investment audiences may not be affected by a strongly negative human interest story – but customers and employees will be.
3. Are you monitoring the media in which the news will break? The local press, for instance, may not be on your hit list for positive message delivery, but they will be the first to pounce on news of redundancies and factory closures in their area.
4. Are there any benchmarks for the exercise? If your organization has been through a similar exercise before, it will be worthwhile comparing the two sets of coverage. The earlier coverage will need to be checked to see if certain media – or particular journalists – will need a detailed briefing.
5. Can the adverse news be used as a vehicle for positive messages about the company? This final point is addressed in detail next.

HARNESSING ADVERSE COVERAGE

One of the most interesting media analyses I have been involved with concerned an international consulting firm which was about to take the step of laying off several hundred staff in various countries. It was just before the start of the 1990–93 world recession; the layoffs were part of a global streamlining exercise in anticipation of difficult times ahead, and the PR team at the company's international headquarters in Europe were determined to present the news to the world in a positive light.

The company's PR programme was designed to deliver six key messages concerning internationalism, quality of service, calibre of staff and others. Its key media ranged from US newspapers such as the *Wall Street Journal* to international business and management titles such as *The Economist*.

The opportunities for the firm to transmit these messages in normal times were relatively scarce: 'normal' coverage concerned contract announcements, application studies, the arrival and departure of senior staff, and learned by-lined articles on the more abstruse aspects of its business.

The analysis needed some kind of a benchmark. We considered looking at coverage of a competitor for this purpose, but we were unable to identify a similar streamlining operation which had taken place in similar circumstances before. So, prior to the announcement, we analysed a selection of our client's own coverage in relatively 'normal' times, taken from different parts of the world where the streamlining programme would have the greatest effect. As expected, delivery of the key messages was positive, but relatively low, and the message bars in the various charts were accordingly flat. The analysis provided an excellent benchmark against which we could go on to judge the success of the announcement of the streamlining exercise.

The IMPACT team then looked at coverage of the streamlining exercise itself, from the same areas. In all areas, we found that volumes of coverage had risen – hardly surprising given the nature of the news. We also found that delivery of every one of the other messages, with the exception of the 'calibre of staff' message, had increased sharply. In some instances, the positive messages were coming over twice as strongly as they had done in the benchmark coverage! To their credit, the PR team were not particularly surprised by the results.

There was nothing magical about the way this coverage was achieved. Much of the coverage was written by labour and industrial correspondents, and business news staff who didn't normally write about the company's affairs. The reference notes on corporate background, and the brief but informative corporate summary in the main body of the announcement were used in much of the coverage. If the company had decided to say nothing and wait for the press to discover the 'bad news', then bad news is what they would have read in their newspapers the following day.

A client once told me that after agreeing the details of a media analysis surrounding an important announcement, she then reread all the media information she was about to issue and decided to have the whole lot rewritten. Why? because it did not contain any of the messages she knew we would be looking for!

It sounds obvious but it is surprising how often this underlying logic is forgotten: if you want the press to say something, it's important to give them the appropriate information in the first place. Many company announcements – especially if they are potential sources of adverse comment – will carry the kind of news which does not look like a natural home for your organization's agreed positive messages. It may need some ingenuity to embed them.

IDENTIFYING ADVERSE MESSAGES

The corollary to this is also worth remembering: if the analyst is not searching for negative messages, they won't be found. The consulting firm mentioned above, for instance, knew some adverse messages delivered on 'calibre of staff' were inevitable so they looked for them specifically.

Let's say that a mythical company Brightco plc is about to announce some gruesome annual results. In answering question 1 in the above list, the communications director may feel that the coverage is likely to convey adverse comment on the company's calibre of management. He or she will know that the coverage will certainly contain adverse comment on the company's financial success and attractiveness to investors.

If the analysis is not already analysing for these messages, the company should consider adding the following messages to the list – and preferably compare its performance against some other competing company who will be announcing its figures at the same time:

- Brightco is a well-managed company.
- Brightco is financially successful.
- Brightco shares are a good investment.

We're expecting adverse coverage, yet the messages are positively stated here. Wouldn't the Brightco PR team be better off measuring the negative message directly (for example, 'Brightco is a badly managed company', etc.)?

Let's take the 'management' message as an example. If we're recording message delivery on a scale of +10 to −10 for each item of coverage, we will find that an item on the results may generate a negative 'Management' message score. But other comment – on allied or completely different topics – could be generating positive scores on this message at the same time.

Financial PR specialists have their own methods of generating positive messages within a 'lower profits' announcement, and the management profile can be bolstered with other news written to put the other side of the management story. Measuring delivery of the 'Brightco is a well-managed company' message may even result in a positive profile overall. It is worth looking on the bright side when you decide what it is you're measuring!

ANTICIPATING ADVERSE COVERAGE IN NON-TARGET MEDIA

Adverse comment has a habit of appearing in the media where you're least expecting it. Companies which trade nationally sometimes ignore the coverage they generate in their local press – coverage they generate simply by being there.

They do so at their peril. Lurking in the shadows of the local media are those dreaded monsters … the disgruntled ex-employee and the plant's next door neighbour. An industrial accident which has been poorly handled by the personnel department, a sacked salesman taking a company to an industrial tribunal, or a down-wind chemistry graduate with analytical gear in his garage can all create teacup storms which can develop into hurricanes.

Think of some of the messages these incidents can generate. We are looking at negative scores on the 'caring company', 'good neighbour', 'good employer' and 'environmentally responsible' fronts. Local journalists are always keen to sell their exclusives to national media to supplement their incomes and the move up from the *Eastleigh Weekly News* to 'News at Ten' can occur with astonishing rapidity.

Local media are often more positive in their reporting of big-name local employers than are their colleagues in the national media, but when the story is a local one, the gloves will sometimes come off. It's undoubtedly worth analysing what the local media are saying about an organization when issues like these are likely to emerge.

We'll now examine three examples of circumstances where adverse coverage can arise, and suggest ways in which the coverage should be analysed.

PRODUCT AND SERVICE PROBLEMS

Quality control can minimize the occurrence of failure, but there is always a chance that one of your products or an aspect of the service you provide can become the focus of the media's anger, criticism or scorn.

In the early 1990s, the UK Government decided to put certain Home Office responsibilities out to tender, and, in April 1993, a private company, Group 4, won a contract to escort and supervise prisoners in transit.

During the first week of the contract, a 21-year-old prisoner escaped from a Hull Court while in the custody of Group 4. Shortly afterwards, another young prisoner kicked his way out of a van *en route* to Lincoln Jail and within a few days a further prisoner was accidentally released after a court appearance instead of being returned to his cell.

On May 8, the same year, Ernie Hogg, a lorry driver from Forfar in Scotland, choked on his own vomit and subsequently died after drinking alcohol while in transit from the Wolds – Britain's first privatized prison – to court in the custody of Group 4. How Mr Hogg came by the alcohol, how he was able to consume so much and why he was left unattended became the subject of a stinging rebuke to Group 4 in a government report which claimed that his death could have been prevented.

Media response was immediate and devastating. Because the idea of privatizing elements of the prison service was at the heart of the Conservative Government's privatization programme (and was therefore highly controversial), there were plenty of commentators and pressure groups such as the Prison Officers Association and the Prison Reform Trust waiting to proffer explanation and opinion. There were over 200 articles in the UK national press dealing with the issue in the 12 months which followed, many of them extremely damaging.

Stephen Shaw is a director of the Prison Reform Trust and his comment on the death of Ernie Hogg in *Scotland on Sunday* is typical:

> It was the lack of experience and professionalism which contributed directly to his death. I know of no other instance when a prisoner has died in circumstances like these. If the escort service had been in public hands I have no hesitation in saying that Ernie Hogg would not have died.

Mr Shaw's damning criticism cites Group 4's lack of experience and lack of professionalism. It also attacks the whole concept of a privatized prison service. The comment will have counteracted any positive messages that Group 4 will have been trying to promote about its security experience and the professionalism of the services it provides.

Why did this piece appear in *Scotland on Sunday*? The publication may not have been on the company's target media list, but the company was on the publication's interest list because the case is full of Scottish angles. Not only was prisoner security a matter of public concern in Scotland as well as England, but the prisoner was Scottish and (as was pointed out in the article) Group 4's managing director was also Scottish.

Controlling an issue such as this one demands the highest level of PR skill. Companies experiencing coverage of this kind will usually need to expand the scope of the media monitoring programme to cover non-target media as well as carefully examining the messages.

EUREKA! YOUR COMPETITOR ANNOUNCES AN ADVANCE

The disposable diaper, the safety match, the word processor and the steamship all have one important factor in common: they created problems for manufacturers of conventional products at the time of their introduction.

When the advantages of using a new product or system are argued cogently and forcefully in the media, the process by which our opinions and behaviour are changed can be accelerated rapidly. As we have seen in earlier chapters, media messages can change the way potential customers think and behave, so monitoring competitor's media coverage becomes of paramount importance at these times.

Analysing your coverage against the competition's coverage for the same old messages month after month probably won't be enough in these changed circumstances. When a competitor produces an unexpected ace card we need to carry out an 'open' analysis to identify the issues and the media involved.

Imagine two manufacturers of high density polyethylene (HDPE) plastic material, slugging it out in a static and closely contested marketplace. The two ranges of products are evenly matched and both attract customers because of their resilience and toughness, excellence of finish and range of colours available.

The situation can be monitored in the press by coverage of messages such as 'strength', 'resilience' and 'attractiveness' in the trade and technical press. But the situation will change radically should one manufacturer introduce a refinement to the production process which makes its product range completely fire-resistant. It is something which one of the companies may not be able to offer.

An 'open' analysis will pinpoint the direction and thrust of the competitor's PR programme. In an open analysis, the cuttings and tapes are analysed for very general messages – not just one's own. The open analysis will also identify vertical market journals, and other media sectors in which the competitor may be seeking coverage.

An open analysis is nearly always carried out on a project basis rather than on a continuous basis, and its purpose is to create or adjust the parameters of an ongoing analysis programme. It can usually be carried out on an informal basis. As a result of the open analysis, the company in our example would probably have added the messages 'safety' as well as 'fire-resistance' to the message list and may have extended the media list to include military and safety/security media.

ANNOUNCING POOR FIGURES

Take most publicly quoted companies and glance at the media analysis charts for the month in which the annual results are announced. They will probably be radically different from the charts for other months. Volumes will be high: often the highest for the year. And *selected* messages will show highs or lows depending on the nature of the results. I emphasize the word selected here.

Announcement of the annual figures and the accompanying chairperson's statement represents one of the most important opportunities in the year for getting positive corporate messages across. And as any experienced financial PR professional will advise, poor figures can be harnessed successfully as well as good ones. The messages such as 'we are financially successful' and 'we are a good investment' will yo-yo with the figures themselves; success in delivering the 'management', 'caring', 'environment' and other messages may be higher or lower depending on the content of the statement accompanying the figures.

Only a certain amount of useful information can be gleaned by analysing a results month for a company taken in isolation. A little more can be gained by comparing with previous months or against a competitor's results month. Much more usable information can be found however in a comparison with an analysis of the company's own last two or three year's figures announcements.

LIVE COVERAGE AND PHONE-INS

Adverse coverage very often occurs when a company spokesperson is caught off-guard in a live situation or otherwise unguarded moment. As a young and inexperienced spokesman for an animal charity, I went live on local radio, prepared for a few mentions of a charity event we were organizing but for little else. After reassuring me that this would only be an informal chat, the interviewer started on air by saying 'Animal activists desecrated the grave of John Peel last night. What's your group's position on this?' The long pause while I gathered my thoughts before expressing my personal disapproval probably did the organization I represented a disservice.

Some organizations – especially central and local government and public utilities – find themselves with more of these live opportunities than most, and for organizations like this analysing them separately is advised. One UK public utility, with whom my own organization has been working for some time, always analyses by various types of media opportunity. Live sessions where the interviewer or the general public are asking complex and open-ended questions usually pose most of the problems. But there is evidence that their ability to handle these situations has improved with the feedback which media analysis offers.

ANALYSING OTHER PEOPLE'S PROBLEMS

One positive element to emerge from competitive media analysis is that it highlights the fact that other companies have media profile problems as well as your own! It may seem ghoulish to analyse another company's adverse coverage, but it does provide real data on the effects of circumstances which could come nearer home at some stage in the future.

Poor figures, product faults, redundancies, and other events all cause adverse coverage as we have seen, and will affect their media profile performance and the media analysis spotlight will help to identify both the cause and the attendant effect.

CONCLUSION

In the above paragraphs, we have examined the reasons why adverse coverage can arise, and we have seen that it is only in some circumstances when adverse coverage is completely 'bad coverage'. In many instances, adverse news can be managed in such a way that it can be used to deliver positive messages.

Many popular analytical techniques such as advertising value equivalents (AVEs) ignore or abuse adverse coverage, encouraging complacency or despair in the organizations they are intended to help and inform. It will be noted that AVEs do not feature at all in the paragraphs above as a way of analysing coverage of this type.

It is often said that the true calibre of the press office emerges when its staff are issuing or responding to adverse news. When there's a factory fire, fraud, the murder of a board director or mass pollution, the calibre of the company itself emerges. It is the coverage which results from this type of event which we will be dealing with in Chapter 14.

14 Analysing Crisis Coverage

There are two kinds of adverse coverage – the kind you know is going to arrive, the kind you can plan for, and the kind you have no control over. Here we enter the realm of crisis communications and the kind of information we can learn about our organizations when media are reporting situations in which backs are very much to the wall.

In the days before Easter 1990, the employees of Sheffield Forgemasters Holdings and its London PR consultancy, Infopress Limited, were preparing for the holidays. The Sheffield based steel firm had just completed a large export order for a chemical plant: little did either firm know of the storm which was to break about their ears.

Customs officials had deduced that a shipment of pipes, manufactured by Sheffield Forgemasters and awaiting shipment to the Middle East might in fact be part of a gigantic gun – the infamous Iraqi Supergun – which had been purchased in component form through third parties for Iraq, from various European companies. Iraq's intention, it seemed, was to use the gun to threaten and bombard one of its Middle East neighbours.

For the next few weeks, Sheffield Forgemasters was rarely out of the headlines. The accusations that the Sheffield firm knew all along that it was a gun, and had somehow evaded the UK Government's export regulations were strongly denied by the firm and by Infopress.

Much of the dialogue over the incident was carried out in the press and media. If the company had done what many other companies would have done in these frightening circumstances and said 'no comment', it is possible that a grave injustice would have been done.

The Sheffield Forgemasters story is just one example of how effective communications can transform a corporate crisis of short duration into a media success. Sheffield Forgemasters' reputation is intact – thanks to a little planning, some very fast footwork and a preparedness to defend the company's actions.

WHY ANALYSE CRISIS COVERAGE?

Crises are not the ideal vehicles for planned delivery of an organization's corporate or marketing messages. Analysing the 'Supergun' coverage for the Sheffield Forgemasters' usual messages, for instance, would have resulted in many neutral scores. But coverage of crises does benefit from analysis for a number of reasons.

First, if corporate coverage is being analysed on a continuous basis, then the crisis coverage should undoubtedly be included. Charts should be examined very carefully to see if the organization's profile has been changed as a result of the incident – either for better or for worse. A factory fire in which sloppy procedures or poor training is cited as the cause will adversely affect delivery of the 'management' message. On the other hand, a row with Government about the illegal export of hi-tech equipment to a hostile nation could inadvertently communicate a 'technological excellence' message very effectively. It could be that the corporate profile of the company becomes seriously skewed as a result of the crisis and corrective action may need to be taken.

The crisis coverage will also usually deserve analysis for its own sake as well – which means separating the crisis coverage from the rest. An open analysis (see Chapter 13) will determine what messages are being conveyed about the company over and above the usual corporate messages. Again, this exercise will determine to what extent the incident has changed the organization's profile and will provide a stimulus to corrective action.

A further benefit of analysing crisis coverage is that the analysis will act as a benchmark against which future incidents of this kind can be judged. The larger the company, the more likely it is that crises will affect them and the greater the need for some kind of crisis communications procedure. The information which media analysis of an earlier crisis can yield provides an invaluable tool for the planning of crises in the future.

MEDIA ANALYSIS AND CRISIS PLANNING

Crisis communications professionals are rarely content simply to wait for crises to happen. Instead, they prepare and plan for the likelihood of particular types of crisis occurring.

An oil company for instance, will need to plan against the eventuality of extensive pollution following an oil spill; an explosives manufacturer will need to plan for an explosion or theft of explosives by terrorists; an accountancy firm will need to plan for a major mistake in an audit leading to a public row with a large publicly quoted client company; a shipping line should plan for the possibility of the loss of a ship at sea.

No two crises are ever exactly the same, but this does not mean that one cannot learn lessons from one incident for application in the future. Analysing old crises in the company's history will show what effect they had on corporate profile. Once this has been determined, compensatory measures can be built into the planning process. It could be for instance that a standby information sheet should be prepared on a company's quality control or security procedures. This could be deployed immediately should the company's quality or security measures come under the gaze of the media in the event of a tragedy.

Crisis communications professionals usually have little enough to go on when the storm breaks, and much of their expertise is in being adequately prepared and being able to move fast. A media analysis of a previous crisis could be just about the only hard information they have to go on in terms of hard data.

If there is no benchmark crisis in the organization's own history, there are always other people's crises to analyse. Crises usually reach the pages of the national press and broadcast media, and relevant material will usually be available retrospectively through public databases such as FT-Profile and Nexis. These databases won't capture all the coverage but they will give the analyst some useful indicators.

An open analysis of a competitor's oil spill, fraud or explosion will identify the points where an organization's media profile, and therefore its reputation, is at risk. And a series of analyses in each of the major areas of risk will spotlight the areas where the crisis communications team will need to concentrate its planning efforts.

COMMUNICATING EFFECTIVELY IN A CRISIS

Once the crisis plan is in place, it will be clear what messages will need to be communicated. Whereas in day-to-day PR the company may want to communicate the excellence of its products, its good citizenship and its responsibility as an employer, the focus of the communication will need to shift to other messages when disaster strikes.

In a crisis, it may well be that the company will be more interested in communicating its management ability, its responsiveness, its integrity and its care and concern for those affected by the crisis. It could be that the central message of the crisis programme will be something even more specific, such as the level of water in a reservoir, the reading of a voltmeter in the plant control room or the presence of a company's finance director in a branch office on a particular day – but foreseeing these is going to present even the most prescient PR person with a problem!

In analysing the coverage after the incident to see how effective the communications has been, the analyst will have to put the existing list of messages to one side for a while and look for new messages in the crisis coverage. The success or otherwise of the communications effort will be determined by how well the team has responded to the new situation – that is, how well it has formulated and conveyed the new messages to the target audiences.

MEDIA CATEGORIES AND CRISES

In Chapter 13, we highlighted the fact that adverse coverage often occurs in media categories which are not on the company's target list. This is even more the case in the context of a corporate crisis.

In the analysis of a crisis, the analyst will need to broaden the scope of the media monitoring to ensure that all the angles are covered. If the company is only monitoring the trade and specific local or vertical market publications, the PR manager will need to broaden the scope of the monitoring programme at the time the crisis breaks. In planning terms, this will mean adding a note on media monitoring to the crisis manual, together with the name, address and telephone number of the monitoring agencies (broadcast and press).

CONCLUSION

Central to the theme of this book is an insistence on the need to allow the communications objectives to drive the media analysis programme. There is no need to depart from this theme when dealing with crisis communications.

Media analysis will be very low on the priority list when a crisis actually breaks, but media analysis can contribute to crisis planning. The following points summarize how media analysis can be used:

1. Analyse coverage of your own earlier company crises, and those of your competitors prior to carrying out detailed crisis planning. If necessary, obtain retrospective crisis coverage for analysis from on-line databases such as FT-Profile and Nexis.
2. After a crisis, always include crisis coverage in any ongoing corporate media analysis, and carry out a separate 'open' analysis of coverage to determine the effect of the incident on media profile.
3. Try to determine in advance of a crisis at least some of the messages you will need to communicate – and look for in the coverage afterwards. They are unlikely to be the same as your usual corporate or marketing messages.
4. Make a note in the crisis manual to review media monitoring agencies' instructions within 24 hours of a crisis occurring so that all relevant coverage can be analysed afterwards.

This chapter concludes our examination of the best ways to analyse adverse and crisis coverage. In the next chapter we return to techniques, and sail very briefly into the backwater of advertising value equivalents (AVEs). These three chapters belong together if for no other reason than that, in dealing with adverse and crisis coverage, AVEs are shown up in their very worst light.

15 Values, Costs, and Advertising Value Equivalents

One of the very earliest types of media analysis – and one still very widely used – is calculating advertising equivalent values (AVEs). The author (who used to do this himself) argues against the technique – primarily because of its inability to deal with adverse and crisis coverage as described in Chapters 13 and 14.

PR would be easy in a world in which there is only positive news, and where journalists always publish the exact words given to them and never have any thoughts of their own!

It doesn't exist, thank goodness. So it seems strange that one of the most popular ways of evaluating editorial coverage resulting from public relations activity has been created for such a world. And the people who calculate spurious editorial 'values' based on equivalent advertising cost think they are living in it.

A brief and guarded welcome to the world of advertising value equivalents (AVEs).

THE CONCEPT OF EDITORIAL VALUE

One of the reasons why advertising value equivalents are still used so widely is because there is a very real need for PR people to calculate the value of the work they carry out for cost-conscious paymasters. The existence of media directories such as *BRAD* in the UK gives the marketing communications professional a ready-reckoner of advertising costs which turns the compilation of a table of impressive looking figures into a simple clerical task.

The AVE practitioner needs just a pile of press cuttings, a media directory, a ruler and writing materials. First, the press cutting is measured in column centimetres; then the media directory is consulted to see how much x column centimetres would have cost if that space had been bought as an advertisement. When the end of the pile is reached, all the advertising costs are added up, and the total is the 'value' of the PR.

The total reached at the end of the AVE exercise is not a true value. It is a cost comparison, for the figures given in the media directory are costs. The editorial coverage obtained only has a value in that it has a benefit to the organization to which it refers. Every item of editorial coverage has numerous readers, viewers or listeners, and the net benefit to the organization is the sum of all the effects which that item has on all of the readers, viewers or listeners involved.

If an article about a new car costing $20 000 results directly in the sale of five of these cars, then the value of the article is a proportion of the profit on the $100 000 resulting from these sales. Perhaps a figure of $2 000–4 000 might result. If an article about an organization's training scheme results in the recruitment of 10 top technical staff, then the value of the article to the organization is a proportion of the financial contribution of those employees over the time they are employed by the organization. This is much more difficult to calculate and is likely to result in a much higher figure.

It would be difficult to track all the effects of a large company's editorial coverage on all its readers, viewers and listeners. It would certainly cost more to calculate than the cost of the PR programme. Fortunately there are far better and much easier ways of working out the end result.

Using tried and tested market research techniques, it is possible to identify the source of sales leads. Direct surveys of target audiences will yield information on the extent to which attitudes and behaviour have changed, and the extent to which media relations activity has been responsible for these changes. If required, this information can be related to the finances of the organization concerned and an agreed value obtained. If a value for editorial coverage is needed, then this is the way to calculate it, rather than through media analysis of the kind we have been describing in this book.

Media analysis gives the communications team much more specific and much more useful information. It is a set of tools to enable communications professionals to manage their programmes more effectively.

MESSAGE STRENGTH – A REMINDER

AVEs represent costs rather than true values, but the reasons for abandoning AVE methods go far beyond this. The main reason why AVEs don't work is because it is a facile method measuring the width rather than the quality: it ignores the content of the editorial coverage itself.

Take two articles of similar length, each reviewing a piece of hi-fi equipment. They are in two rival publications with identical advertising rates. In the first article, the item is headlined 'A mid-range hi-fi system' and the piece goes on to discuss the equipment in accurate but unemotional detail. In the second, the headline claims 'Samsung's new midi is a world beater' and after enthusing over the technical details, concludes by urging its readers to go and buy one immediately.

146

Under the AVE system, the first article is assigned exactly the same 'value' as the second, even though the message strength in the second is so much higher. Media analysis, as we have seen, needs to distinguish between items which vary in message strength.

ADVERSE, NEUTRAL AND POSITIVE COVERAGE

AVEs are also very poor at dealing with adverse, mixed or neutral coverage. In the hi-fi example given above, take the case of a review in which a system is described as being of 'very good sound quality but extremely pricey for the specification'. The item is strongly positive on 'quality', but negative on 'value'.

This item will place the AVE practitioner in a dilemma. Should the item be assigned the full advertising value, should the item be ignored, or should the advertising equivalent be subtracted from the total? Unfortunately, the client is at the mercy of the practitioner here, and all have different rules.

Strongly adverse coverage presents even more of a problem. There have undoubtedly been many instances where items which are negative on all messages have been 'evaluated' in advertising equivalent terms; the 'value' added to the total for a campaign or for the month and the client organization is consequently misleading.

We have established that advertising equivalents are not much good at analysing coverage in which there is negative message content. So is the AVE method safe for analysing positive coverage? Unfortunately not.

During his 1994 presidency of the UK's Institute of Public Relations, Mike Beard described the effect of a few lines of coverage in the Lex column of the *Financial Times* in which his employer Taylor Woodrow was described as being in 'safe hands' after a period of difficulties. The effect was immediate and dramatic, and had immense benefit (and therefore value) to the company. To have applied the AVE method to those sentences would have resulted in a 'value' of merely a few hundred pounds.

AVEs AND NON-ADVERTISING MEDIA

One of the most potent UK media on which to air news and comment is the BBC Radio 4's early morning 'Today' programme. As well as being highly influential in its own right, it also tends to set the news agenda for other media in the following 24 hours. Among the huge number of listeners which the programme reaches are influential AB business people and opinion formers.

The 'Today' programme presents the AVE practitioner with a further problem, for the simple reason that it is impossible to advertise on any BBC programme, thus rendering any AVE calculation meaningless and valueless. The same problem arises for BBC television news and feature programmes, in editorial-only newsletter media and in any other media where the medium's revenue is gained through means other than advertisements.

AVEs AND MULTIPLIERS

Despite all these disadvantages, the practice of calculating advertising value equivalents persists. And despite these drawbacks, the practice has been super-charged by some practitioners to yield even more outrageous results than the basic AVE method.

On the premise that editorial copy is of more value than advertising copy (an incorrect assumption in itself) some practitioners multiply their AVE totals by factors of three or seven, resulting in even more astronomic AVE totals.

Editorial coverage can certainly be of more value than advertisements of the equivalent space. But the converse is also true, and there is certainly no simple mathematical trick to link the two. A journalist will often rewrite a story to such an extent that desired message content is minimal: in societies where journalists enjoy relative editorial freedom, PR practitioners will only ever be able to provide and suggest, never to dictate. One of the key skills of the PR professional is to transmit messages through the editorial filter that journalists represent; one of the key skills of the media analyst is to measure how successful they have been in achieving this.

MEDIA ANALYSIS AND PR PROGRAMME COSTS

At the outset of this chapter, I introduced the idea of editorial coverage having a monetary value. A further parameter also deserves analysis, and this is the cost of generating editorial coverage.

It is highly instructive to calculate the total cost of an organization's media relations programme including salaries, distribution and media monitoring services, overheads such as the cost of premises and computers and the additional cost of retaining external PR consultants. The monthly cost is relatively easily calculated.

Armed with this information, it is a further simple task to compute the cost of achieving the stated objectives of the programme – provided they are accurately defined.

A press office tasked with delivering five key messages (see Chapter 5) might, in one month, achieve scores for each of these messages in each of three media categories as shown in Table 15.1.

The total number of message points delivered is 676. If the cost of running the PR department during the month was $20 000, then the cost of delivering each

August message scores	National	Trade	Regional
'Success'	23	62	131
'Environment'	0	23	78
'Management'	54	59	41
'Responsiveness'	0	27	64
'Citizenship'	11	-6	109
TOTALS	88	165	423

Table 15.1 Message scores for five key messages in a single month

message point is $29.6 – an intriguing figure, and one which a good manager will want to minimize.

The figures won't be highly accurate, because much of the PR work carried out in one month won't bear fruit until the next. Also, the difficulty in delivering message points via powerful national media will be greater than the difficulty of generating message points in the trade press: the calculation should take account of this. But, in the context of the company's own experience, the figure is a real management indicator and one which is of considerably more relevance than the notorious AVE.

CONCLUSION: WHY AVEs DON'T WORK

Media relations is a complex web of different disciplines, and it is only in the most sales-orientated media programmes that communications objectives can be defined in purely monetary terms. This in turn means that the results of media relations efforts cannot usually be defined in monetary terms either.

Advertising value equivalents (AVEs) represent an early effort to assign spurious monetary values to media relations activities. They are based on how much it would cost to buy an equivalent advertising space, and are flawed in concept because:

1. The AVE is an equivalent cost, not an equivalent value.
2. The AVE takes no account of message content.
3. The AVE cannot evaluate neutral or negative coverage.
4. There is no AVE data available for media which do not accept advertising.

By the time further editions of this book appear, it is to be hoped that the practice of calculating AVEs will have disappeared and that these comments on the practice will no longer be necessary.

The calculation of message delivery cost is of much more value to the PR manager. Keeping this as low as possible will encourage the PR virtues of keeping costs down and maximizing message delivery effectiveness. Achieving this latter virtue will necessitate making the best possible use of the space that is available in terms of headline geometry, page and position on page. It is towards the treatment of positional data that we turn the spotlight in Chapter 16.

16 Positional Data

Some media evaluation systems rely heavily on recording the position on the page, the page number (for printed media) and the timing (broadcast media) of the item concerned. All contribute to the extent to which an item impacts on a target audience. But the cuttings agencies whose roles are outlined in earlier chapters don't usually record this for the benefit of the evaluators. The chapter starts with a plea for the agencies to change their ways.

One of the traditional complaints of public relations people over the years has been the inefficiency of their monitoring agencies. I know that the more reputable press cutting and broadcast monitoring agencies actually do a better job than they are given credit for – but I have a complaint: some agencies record the page number and position on the page of the press cutting if asked, but most don't.

If we accept that media analysis can be helpful to the public relations business, the press cuttings agencies in particular aren't helping either the PR professional or the analyst when they fail to record positional data associated with the material they have extracted.

The physical location of a published or broadcast item in space and time has a dramatic effect on who it reaches and how effectively it delivers the information contained in it. An item given to a national newspaper late in the evening will miss the first edition and the early morning commuters who may have been intended to read it; an article on page 15 of a broadsheet newspaper will be read by fewer people than an item of exactly the same size appearing at the bottom of the front page.

Recording timing, page and position is a natural job for the press cutting agencies to take on. Media analysts aren't usually geared up to deal with high volumes of newspapers and magazines, and as analysis becomes more popular, there are undoubtedly going to be opportunities for the agencies to provide more detailed information for a slightly higher fee.

Here are some of the positional parameters associated with press and broadcast coverage which affect impact on audiences. In common with each other though, they cannot be taken into account in analysis unless the details are recorded as they are extracted.

SPECIALIST SECTIONS

Specialist sections for professions, industries and special interest groups can play havoc with the mathematics underlying media analysis as is shown by the following example.

A recent issue of the UK newspaper the *Independent* carried an article about a new scheme by the Royal Bank of Scotland whereby companies could spread the cost of their annual accountancy bill over six or ten months rather than having to pay it in a single annual payment. The item was in Section II of the newspaper, on page 30, in the accountancy section.

The item would have been of interest to a number of directors of companies – especially small companies – but how many of this group even look at, let alone read the accountancy section? An item of the same size and identical wording in the business section would have reached more people and may have had a more beneficial effect. Any computation which takes into account the whole circulation of the newspaper, and which assumes the item reached them would be a nonsense.

The Royal Bank may, on the other hand, have been trying specifically to reach accountants, in which case this begins to look like a much more effective exercise. Newspaper readers are not particularly loyal, and the readership of the *Independent* among accountants peaks on Tuesdays, the day the feature is published.

Special sections attract some readers, and repulse others. An entire generation of public relations people bought the *Guardian* from the 1970s onwards so that they could read the newspaper's 'Creative and Media' section which appears on Mondays. Some bought it despite the publication's left-of-centre stance and despite the fact that they may have preferred to read *The Times* or the *Telegraph* on other days of the week.

EDITIONS

If special sections cause problems for media analysts, early and late editions can be a nightmare.

Despite the best laid plans, there are always going to be days when there is an assassination attempt on the president of the USA, a party leader dies of a heart attack or some other unexpected item of news displaces an item about your organization from the front page. A late breaking development in world news can displace your story from all but the first edition, with a consequent diminution of the effect on target audience.

A published item sometimes does not have the expected effect in terms of interest, enquiries and comment, and the PR professional can always check to see if the item was cut in later editions. But the media analyst dealing with hundreds of cuttings has rather more fundamental questions to ask about whether the information provided to clients is accurate. The analyst will be haunted by the possibility that a selection of key press clippings in a given month may have featured in only a subset of the full circulation – as a regional, early morning or late evening edition.

PAGE 1 OR PAGE 21?

If you have tried opening a broadsheet newspaper on a very crowded bus or train, you will know how important a front page position is when it comes to placement. Sometimes it's just impossible to read the inside pages without elbowing your fellow passengers in the face, and so you have to stare at the front and back pages for long periods.

But physical constraints are only part of the problem. Newspaper and magazine readers tend to browse rather than read serially, and each person browses the pages in a slightly different way. A sports fan, for instance, may encounter a sponsor's name in a match report without even noticing an item on the business pages – an item suggesting, perhaps, that the sponsor is in serious financial difficulties.

Some homespun media evaluation systems assign simple weightings to items appearing on page 1 or at the top of a page. The reality is more complex: the effect the item has on the audiences can't be expressed in simple numerical terms unless the readership data is accurately known.

HEADLINES

Headlines can also change the effectiveness with which your messages are reaching (or missing) the audiences you are targeting.

A good headline can deliver a message very powerfully, even to a browser who has no intention of reading the article beneath it.

Here are some examples from the UK national press. The introduction of ombudsmen has given the headline writers some marvellous opportunities to exercise their skills. Every time an ombudsman's report is published, there is a ready-made news story, but the headlines vary considerably from story to story. Sometimes the organization concerned is let off lightly, as is the case in this item from the business pages of the *Glasgow Herald* from 17 August 1994:

PENSION SCHEME WORRIES OMBUDSMAN

There's no clue from the headline which company's pension scheme has caused the ombudsman to worry, and the word 'worry' is by no means the strongest which could have been used.

The *Independent* carried a further article on 14 July 1994, in which the National

Health Service ombudsman was quoted:

FRESH SURGE IN HEALTH SERVICE COMPLAINTS: NHS OMBUDS-MAN 'RATHER FED UP' WITH REPEATED MISTAKES

Here, the language is again muted but the organization is clearly identified for the reader. In four earlier articles however, all relatively short, the language was far stronger and there can be no doubt at all over who the NHS ombudsman was criticizing:

OMBUDSMAN CRITICIZES 'PITIFUL' NHS MANAGERS (*Glasgow Herald*, 8 July 1994)

SAVAGE REBUKE BY OMBUDSMAN FOR FAILINGS IN HEALTH SERVICE (*Daily Telegraph*, 8 July 1994)

NHS ATTACKED OVER 'SHABBY' PATIENT CARE (*Independent*, 8 July 1994)

REFORMED NHS IS AN UNCARING SHAMBLES, SAYS OMBUDS-MAN (*Evening Standard*, 7 July 1994)

There can be no doubt that the wording and strength of the headline has strengthened the delivery of the messages in the article as a whole.

RADIO AND TELEVISION: PROGRAMMES AND TIMING

The concept of total circulation, as applied to newspapers and magazines, is a useful one when calculating message penetration, but the audience of a television or radio network waxes and wanes with the timing of the broadcast and the subject matter. Thus the disloyalty of newspaper readers is as nothing compared with that of viewers and listeners. While ITN's 'News at Ten' will attract millions of viewers, an item on Freescreen, broadcast on the same wavelengths in the early hours of the morning, is likely to attract a handful of insomniacs and shiftworkers.

Headlines have no equivalent in radio and television. Because broadcast times are fixed, listeners or viewers may only catch the beginning, middle or end of a programme and will be unlikely to have the opportunity to listen to the remainder of the item later. They won't have their video recorders set all the time, and aren't therefore likely to be influenced by messages transmitted in the other parts of the programme.

Audience data for broadcast media need to be calculated on a programme by programme basis. Fortunately, these figures are obtainable from the Broadcasters' Audience Research Board Limited (BARB).

USING EDITION, PAGE AND POSITION DATA

All the variations, complications and contributing factors listed above will have an effect on the success with which an organization's messages are delivered to its target audiences. The extent to which the analysis should be adjusted to allow for these variations however will depend on the reasons for carrying out the analysis in the first place.

Table 16.1 shows the main parameter which each variation affects, and there is a suggestion alongside each to show how the analysis should be adjusted to compensate. If the main reason for the analysis is to ensure that the correct messages are being transmitted, it may be that the analyst will only need to adjust for headline data, page number and position. If the purpose of the analysis is to determine as closely as possible the extent to which the messages have reached the target audience, however, some further adjustments will need to be made.

Variation	Analysis parameter	Suggested adjustment strategy
News page/feature?	Audience	Adjust readership data[*]
Early/late edition?	Audience	Adjust readership data[*]
Regional edition	Audience	Adjust readership data[*]
Page number?	Audience	Adjust message score
Position on page?	Audience	Adjust message score
Size of headline?	Message	Adjust message score
Data in headline?	Message	Adjust message score
Programme audience?	Audience	Determine audience data

[*] if available

Table 16.1 How media analysis data can be adjusted for varying editions, page number and position on page

Determining readership data (as opposed to simple circulation data) and adjusting this for special sections, late editions and regional variations will take some time as it is likely to involve contacting publications on a one-to-one basis and is therefore likely to result in a considerable rise in the cost of the analysis.

The location of an item on a page, its position in a newspaper, the time it is broadcast are all likely to have an effect on the numbers of people an item reaches. We have found that the geometry and content of the headline, however, affects the message content of the item itself.

Another factor which affects message strength and delivery is the illustrative material which accompanies an article and the visual and aural content of a television or radio programme. Determining how these elements of the coverage affect message delivery requires the use of different judgemental skills and techniques. In Chapter 17, we will be leaving the written and spoken word for a short while, and entering the world of photographs and illustrations.

17 The Role of the Picture

Is a picture worth a thousand words? The answer is not a simple 'yes' or 'no'. We put forward the idea of evaluating a picture in terms of the delivery of the overall message. If an illustration conveys a message powerfully, it may be worth a million words; if it says nothing, it might as well not be there.

A picture can transmit a message with a powerful impact unattainable by mere prose, but many media relations professionals use pictures poorly, choosing the wrong picture to illustrate an article.

Most of us have been affected by a photograph of a basket of puppies, or an abandoned baby gorilla taking milk from a bottle. Many of us will have been brought to tears by a newspaper picture of a child wounded in war – a war which perhaps had not touched us previously. It is not for nothing that the West's relief agencies unashamedly use pictures of starving children with bloated stomachs to tug at our purse strings.

Pictures are powerful medicine, with both benefits and dangers. They convey reality directly, without the filter of language, and they can bring situations and issues to our attention in a direct way, with no need of explanation.

Pictures also pose a challenge to the PR profession, however, and the way pictures are used in the media can be a useful measure of a PR team's professionalism and influence. I have included a chapter on pictures because their treatment can bring a range of problems to the media analyst, and because I believe photographs, cartoons and diagrams deserve the analyst's close attention.

IS A PICTURE WORTH A THOUSAND WORDS?

Only once has a company suggested to me that a picture should be given a 'word equivalence' of 1 000, and I suspect the person making the suggestion was only half serious.

The truth is that illustrations can be worth much more or much less than a thousand words. Many PR people use pictures as editorial embellishments only, and select the subject matter, style and medium without reference to any communications agenda. Others use pictures as the fulcrum of an entire campaign.

The contractual handshake is a classic situation which PR people love to exploit. There seems to be a compulsion among PR people to photograph overweight, pin-striped managers shaking hands with each other: sign a deal, anywhere, and a PR person will be lying in wait to take a photograph and send it to the newspapers. The characters may be unphotogenic, the subject may be boring and obscure, but of course a picture is worth a thousand words – and a photograph there must be.

Contrast this with the photograph taken of one of the most memorable handshakes this century, on the lawn of the White House when the Palestinian leader Yasser Arafat shook hands with Israeli Prime Minister Rabin in the presence of President Clinton. The handshake signalled what was hoped to be the beginning of the end of the conflict over the future of the Palestinians.

The White House handshake was significant because the faces were wellknown, and their fame was at least partly due to their owners' well-documented mutual opposition and hostility towards each other. Seeing the two sharing a public gesture of friendship and co-operation brought readers and viewers up with a start. The picture told us that something momentous was going on – and there was no need for words.

Millions of pounds are spent each year on boring handshake pictures, but this is nothing compared with the money spent on unusable product pictures. Editors are bombarded with product pictures because companies think that the inherent virtues of the product will leap out through the lens, and into the hearts and minds of the readers. It's more likely, of course, that the picture will leap into the editorial waste paper basket – and the few that are used often contribute nothing to the story and nothing to the promotion of the product.

But even product pictures can be made to communicate a message. To use an example referred to in an earlier chapter, a photograph of a pile of granules will not tell the reader anything about the properties of a flame retardant plastic; a picture of a blackened component, barely smoking in the concentrated flame of a bunsen burner most certainly will.

TRACKING VOLUMES AND MESSAGES IN PICTURES

Media analysis can tell a PR team how well messages are coming across in media pictures. Their frequency and their size can be charted to measure any effect on the attainment of communications objectives. But just as volume of words by itself doesn't represent a useful measure when it comes to measuring the effectiveness of text, volumes and frequencies by themselves aren't a great deal of use when it comes to pictures.

In a mature programme in which pictures play an important but non-pivotal part, the contribution of pictures can be calculated by allowing for picture coverage when carrying out a word count. In other words if there is a 400-word item in a national newspaper accompanied by a picture the same size as the text, the analyst should record a total word count of 800.

Message scores can be accounted for in an analogous way, adjusting the message score of the item as a whole if the picture adds a positive (or perhaps negative) angle to the story. The score for a corporate message like 'Company A is a key supplier to education' for instance, will be boosted by an accompanying picture showing the company's products in use in a classroom. A picture of a row of pickets outside a factory, on the other hand, may detract from an otherwise positive article about a local employer.

TRACKING PICTORIAL COVERAGE SEPARATELY

In the late 1970s, when King Henry's flagship *The Mary Rose* was first discovered on the seabed in the Solent near Portsmouth in England, a television camera was lowered to the excavation site, and footage and stills of cannons and bulwarks were syndicated to newspapers all over the world. It was a first – and the pictures conveyed an excitement which prose alone couldn't communicate.

If a series of photographs, cartoons or diagrams have a special function in a programme, track the illustrative content separately. The discovery of *The Mary Rose* event was a good example – and the unveiling of a new car design, a fashion event, or a high-speed photo of a dummy crumpling alarmingly in a poorly designed safety harness are others. They're all examples of media information where the picture can do a job which probably can't be done by a press release, and its contribution deserves its own thread of analysis.

One good reason for analysing illustrations separately is the expense of obtaining them. If, after analysis, it's found that the pictures are contributing nothing in the way of message content and aren't helping the items get published, the strategy should be changed or abandoned.

It is easy to waste money on illustrations. A good cartoon by a known-name cartoonist will cost hundreds of pounds; a top-class photographer's bill for a day's work may cost thousands of pounds; a colour diagram of a new manufacturing process may keep a draughtsperson off the next project for a week. The money will be well spent if it delivers the required message strongly; it will have been a waste if it's unused or, as is annoyingly often the case, used but not attributed.

PHOTOS: ATTRIBUTION AND NON-ATTRIBUTION

Newspapers and journals derive their illustrations from a variety of sources. If a journal uses a library picture or a picture from some other source to illustrate an article about a product, a company or an organization, the analyst should incorporate that picture into the analysis.

It's so tempting to be delighted when you see *your* picture in an article, and to ignore the ones from other sources. You organized the shoot; you briefed the photographer or the cartoonist. The trouble is, it's the effect on the reader that counts and the reader probably doesn't care where the illustration has come from.

A picture is sometimes sent to a newspaper or magazine and stored for future use. When it is eventually used it may reappear as a backdrop for another article or appear out of context in a round-up feature. If there is no attribution in the caption or text, it can't contribute to any product or company message for which it may have originally been intended. Its value to the newspaper may be high, but its value to the company is zero, and is not worth analysis.

PRESENTING PICTORIAL DATA

The analyst has the choice of incorporating pictorial data into his or her routine analysis or producing a special set of charts which single out the contribution made by the illustrations. The objectives of the programme, the subject matter, and the budget should contribute to this decision.

If the illustrations are delivering a significant number of message points, it is better to track them separately. Tracking them against changes in attitude and behaviour among the audiences will also be worthwhile. It may be that it is the pictures, not the words which are persuading the hi-tech companies to include your town on their short-list for a new manufacturing plant, or the diagram which is attracting licensees for a new process.

This chapter concludes our study of media analysis techniques and applications. The next decision communicators should address is a simple one: when should the analysis begin? In Chapter 18 we suggest that this should be earlier rather than later.

18 The Corporate Environment

Thousands of companies have decided that they intend to analyse their media – soon!
They are waiting until recent events have settled down, until the budget becomes
available, until the current round of corporate change is out of the way. We argue the
case for starting media analysis now – after all, your customers probably don't know
about the corporate changes your company is implementing, but they still have money
to spend.

Most organizations that I know are in a constant state of change. People are
changing; divisions are being merged or disbanded while others are being
formed; new management information is required; and new performance
standards have to be met. It is hardly surprising, therefore, that when the idea of
media analysis is introduced it never seems quite the right time to start.

The pace of change rarely slows down. When today's crisis is over, there's
always another one looming. Next week, we tell ourselves, or in three months' or
six months' time, the time will be right and we will be sailing on untroubled
waters. Perhaps that is the time to start our media analysis? Perhaps, on the other
hand, the pace of change will never slow and the right time will never arrive.

Media analysis is at its most useful during periods of fundamental change. It's
needed during change for two reasons. Not only can media analysis methods be
used to monitor existing media profile while internal reorganization is taking
place, but if there are external implications, the results can be used to ensure the
change is managed successfully. We'll deal with these two aspects of media
analysis in this chapter – but first we need to examine (and discard) some of the
excuses for not implementing it straight away.

EXCUSES FOR DELAYING THE START DATE

I'M TOO BUSY RIGHT NOW. . .

There's an old adage which suggests that if you want a job done well, you should
give it to someone who is already busy. That could well be you! Obviously, there

are seasonal changes in business, and nobody would suggest starting analysis on the day you issue the annual results, for instance. But there's nothing against scheduling the start of the process in a week or a month's time – and you can write a diary note to yourself even during the company AGM.

In a company of Times Top 500 or Fortune 500 proportions, you will probably need to schedule half a day to draft the messages and set up a series of meetings (or add items to existing agendas) with those people with whom you'll need to agree the measurement parameters. There's time for that level of activity in most people's diaries. And once it's arranged, the process has started.

The key judgements about message delivery are best made by an outside party, so it could be that once the process is under way, the time commitment will turn out to be far less than expected (see Chapter 7).

I'M WAITING FOR MY NEW GRADUATE PA TO START. . .

This is a classic excuse, and a common one. There are implications that the manager feels that media analysis is going to be difficult (and perhaps tedious). There is a further implication that the measurement process won't reach the heart of the organization.

Media analysis needs very senior input at the start. And it needs the person who is to manage it to know the culture and the dynamics of the organization intimately. If you are severely stretched, by all means wait for the new PA, but give him or her something else to do – and you use the time freed up to get the media analysis off the ground, making sure that you are measuring against real objectives, not an academic standard of little or no significance to you.

THIS PERIOD IS UNUSUAL – IT WILL DISTORT THE RESULTS. . .

Another distressingly common excuse. It's a little like saying 'I don't think we ought to map this bit of the Himalayas because it is too mountainous.' No matter whether you are launching a new division, sacking your finance director, or attacking a new marketplace, the media profile for the period will supply you with important feedback about the effects the changes are having on your audiences – and you ought to know about these.

There isn't really a 'normal period' in an organization's development. A month is a collection of unique events, and if you wait for a 'normal' month you could be waiting for ever.

THE MESSAGES AND AUDIENCES ARE CHANGING. . .

Of course they are! The term 'dynamic organization' means an organization which is moving and changing, and sometimes change means changing direction as well as increasing pace. Managing a dynamic organization means reviewing objectives, messages and audiences constantly.

An imminent change of messages from 'We are a US-based company' to 'We are an international organization' is an excellent reason to measure both messages now – to see how much work there is to do. A change of audience implied by an attack on a new marketplace is an excellent reason to look at the new target media before you announce your move: it will provide you with some useful benchmark information.

WE'RE WAITING FOR SOMEBODY ELSE. . .

A delay while somebody elsewhere in the organization provides information is often used as an excuse to delay the start of a media analysis programme. Sometimes it is the marketing department who need to identify vertical market audiences, but more often it's a wait for someone at a senior level to approve the draft messages or target media.

The information needed for media analysis is the kind of information which should form the backbone of the PR or communications programme, and should be readily available. A suggestion that you would be quite happy to start the programme with your own ideas and consequently without their cooperation is often enough to gain enthusiastic support from your seniors.

THERE'S NO MONEY IN THE BUDGET FOR MEDIA ANALYSIS. . .

This is easily the most widespread and most plausible excuse of all. The reason why there is no cash for media analysis is usually because nobody has *asked* for cash for media analysis. Because media analysis is a relatively new discipline, there is no tradition of budgeting for it, so new money must be found.

The money may be made available following a direct appeal to senior management, but very often the cash can be allocated from another area. Companies who budget independently for market research may want the funding for media analysis to come from this separate budget rather than extend the marketing communications or public relations budgets. We explore this question in greater detail in Chapter 23.

THE ULTIMATE EVALUATION SOLUTION WILL ARRIVE SOON. . .

Just as Godot never manages to arrive in Samuel Beckett's famous play, don't wait for the 'ultimate PR evaluation system' to arrive. Media coverage must be analysed if a public relations programme with a significant media content is to be evaluated. Every element in a PR programme needs to be evaluated – but there are no short cuts to PR programme evaluation available now, nor are there ever likely to be any.

A research survey carried out among PR people by Tom Watson (1992)* indicates that PR people are convinced that computers and software will eventually provide an evaluation solution. Comments at conferences and seminars often indicate that there is a yearning among PR people for a system into which they can place their entire PR output – media and non-media – and await a result.

People who provide media analysis are often criticized for 'not being able to analyse the non-media elements of the programme'. Who, going into a car showroom, complains because they don't sell aeroplanes there? And remember that in 1970 there was no media analysis being carried out at all.

IT'S NOT MY JOB. . .!

Media analysis can be anybody's job. Ideally, as indicated elsewhere, it should be the responsibility of the director of communications or the public relations director. If it is not being carried out at a senior level, there is an opportunity for more junior staff to take the project on.

The individual who specifies and manages media analysis is confirming the communications agenda, and will be in a position to monitor corporate progress against objectives. It is a position of considerable influence and power. The senior person who passes the job to someone more junior does so at his or her peril.

UNDERNEATH IT ALL, I DON'T WANT TO BE MEASURED. . .

An honest excuse which is rarely voiced, but one which undoubtedly underlies the reluctance of some organizations to become involved in media analysis.

There is no need to fear the results of media analysis provided it is used as it should be – as a management control mechanism. Good media analysis measures agreed parameters in all media coverage surrounding an organization, not just the coverage generated by the organization. It therefore need not and should not be regarded only as a measure of PR performance.

Setting up a measurement system is a bold and confident move which will bring recognition and reward in most organizations. From the consultancy viewpoint, even problems thrown up in media analysis have their advantages: a drop in that part of the profile associated with a key message will usually require a PR solution – which in turn will generate the need for more PR activity.

INTERNAL CHANGES – KEEPING AN EYE ON THE BALL

Try naming five operating divisions of Kodak. If you aren't employed by the company, and don't do business with them, you'll find it tough. Ask yourself where the

*IPR Journal, November 1993.

corporate headquarters of ICI is: is the company based in London? Or Billingham? Or Teesside? Or perhaps Welwyn Garden City or New Jersey? We still continue to buy film from Kodak, and ICI will carry on supplying the world's chemicals, agriculture and garment industries in huge quantities regardless of our ignorance. The fact that we don't know these facts doesn't really matter to us, and it doesn't matter to them.

An office move, or the formation of a new division will have little impact on a company's target audiences. It may have cataclysmic effects on the public relations department however. While literature is being changed, new letterhead produced, new lines of communication being established, it is all too easy to neglect ongoing corporate and promotional work. Press calls can arrive and remain unanswered when we've got other things on our minds; projects are all too easily put back or shelved when there are other, seemingly more important, tasks to attend to.

Media analysis is a useful mechanism for monitoring the way the company is seen in the media at times when these changes are occurring. If there has been a shortfall, it will show up and will need to be corrected at a later stage. If the workload has been maintained, the charts will provide no unpleasant surprises. The discipline of media analysis can be used as a management technique to ensure that we keep our priorities in the right order.

MEDIA ANALYSIS DURING PERIODS OF HIGHLY VISIBLE CHANGE

During a period of internal changes the attention level can be allowed to drop, but highly visible external changes such as a takeover or a launch into a new marketplace demand high levels of activity from communications staff.

Far from putting off the introduction of media analysis during periods of change such as this, the director of communications should ensure that the analysis covers the activities in question. The communications team can learn a huge amount about the dynamics of a marketplace, and about its own place in that marketplace by analysing the media after it has made its move. Here are a few examples.

CONTESTED ACQUISITIONS

An acquisition – especially a contested one – can change the perceptions of both the acquisition target company and the predator. During the slanging match which often precedes a contested acquisition, the image of both can be seriously damaged, to the detriment of both companies. Talking the price down in private is one thing, but when the dialogue spills over into the daily and weekly trade press sales audiences, the local community and, most important of all, employees can also be adversely affected.

Both companies involved should analyse media reports of the takeover and take steps to correct false and damaging perceptions conveyed by their opponents. It is advisable to review messages and media categories vigorously during these circumstances. At these times, look for messages such as:

'XXX is successful.'
'XXX is well managed.'
'XXX is trustworthy.'
'XXX is a good employer.'
'XXX is a market leader.'

The infighting can be fast and furious, and the weapons can be changed in the space of a few hours. Media analysis probably needs to be carried out on a daily or weekly basis: a monthly report will be an interesting record of events but such an analysis will not contribute much in the heat of battle.

Analysis of the international public wire services (for example Reuter, AP, Press Association, AFP) and the paid-for press release distribution services (UNS in the UK, PR Newswire and Business Wire in the USA) can be highly informative during a contested acquisition. My own company, Infopress, has been involved in monitoring the wire services during acquisitions and has on occasion been able to neutralize a damaging story before it hit the pages of the newspapers the next day by issuing a strongly worded rebuttal less than an hour after a predator's wire item appeared.

Simple product and corporate coverage will also need to be analysed during this time. Phrases such as 'Beleaguered engineering company ...' and '... acquisitive fashion accessory manufacturer' can alter significantly the tone of an otherwise positive or simply informative piece of editorial copy.

SENIOR MANAGEMENT CHANGES

Most senior management changes go unannounced, or merit no more than a line or two in the trade press with a photograph and some biographical details.

When, however, a well-known individual with a background in Government or some other highly visible record is appointed or departs, the effect can be a doubling of the volume of coverage for a short period and a sudden change in the message delivery performance – for better or for worse.

Monitor these effects so that the effects of future arrivals and departures can be anticipated and if necessary communicated to the board before the next round of senior staffing decisions is taken.

NEW MARKETS

When a company enters a new marketplace – either geographical or industry sector – with a new range of products or services, both the messages and the media categories will need to be reviewed. A product launch or key change in policy like this provides the PR team with a once-only opportunity to build a useful profile in a new media sector. A little time and money spent during this time will be a good investment.

Extending the scope of the monitoring to encompass the new journals is an obvious step. The product USPs (unique selling points) and customer benefits will have been reinforced in the launch material and it will be necessary to look for these in the media coverage which ensues from the launch.

MEDIA ANALYSIS – A USEFUL INDICATOR DURING CHANGE

A healthy and dynamic organization is constantly changing. Far from being a reason for delaying the introduction of media analysis, a period of change should be a reason for bringing it forward. An ability to adapt to change is one of the key qualities which enables organizations to survive, and media analysis will give high quality information about its external effects.

For a moment, think about a member of one of your key audiences, perhaps a customer or business partner, and think about the information they will be receiving about you. Answering the following questions should help you decide the timetable for the introduction of media analysis.

1. Do I need to know how effectively I have been communicating with our audiences this month?
2. Do I need to know what messages about my organization are being conveyed to our audiences via the media this month?
3. Is anything likely to happen this month, over which I have limited or no control, but which will result in media coverage about us?
4. Are our audiences this month the same audiences as they were last month, and are our messages the same as they were then?

If the answer to any of the first three questions is yes, then the time is right for you to commence media analysis.

The first step is to decide on the target audiences and media categories and ensure that you are collecting and keeping the media coverage itself.

The next step is to set out the measurement parameters (see Chapter 3) and to gain the agreement of those who will be involved in generating the coverage. You should also decide on the type of approach you need (see Chapters 7 and 9).

If the answer to question 4 is no, it is likely that you are in the midst of a seasonal fluctuation or some other change of direction. Good media analysis is flexible and responsive and the system you use should be capable of adjustment to the needs of the new situation. Even if the priorities are changing very rapidly indeed (for instance in the case of a contested acquisition as suggested above), it will be possible to adjust the parameters of the measurement to cover all the angles.

With the media analysis programme under way, the communications director will now want to turn his or her attention to the direct measurement of opinion, perception and behaviour. It is the correlation of these two empirical measurements which will enable the PR team to understand and anticipate the changes which take place in the organization's communications environment.

Part III
Media Analysis in Perspective

19 Direct Measurement of Opinions, Perceptions, Reputation and Behaviour

Perhaps the unique and most important task of media analysis is disentangling editorial message data from advertising message data as it arrives in the minds of your audiences. As such it needs to be carried out in parallel with some kind of direct measurement of the opinions, perceptions and behaviour of your target groups. The author introduces the concepts, explains how they work and refers to some companies who do it.

Without intermediate research such as media analysis it is usually impossible to tell which element of an organization's communications mix has resulted in an observed change of visibility, knowledge, opinion or behaviour in a target audience.

The converse is also true: you may know that your message has appeared in the media, but you won't know for sure that it has reached your target audience until you use audience research to check that it has arrived.

Audience research is a natural partner for media analysis and neither can be interpreted reliably in a media relations environment without leaning heavily on the other.

Some PR people (and it must be said, some advertising and direct maketing people as well), have been less than honest in interpreting the results of audience research. For some, launching a modest PR programme alongside a creative, energetic and expensive advertising campaign is a safe and rewarding exercise. Measure brand recall before and after the launch programme, and Bingo! – the recall figures have shot up. Did the changes occur as a result of the public relations work? Perhaps not, but some claim the result for themselves. I call this practice 'ad surfing', and I suspect a number of prestigious PR industry awards have been won by practitioners of the sport.

Using media analysis alongside audience research will inhibit the surfers from entering their work for awards they don't deserve. More importantly, the techniques used in harmony can help a marketing communications professional to unravel the tangled causal skein of a multi-threaded programme and reveal what activities have been responsible for what results – revealing where the money should be spent to best effect in the future.

AUDIENCE RESEARCH IN PR – SOME APPLICATIONS

The public relations professional will be no stranger to audience measurement techniques. But in many instances the professional's primary concern is to mould opinions rather than to measure them.

The PR-driven survey is a technique which has been widely used for the past 30 years. In this technique, a survey is carried out which demonstrates the lack of a product or service, highlights an underlying attitude or opinion, or perhaps demonstrates a high level of ignorance on a key subject. The results of the survey are quickly published to the amazement of journalists, readers and viewers. Then a few weeks later a product is announced which fills the need, a manifesto is published which agrees with the opinion, or a book is published which fills the information gap.

The PR-driven survey prepares the ground for a rather more hard-nosed, sales-orientated promotion, raising the visibility of the sponsoring organization and associating it with an issue or problem which it has a vested interest in solving. There is nothing wrong with the PR-driven survey. But in its naked form it is not the kind of survey which is going to help a PR professional to formulate and track PR key programme messages. It is this area of rather more fundamental importance which we need to explore now.

Fortunately, the research methods of the PR-driven survey are borrowed from pure audience research, and the suppliers of expertise are likely to be the same. In coming to use audience research for the first time, the PR professional who has commissioned a PR-driven survey will be on very familiar ground.

AUDIENCE RESEARCH AND MEDIA ANALYSIS WORKING TOGETHER

Audience research and media analysis can be designed to complement each other exactly, and in seeking to establish a causal relationship between media relations activity and achievement of communication objectives, the analyst will be seeking to establish a correlation between the two.

Like any other research exercise, a survey of visibility, knowledge, opinion and behaviour among target audience needs careful planning and preparation. Looking up Audience Selection, MORI or NOP in the telephone directory is something you don't need to do straight away. It's far more important to work out in advance exactly what you want to measure. As will be seen later, it could be that you won't need external help at all.

Let us deal with corporate and brand visibility first. Media analysis gives us frequency of use of the company or brand name, and in looking for a correlation, the audience researcher will be looking for changes in spontaneous and prompted recall of that name in the audience research. A close link between the two will indicate, but not necessarily establish, the causal relationship which is sought.

CHOOSING AN AUDIENCE RESEARCH METHOD

It is the communication objectives and the messages embedded in them which are of key importance in choosing an audience research method. In Chapter 5 we identified three types of message corresponding to changes in audience knowledge, opinion and behaviour. If the objective of the programme is to change one or more of these, then it is these changes which the PR professional will need to measure, and it is these results which will need to be compared with the media analysis.

Classic audience research offers an impressive and reassuring range of measurement possibilities. Most companies' own records also offer useful audience research possibilities and these low cost options should never be ignored. In the following pages, we will be touching briefly on:

- Telephone surveys
- Street surveys
- Omnibus surveys
- Focus groups
- Self-completion questionnaires
- Regularly published industry surveys
- Yearbooks
- Sales and enquiry figures and statistics.

It is not within the scope of this book or this chapter to cover any of these in detail. Those wishing to explore audience research more thoroughly would be well advised to obtain a copy of a more specialized book on the subject (for example, *The Consumer Market Research Handbook* by Robert Worcester and John Downham). Let us instead re-examine three of the examples given in Chapter 5 and suggest some of the audience measurement options which would be suitable for each one.

1. MEASURING AUDIENCE KNOWLEDGE

In the example of a plastics moulding manufacturer serving the toy and electrical industries, one of the knowledge messages the manufacturer was keen to transmit to its business audiences was '30 per cent of our output is manufactured from recycled plastics waste'.

A dedicated (and expensive) telephone survey would of course establish a company's environmental credentials in the minds of the audiences in each of these two industries, and the chosen research firm would be able to advise on the smallest number of interviewees to form a large enough sample to obtain representative results. But companies in the business-to-business sector, like our mouldings manufacturer, would need to think carefully about the economics of such an exercise before implementing it. The cost of the research exercise may

173

outweigh the benefits of gaining that knowledge – of which more later.

It would almost certainly be more cost-effective to add a question on environmental matters to a much more general research study on knowledge and opinions of the company and its competitors. This could be based on a telephone survey or a series of in-depth, face-to-face interviews. Such a study could cover subjects ranging from purchasing and specification policy to the audience's knowledge and interest in industry issues.

If the media relations programme has been a success, and if the research is well designed, it is likely that confirmation of successful message delivery will emerge in the replies without prompting. The company's own name may feature in answers to 'open' questions such as 'Name a plastics mouldings manufacturer you admire'; the company's environmental practices will emerge, perhaps, when the interviewer probes for reasons.

Participation in a broad spectrum corporate or product-orientated research study is a good method of determining delivery of knowledge messages, but such studies are beset by two basic problems.

1. The study will often be 'owned' by the marketing department rather than communications and public relations, and any opportunities to control the content and scope of the questionnaire will be very limited. Perhaps the effectiveness of delivery of only one or two messages can be determined.
2. A related problem, concerning audiences. If the recycling message in our example was directed at environmental officers or end users, a detailed interview with a plant manager or an engineering director will not give us the information we need and will therefore be of little use.

Consumer audiences, especially those associated with big-name consumer brands, present the researcher with different difficulties. Brand positioning, the PR programme, the advertising programme and the research programme should together form part of an interlocking logical structure in which the media relations programme forms a relatively small part.

If media analysis and consumer research are going to be used together to construct a full and accurate picture of message delivery to those consumers, the programmes will need to be planned in tandem. Knowledge and opinion messages are designed to enhance or otherwise change the way in which a member of an audience thinks about a company, an organization or an issue. By measuring some specific messages in the media and a set of closely related attributes in audience research, the analyst will not need to rely on interpolation to deduce results – results which will be unreliable and only marginally useful.

Where it is necessary to measure audience knowledge, an organization will need to use the services of a reputable market research company or trusted independent researcher unless a regularly published industry survey happens to highlight the answer to the questions, thus enabling the researcher to track the levels of audience knowledge in which a change is sought.

2. MEASURING AUDIENCE OPINION

There is a fine line between knowledge and opinion messages, but they present different problems to the audience researcher. Take the opinion message we used as an example in Chapter 5: 'It's good to live in a town where IBM has an office.'

To have an informed opinion on this statement, a member of the local community must first know that IBM has an office there. This can be established by a telephone survey or street survey of the local community. But having established this knowledge, the researcher may need to delve deeper. The survey may have established whether the interviewee agrees with the message in our example, but neither the telephone survey nor the street survey are the ideal way of exploring the complex set of ideas which may lie behind such an opinion.

Many local people will know someone, or even be related to someone who works for a local IBM office, and this will affect their opinions of the company. Another interviewee may be involved in a community scheme sponsored by the company, and again, his or her views will be coloured by this. Yet another may be a customer or supplier. Are their opinions modified by local media coverage? The answer will not be found using simple quantitative audience research techniques: it will probably require a less simple and more expensive study.

Possibilities might include detailed face-to-face interviews, or a focus group session in which the interaction between a number of people can be studied. A more informative picture will be obtained by comparing media analysis results with the secondary information which results from this more open and investigative approach.

There may be short cuts in obtaining audience opinion data. Occasionally, an off-the-shelf industry survey may give some of the answers needed by the researcher – at a much lower cost than the cost of conducting tailor-made research.

If the messages are very simple and straightforward, some message delivery data may be obtainable from omnibus surveys in which a number of different companies participate, each 'owning' two or three of the questions. These are relatively cheap to participate in as the agency's overheads are shared between a number of different clients. The research companies have probably already been actively marketing the omnibus in the sector you are working in and their offerings are likely to be well known. If not, a telephone call to each of the big market research agencies will probably give an indication of what is available, and at what cost. One omnibus which is particularly well known is the Audience Selection's Key Directors Omnibus, enabling organizations to test the opinions of this important group.

Where the messages are detailed and precise, however, these lower-cost options are less useful. A published survey of the computer industry probably won't state whether there has been an opinion shift among systems managers towards token ring networks. A question in an omnibus survey is not the ideal opportunity to ask a chief executive to guess what proportion of turnover ICI spends on R&D: his or her answer may be 'polluted' by the question he or she has just been asked about European legislation on bananas.

3. MEASURING AUDIENCE BEHAVIOUR

It is usually much easier and less expensive to obtain information on audience behaviour than it is to measure knowledge and opinions through audience research. As many communication programmes are action and behaviour orientated, this is good news for the communications professional with limited funds at his or her disposal.

Changes in audience behaviour can often be tracked without resorting to direct contact with the audience at all. Sales figures, for instance, can be compared to product messages in the media; an election result will tell a politician whether campaign messages have been delivered successfully – a comparison with media analysis of coverage during the campaign will make useful and interesting reading for the future.

The interpretation of behavioural data can be tricky, however. The purchase of capital equipment, for instance, will probably be preceded by a period of enquiry, trial and negotiation, and the sale itself may take place years after the sales lead was first received. Any month-by-month comparison between 'sales' and delivery of the 'product quality' message in the trade press will therefore probably be spurious in these circumstances.

Sales of lower-price, fast-moving consumer goods (fmcgs) do not have this time problem; with fmcgs the difficulty is in disentangling the influence of PR from the influence of the advertising campaign running alongside it: we are back to the 'ad surfing' problem referred to earlier. Fortunately, the advertising industry has developed a battery of techniques for measuring the effectiveness of its advertisements. Some of them are applicable to media relations.

Media relations is often used to persuade an audience to do something – like buy a product, give money to OXFAM or vote for Ms X. Occasionally, media relations is used to persuade an audience not to do something – like smoke cigarettes, sell shares, club Canadian seals or indeed, vote for Mr Y.

Share price data is available in newspapers each day and is the easiest to obtain of the above. Election result and opinion polls will tell the campaigner how successful the campaign against Mr Y has been. In Chapter 5, we highlighted the message 'Stop smoking or you'll die' as an example of such a message. Regional smoking data are more difficult to obtain than share prices, but are available from the Government and are published occasionally in the press. Tobacco companies also collect data on smoking, but don't often publish their own sales statistics, making a detailed correlation difficult.

Again, there are some short cuts which can be taken. Industry yearbooks and handbooks are a useful source of data on audience behaviour. The pattern of consumption of margarine, the growth of PBX switchboards and accident figures are all available for correlation if needed – and if relevant. A good first port of call for a researcher requiring this kind of detailed data is the relevant Government department. Trade associations and other representative industry bodies are also often useful sources.

THE MEASUREMENT OF CHANGE

The advantage of handbooks, omnibus surveys, other off-the-shelf research options and the examination of internal sales and enquiry records is that all are usually available regularly, enabling the media analyst and the audience researcher to construct 'before' and 'after' pictures at relatively low cost.

Their value in obtaining meaningful correlation with the media analysis varies enormously, however. A handbook published anually will only give an indication of the nett, cumulative effect of communication activity over a year; sales and enquiry statistics however are usually available on a much more regular basis and they present more opportunities for finding useful correlations for product related messages.

Media analysis techniques are better at measuring change than they are at measuring absolute values, and the same applies to audience research and direct observation of audience behaviour. Consider a company which has sold 500 television sets a year for the past five years, and then carries out an intensive product PR campaign. If the company then sells 750 sets the following year, it is likely that with all other things being equal, the PR has helped to sell those extra 250 units.

On the other hand, a company which launches a television with a PR programme and sells 250 units in the first year cannot say with any degree of certainty how those sales were generated.

The certainty increases if the monthly pattern of sales closely follows the media analysis charts – for instance the volume of coverage trend chart, or the charts tracking delivery of key product messages.

Monthly or weekly trend data can establish a pattern of message delivery for a period, and this can be correlated with sales and enquiry records for the same period. A geographical comparison can also be made. If the behavioural data is only available annually from a yearbook, an industry survey or annual reports, detailed monthly information will not be available for comparison. Less can be read into the correlation, and there will be nothing to compare the monthly pattern with.

The principle of measuring knowledge, opinion or behaviour before a media relations campaign and examining it again afterwards is valid whatever audience or other behavioural data is available.

AUDIENCE RESEARCH IN MESSAGE FORMULATION

So much for the role of audience research in establishing the relevance and significance of media analysis. Direct measurement of audience knowledge, opinion and behaviour also has a bearing on the parameters of the media relations programme (and therefore the media analysis programme). In addition to telling us how well we've been delivering the key messages, audience research can also tell us what these messages should be.

In Chapter 8, we examined the role of the communications audit in establishing the overall direction of a public relations programme. External audience research has a vital role to play in the audit. Even where a full communications audit is not needed, however, the communications professional will want to become involved in any research in which the organization's audiences are asked about their knowledge, opinions and behaviour.

Audience research can establish many key facts about a planned public relations programme from the importance of corporate visibility ('I'm happier dealing with a smaller company than a larger company') to the identification of totally new messages ('I need to know more about new European legislation on livestock movements').

Once the broad strategy and the basic messages have been agreed on they can be refined using qualitative research. Attitudes, opinions and key messages can be explored in focus groups and the communications strategy given a final polish.

Audience research – qualitative and quantitative – also offers good opportunities to review existing practice and existing messages. The results may indicate that a message of earlier importance ('All our instrumentation is based on digital technology') is fading into the background because it has lost its ability to differentiate. Issues also change: the sale of high technology to the former Eastern bloc is welcome now, rather than abhorrent and illegal as it was in the 1970s and 1980s.

WHO SHOULD CARRY OUT AUDIENCE RESEARCH?

The market research industry is complex. It is formed of large, multi-faceted agencies offering a comprehensive range of services, lone operators offering deep industry specialization and all points in between. An organization using audience research for the first time would be well advised to go to a large generalist market research agency until specialist staff can be hired or until existing staff have learnt the ropes.

In choosing an agency, the following checklist of questions may prove helpful:

1. Does the agency offer a wide range of services or is the agency specialist in a particular technique? Will it force us down a particular route (for example, qualitative rather than quantitative) even though it may not be best for us?

2. Is the agency experienced in our sector? Like PR consultancies, market research companies earn their reputations through experience – a big consumer-orientated firm may be in deep water when it comes to a closely focused business-to-business assignment, and vice versa.

3. Do we communicate well with the agency team? Find out in advance who you will be dealing with personally – and it's vital that you get on well. Misunderstandings can be expensive.

4. How much will it cost? This sounds obvious, but overruns and extra questions all cost money. It is easy to overlook them when you need the results in a hurry. A ball-park estimate which just falls within your budget can be out by as much as 100 per cent. If you are acting through a PR consultancy, don't forget to budget for its commission; if agreed in advance, it might be possible to get this billed direct, thus eliminating a significant extra cost.

5. When will you receive the report? Agree the timetable at the outset, otherwise your PR programme could be delayed or get off on the wrong foot, and need adjustment later.

6. What form will the results appear in? And in particular, do you just need only fieldwork or are you looking for an analytical report based on the tables of data? It is easy to jump to conclusions if the data is not fully understood.

7. Have I briefed the agency thoroughly and unambiguously? Prepare a written agency brief even for a simple assignment. If after briefing the agency there are still areas of doubt, cover these in a following letter – a step which again may save arguments later.

8. How many copies of the final report are needed? Ask this of colleagues in other departments before commissioning the report: a key person you hadn't thought of may also need the data.

9. Is this going to be a regular exercise? If you are going to repeat this survey year after year or every six months, it may be possible to obtain a reduction in cost by committing the organization to two or more, now.

FITTING IT ALL TOGETHER

Once the audience research is available to drop into position alongside the results of the media analysis, detailed comparisons can be made and conclusions drawn. The two sets of data can be appreciated most effectively by graphing them manually or by entering them into a spreadsheet with graphic capabilities.

Sometimes a direct relationship between the two will be obvious. Sometimes it will be difficult to detect and the results will need to be analysed further using statistical techniques.

In the next chapters we discuss the applications of media analysis in a dynamic corporate environment. We examine two ways of looking at the results: as a feedback mechanism to fine tune a media relations programme; and to justify a media relations programme or the expenditure on which it relies.

Backed by audience research, media relations is even more potent, both as a programme control mechanism and as a persuader. With audience research, the importance as well as the magnitude of successful message delivery can be demonstrated; while media analysis can show that the desired communication has taken place, only audience research can demonstrate the effects it has actually had on the audience, in detail.

Perhaps more significantly, a single examination of the effects of a media relations campaign on an audience will enable the PR professional to anticipate the effects of future media relations activity when only media analysis data will be available.

AUDIENCE RESEARCH AND COSTS

In this chapter we have examined various ways in which we can analyse the effects of different categories of message on our chosen audiences. We have found that the experience which many PR people have gained in managing PR-driven surveys will be useful in managing the more fundamental discipline of choosing and refining messages, and in tracking their effect.

We have found that researching audience knowledge and opinions can be a good deal more expensive than researching audience behaviour. Both need to be considered. Pete Cape, a director of Audience Selection, is of the opinion that it is almost impossible to over-research a project. But, he states, there comes a point when the extra cost needed to research a subject a little more thoroughly outweighs the benefit of the extra thoroughness. When that point is reached, the client must call a halt; finding the right point is a matter of fine judgement and experience.

In conclusion, I'd like to return to a point made in the first part of this book about the nature of public relations. If public relations is concerned with the establishment of 'mutual understanding' then the evaluation of media relations must involve the analysis of audience attitudes, opinions and knowledge alongside media analysis. If, on the other hand PR is concerned mainly with persuading audiences to do something, or otherwise act in a different way, then we should put more emphasis on the correlation of our media analysis with audience actions; analysis of knowledge and opinions will only be of intermediate importance.

I believe that there is room for all the direct audience research methods in the science of media analysis and evaluation.

In the next chapter, we leave the market research industry for the cyclical nature of decision making in the communications function – and the role that media analysis plays in it.

20 The Feedback Process

With the building blocks in place, the author now introduces the concept of feedback in two situations: a situation in which expenditure on PR needs to be justified, and the management of a programme or project. The communications business needs a communications production line, with design, production, testing and quality control. Why has the idea of testing communications strategy and techniques lain undeveloped for so long? Now that media analysis is here, the author argues, there's no excuse for ignoring it.

Some organizations are large enough to employ as many people, and spend as much money in their communications departments as quite a considerable company in its own right.

Put the entire staff of Barclays Bank's corporate affairs and public relations department into a single building and that organization by itself could be the largest employer in a small town. Take the UK Government's information service as another example. In Britain, the Central Office of Information (COI) acts as an information resource for most UK Government departments: with a string of regional offices, the COI is almost an industry in itself.

Communications is big business. Even small private companies spend large sums of money on communicating with the rest of the world – and the activity needs to be controlled, both financially and technically, just as carefully as production, accountancy, and research and development.

THE PRINCIPLE OF FEEDBACK AND COMMUNICATIONS

The principle of feedback is inherent in the control of any corporate function, and it applies to corporate communications at two distinct levels.

THE CORPORATE LEVEL

Let's consider the corporate and financial level first. It's logical for an organization to establish a system to ensure that it is achieving the very best value in terms of 'communications output' for the money it's spending on communications. If it finds it's not receiving this value, the infrastructure of the budget and the level of investment can be adjusted to ensure that the situation doesn't continue.

There aren't many firms spending large budgets on open-ended research and development which doesn't offer some kind of corporate payday at a future date. There certainly aren't many production lines which continually produce goods which don't get sold: the years of recession have taught us that these are luxuries most firms can't afford. Yet many companies continue to spend, and continue spending on their public relations work without the knowledge that good quality feedback can give them on how effective it's been.

Most of the building blocks for such a financial control system should already be in place. The organization can keep track of the money spent on literature, salaries, postage, stationery, telephone calls, consultancy and other expenses associated with communications. Then of course the organization should measure the quantity and quality of the output – and they can find out what they're getting for their money.

THE PROGRAMME MANAGEMENT LEVEL

The second control level is the programme or project management level. It's logical for the PR manager to set up internal controls in the PR department to optimize the processes being used. Information about what is working satisfactorily – and what isn't working so well – can be fed back into the system design to make it more effective.

The two levels are strongly linked. And media analysis has equally significant parts to play in the big corporate picture and in the day-to-day management of the programme.

CLOSING THE FEEDBACK LOOP

The big problems to date in controlling the communications programme have been in selecting the parameters which represent 'communications output', establishing a method of monitoring them reliably and repeatably, and incorporating them into the two levels of the management process outlined above.

It must be stressed that media analysis only provides part of the answer. In very few communications departments will the quantity and message content of newspapers, radio and television be the only applicable measure to use. Separate measures must be employed for other departmental functions such as literature production, parliamentary and investor relations. But the media element has been the fly in the measurement ointment for a long time. Now that it's here, we have reached a point where the feedback loops – at each level – can be closed at last.

THE PR FEEDBACK LOOP – GAINING CORPORATE CONTROL

To establish a feedback loop giving organizations better control over the PR process, the board and the PR department need to agree which parameters represent the department's output. Benchmarks can be established for each departmental function, and this can now extend to media relations.

Media relations benchmarks can be message scores for general messages such as 'Obtain a better "quality" profile than our competitors', or very specific message orientated goals such as 'Increase number of "environment" message points from 250 to 500 over the course of the year'. We've already explored the idea of graphing departmental expenditure against key message scores as an alternative to the outmoded AVE (Chapter 15). The principle of using message delivery scores as a unit of departmental output is suggested here.

It is unlikely that a single message score could be used as an absolute measure of PR department performance without reference to other factors. As has been pointed out in previous chapters, a chemical spill over which the PR department has no control can ruin the department's delivery of the 'environmentally responsible' message; the strength of delivery of any message relating to 'financial success' can be boosted by good year-end results even if their announcement was poorly handled.

It should be possible however to relate total scores for a portfolio of messages across a wide spectrum of activities to the cost of delivering them. Alternatively, there is the option of dividing departmentally generated coverage from that which has arisen from other sources – a task of analysis which is relatively easy to perform. It is up to the individuals involved to negotiate and eventually agree which are the fairest and most meaningful parameters covered in the analysis which can be truly said to represent 'communications output'.

A further application of media analysis which extends beyond the orbit of the PR department is in personnel management. I know of a number of instances where the results of media analysis are used as personal performance indicators for members of the PR team. In one instance (see Chapter 9) each PR team member has been made 'champion' of a particular message: it's his or her job to put that message across each month. The degree of success or otherwise can contribute to the career appraisal process.

THE PR FEEDBACK LOOP – PROGRAMME CONTROL

The media analyst's report data has an even more direct relevance to the management of the programme itself in the department or consultancy.

As the months go by, the user of media analysis, whether it's the director of communications or the PR manager, is receiving feedback on volume of coverage, brand or corporate visibility, and message delivery across a broad spectrum of media and messages. By relating results to activity, the manager can establish which activities are delivering the goods in the areas where they're most needed. At this tactical control level, media analysis is a potent management tool.

Bass Brewing's External Communications Manager Lesley Allman describes how she uses the IMPACT media analysis service in an article in the *Financial Times*:

> If the tracking studies show that a message such as 'Bass offers quality brands' is being expressed less frequently in the press, the company will try to remedy the trend by, say, making extra efforts to publicise awards won by its beers[1]

Sometimes media analysis will expose a flaw – or an opportunity – in the strategy, rather than in the way it is being implemented. In one recent example of this, a media analysis user in the travel sector found that it was unable to deliver two key messages about its service via classic media relations techniques in local media. However, media analysis revealed that one of its competitors was succeeding in delivering them rather too well: the analysis showed that the competitors' messages were appearing in competitions and advertorials. As a result, funds were switched to the same techniques, and much better results were obtained in the next period.

Figure 20.1 outlines the simple feedback process as it applies to PR programme management. Communications objectives drive the strategy and the implementation route chosen to support that strategy. When the results are analysed, the information can be used to modify the implementation of the programme as was the case with the Bass example given above, or to modify the strategy itself, as was the case with the travel company just mentioned. There is a third loop in the diagram however, because media analysis can sometimes result in the all-important communications objectives being changed.

Open analysis often reveals the need for a change of objectives. Competitors sometimes reveal a subtle change of direction only in their media coverage, and a company will need to introduce a new facet to the thinking behind its PR programme to cope with it.

Analysis may also reveal the complete impossibility of delivering a particular message by any means at all. One company in the information technology sector wanted to be seen as a group of gentle, friendly people. However, it had a rapacious appetite for acquiring other companies in the sector and however hard the PR team tried, the very opposite of the desired messages kept appearing in the press week after week.

By attempting to promote the 'friendly' message the company was, well, lying through its PR teeth: eventually they gave up trying, and the move does not seem to have had any adverse effect.

---

[1] 8 September 1994.

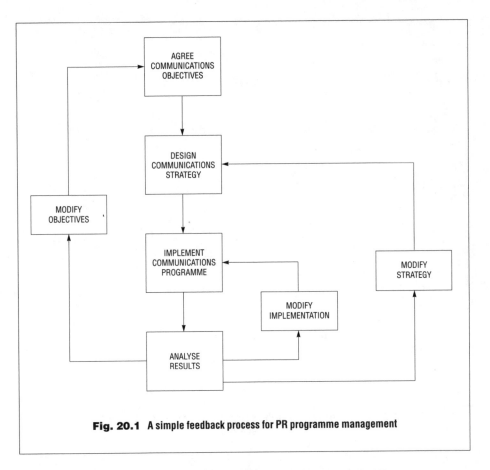

Fig. 20.1 A simple feedback process for PR programme management

MEDIA ANALYSIS AND THE COMMUNICATIONS CALENDAR

Analysis can provide valuable feedback to the management processes at various stages in the management cycle of organizations.

ANNUAL BUDGET ANALYSIS

A media analysis report is very often used to support a budget allocation request, when a PR department head is attempting to justify his or her planned expenditure for the next year. In these circumstances, the analysis is likely to be carried out annually, and cover the whole of the previous year. The whole year's coverage can be treated as a single entity and analysed for message delivery efficiency, or a trend report can be produced spanning 12 months of PR activity. Using the trend analysis technique, the rate of change over the year and the trends in individual messages can be determined. Volumetric peaks (at times such as the emergence of the annual results) can be analysed for last year – and planned for the next.

Most spreadsheets available offer a line-of-best-fit capability (Figures 20.2 and

185

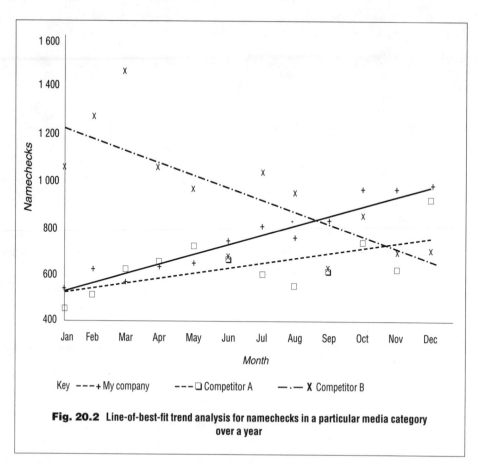

Fig. 20.2 Line-of-best-fit trend analysis for namechecks in a particular media category over a year

20.3) which will demonstrate very clearly indeed whether the trend in volumes, visibility and delivery of individual message is rising or falling. Care must be taken not to read too much into these purely mathematical techniques, but the unambiguous form of the charts can tell a purse-string holder a story of advance (or retreat!) clearly and concisely.

Some PR teams use media analysis only as a post-mortem technique, to demonstrate how well they have done and stake their claim for next year. It's a reasonable application, but not many PR teams can justify the expenditure of significant proportions of their budget on self-justification. It's important to note that this data will come as a bonus if media analysis is carried out on a monthly basis for programme management purposes: there's no need to analyse the same data twice.

While we are talking of budgets, it is worth noting here that PR budgets should also include an element of expenditure on the media analysis itself – but we'll be dealing with that in Chapter 23.

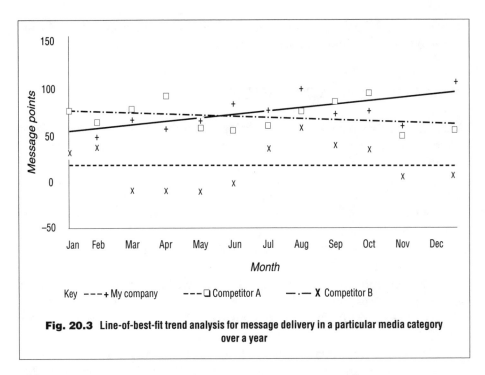

Fig. 20.3 Line-of-best-fit trend analysis for message delivery in a particular media category over a year

MONTHLY PR PROGRAMME ANALYSIS

Programme management data can be on a quarterly or weekly basis but is most often needed on a monthly basis.

The monthly media analysis report has an appropriate place in the monthly planning meeting, the quarterly review meeting or in a consultancy's regular client report. They can be used to summarize the results of PR activity, to pinpoint issues as they arise, and to keep a media-wary eye on a competitor. We've already shown how a media analysis report can be a stimulus to future activity: it's important to ensure that actions are taken as a result of the information emerging from media analysis. This is best decided in a meeting of the participants rather than as a few sheets of paper sent through the post and filed.

A media analysis report may be received and studied in detail once each month, but it is essentially part of a continuous process, and is analogous to a quality control station in a production line. No production engineer worth the name would design a process control system without quality control and testing built-in. I wonder how it is that the PR business has managed to escape the need for one for so long?

Some rapidly moving situations demand weekly or even daily analysis. We have already dealt with the application of media analysis in crisis management and in contested takeovers. The tendering for and negotiation of public contracts sometimes involve several organizations jockeying for position very publicly, using the press and broadcast media as weapons of assault and defence. In these circumstances, a weekly analysis may indicate the need for a sudden and telling change of direction for one of the organizations involved.

MEDIA ANALYSIS AND CORPORATE POLICY

When used as part of a management feedback process either at the corporate or programme management level, media analysis can have a profound influence on an organization's policies.

At programme level, monthly analyses can highlight flaws in communication and in information provided which suggest alternative methods.

As we have seen above, it can also be used as a method of justifying expenditure on communications at a corporate level.

But media analysis can have a far more significant effect than this in the formulation of corporate decisions. As an indicator of corporate reputation and success, media analysis can ask questions like 'Shouldn't we be going upstream into our suppliers' territory?' and 'Wouldn't we be better off getting out of aerosol production altogether?'. It can suggest significant changes – like hiring a quality manager.

Media analysis is another strand of management information which when used with other reports can enable directors to solve problems by triangulation. That is why boards are eagerly examining media analysis reports – a phenomenon examined in more detail in Chapter 24.

But while the board is pondering over the long and medium-term opportunities and problems, the report may have thrown up more pressing problems for the communications team to deal with. We'll indicate some ways of solving them in Chapter 21.

21 Trouble Shooting

We now examine the return loop of the feedback process as described in the last chapter, and examine some situations where media analysis has shown up cracks in the corporate mirror. Some strategies for tackling problems thrown up in this way are suggested, including creative strategies (for example, brainstorming and synectics techniques) and the role of the strategic advisor (for example, PR companies, management consultants) is explored.

It's a good feeling to look back over a year's public relations work and see all the message delivery charts indicating positive results, the visibility charts indicating a growing awareness of company and products, and see your competitor's parameters declining as the year progresses.

A time for a pat on the back? Perhaps. But not a time for complacency, because there has never been a perfect public relations programme and there's always room for improvement. Sometimes, of course, even a pat on the back will not be appropriate – because sometimes the results are going to be appalling and showing every sign of getting worse.

Organizations often behave very illogically in the face of a poor public profile. Reactions can range from ignoring it, doing more of the same, or transferring control of the PR department to someone who will take a 'tougher line'. The tougher line sometimes takes the form of clamming up altogether or taking inappropriate action such as suing a newspaper or magazine – the PR equivalent of shooting the messenger.

POST-MORTEM OR CONTROL INFORMATION?

Corporate panic sets in when an organization does not understand the mechanisms underlying a poor media profile. A poor profile will induce inappropriate response when the control loops explained in Chapter 20 have not been appreciated.

If a process in the plant is running too hot, the production manager won't be sacked – he or she will just turn the thermostat down. But when the pressure in the media relations department begins soaring, there are some organizations that don't know which button to push. This chapter looks at some of the problems which can be revealed by media analysis and suggests the initial steps needed to deal with them.

WHO GETS TO KNOW ABOUT THE PROBLEMS?

The first question the communications director will need to answer on seeing the adverse charts is who should be informed. It's likely that if the charts are terrible, most of his or her colleagues will already know something about it. On the other hand, a gradual diminishing of visibility or the steady rise in the 'quality' message for a small but energetic competitor may go undetected.

The decision about who to tell depends on the nature of the problem. Sometimes it's a small control problem and it can be dealt with by the department without troubling other, more senior colleagues. On other occasions, the problem has much wider ramifications and the communications director will need to gain the support of colleagues outside the department. Sometimes, of course, it will be something other than a PR problem which has caused the dips in the charts and the task of solving it will need to be handled by others.

It's unwise to overreact to a single month's scores as coverage can be highly seasonal for a start – and not just in the holiday industry either. Issues of magazines are thin in August and December and there is a natural seasonality to the coverage of publicly quoted companies with natural peaks when they publish their annual results.

It is quite likely that for a company generating 100 cuttings per month on average, the volume of coverage in one month can be half the coverage generated in another. There can also be a dramatic change in message score between one month and the next. It is important, however, to understand why it has happened when it does.

If the volume of coverage is dropping month on month and the organization and the media attention that it was getting a year ago simply isn't happening now, then it will be necessary to look into this long-term effect rather more closely. Similarly, if message scores are showing a deterioration over, say, three or four months, or if a competitor's message is seen to be rising over a long period, then corrective action will need to be taken.

There are several types of problem which can be revealed by the charts and they can be grouped loosely into the following broad categories:

● Too little visibility
● Failure to deliver a message
● Reputation suffering as a result of company policy
● Communication objectives unrealizable.

Let's consider these one at a time.

TOO LITTLE VISIBILITY

Low corporate or brand visibility is a phenomenon which may well not be a problem at all, of course. And it is certainly not within the scope of this book to explore classic PR techniques for raising profile when it's needed. An examination of one or two of the internal reasons why the organization may be becoming a paler shadow of its former self is a good idea though.

Trying to answer the question 'Why aren't we being written about?' by perusing the little coverage which was obtained probably won't reveal useful answers very readily. Examining the charts associated with competitors and with the coverage obtained when the organization was very much more visible probably will.

An evolving, fast-moving and dynamic organization will generate media coverage about itself almost without trying. An organization which is hiring new staff, and announcing new products and services on a regular basis will attract attention from journalists and editors and other influential opinion formers – people who will in turn generate their own very visible wake.

The question 'Why aren't we being written about?' now becomes 'Why have we stopped issuing product information?' or 'Why haven't we hired anybody recently?' or even 'Aren't we getting a bit complacent as an organization?'

There may be simple answers to these questions. If a marketing department is holding up the publication of product information, they must be told what's happening to the profile as a result of its delay. Perhaps the chief executive wants to keep the formation of a new Division under wraps in order to 'surprise' competitors. They'll need to be informed of the short-term consequences of this decision.

So the volume of coverage and namecheck charts may be a simple stimulus for change within the PR department, but they can also be a powerful tool for engineering change within the organization as a whole.

To make an even more powerful point, the communication director may be able to correlate changes in visibility with changes in organizational performance – sales being a particularly powerful indicator. If a relationship between visibility and sales performance can be proved (and it often can), an obstructive sales or marketing manager will risk the imposition of corporate silence at his or her peril.

FAILURE TO DELIVER A MESSAGE

Communicating a corporate or marketing message requires an act of will on the part of the PR professional responsible. As has been stressed in Chapter 13, if you don't integrate quality values and quality statements in the material you give to the media, you shouldn't be surprised when you discover that they don't appear in the cuttings.

The news may not be as bad as you think. Message scores will sometimes begin to decline at the end of a campaign, when a message stops being quite so urgent, or when there is a change of press office personnel. Communicating 'product reliability', for instance, will be of vital importance for the months after a series of visible and damaging product failures – but scores may begin to slide after a trouble-free year when the press office has had other urgent things to do. Does this decline really matter? Priorities change, of course, and the question is one that only the communicators themselves can answer.

A simple content analysis of the material being issued will be enough to determine whether new personnel, changes in policy or downright carelessness are responsible for the appropriate messages being de-emphasized or missed out of the source material altogether.

Sometimes a decline in message delivery comes from outside the organization. If negative message content is penetrating the profile from external sources, the matter should be of much greater concern. That's why the regrettably widespread practice of 'evaluating' only the coverage which the organization itself generates is so short-sighted. Readers will regard the newspaper or television programme as the source of the material they read or see, and do not care whether it has been placed by a clever PR department, an aggrieved ex-customer or an aggressive competitor.

Adverse coverage is within the department's area of responsibility, and it needs to be dealt with swiftly. Media analysis will reveal the source of the problem; we look at brainstorming later in this chapter.

REPUTATION SUFFERING DUE TO COMPANY POLICY

Adverse coverage – and the poor reputation it helps to generate – is very often a direct result of other departments' policies and actions. I have introduced elsewhere the idea of critical mass: it's usually the larger organizations, above the critical line, that we are concerned with here.

If the communications director determines from media analysis that poor (or negative) message delivery is directly attributable to corporate policy or other departments' actions, there are some serious decisions which need to be taken.

Take it straight to the board? Hand in a letter of resignation? Spring it on colleagues in a management meeting? Ignore it? These are some of the possibilities which may spring to mind, but as in all instances where the dissemination of internal information is concerned, the right course of action is likely to need careful thought beforehand.

Perhaps the easiest solution is to ignore the situation, but in the long-term this is no solution at all and very dangerous. A poor profile on environmental matters, or a profile resulting from articles showing that a company is not caring for its staff are typical of the kinds of situation over which the PR team has little or no direct control. But they are aspects of the organization's reputation, and as such they can land the organization – and the PR team – into trouble.

Let's take an environmental problem as an example.

EXAMPLE: SMELTCO – A SMELTING COMPANY

A series of complaints over smoke emissions have reached Smeltco's local press and are beginning to creep into the national and trade press. This has resulted in the company's 'environmental' scores taking a sharp dive in the company's media analysis charts. They've been lower every month for five months now, and the cumulative score totals now bear a minus sign.

The company hasn't changed its smelting processes, but there is evidence that the local community is more and more sensitive to the emissions Smeltco's local plant is producing – especially following the establishment of a highly proactive environment group in the area where the plant is situated. The chief executive feels that the PR team ought to have somehow put a stop to this group's embarrassingly public position and stopped the local media hounding the company – he's suggested threatening the press with a withdrawal of local advertising.

The PR team has gone as far as it can in briefing the press on the need to keep costs down, on the importance of local jobs, and the harmless nature of the smoke emissions. The fact that the emissions are within statutory limits has been underlined, but after the first two weeks the company line seems to have been dropped in the articles.

This is the time for the communications director to meet the plant manager and discuss the problem on a one-to-one basis. The charts can provide the basis of the discussion, especially if the scores can be compared with scores from a previous period when the problem did not exist. In the privacy of a small meeting room, the plant manager admits that it's a lack of funds which prevents the furnaces from being equipped with the latest technology – technology which would get rid of the problem altogether.

The board is responsive to a joint report from this meeting – a report which includes the relevant message delivery chart. The board agrees to a request in the report for funds for emission control technology. A simple request from the plant manager and an observation on 'environmental profile' from the communications department earlier had had no effect at all.

Imagine what could have happened if the communications director and the plant manager had not made a joint approach. The emissions would have continued and Smeltco's reputation as a polluter would have begun to tarnish the company's otherwise good reputation with customers. The communications director would have earned an internal reputation too – as a lone voice who moans incessantly and who appears unable to deliver the company's views to the media and local people.

The chief executive may have ended up insisting on the withdrawal of advertising, and war would have been declared between the media and the company. With no real need for professional media relations help, the decision may have been taken to close the PR department.

Exaggerated? Perhaps – but limp reactions to other departments' problems which nevertheless affect a company's reputation can give rise to drastic results like this.

COMMUNICATION OBJECTIVES UNREALIZABLE

In Chapters 5 and 8 we pinpointed some of the ways of choosing messages and how we can define the underlying communication objectives. It's of key importance to get these right – the media analysis can make very depressing reading indeed when the results are unrealizable.

It's easy to get them wrong. The straw poll among staff which we suggested in Chapter 5 shows how many worthy objectives there are and how many messages there are to promote. Spend time getting them right.

Take the simple message 'We are market leaders'. For some reason, companies are very often determined that they want to promote this message about themselves. Most customers I have met want to buy the best product or service at the lowest possible price, and some would actually prefer to deal with a smaller operation than a larger one. But corporate pride must be satisfied, so they've got to be seen as market leaders.

It's especially difficult to promote a leadership position when your company is some way down the league table. Yet some companies still want to be seen as market leaders – even to the point of stating that they are when they manifestly aren't.

Promoting a company as leader (when in fact it's fourth); promoting a company as good employer (when it is demonstrably exploitative); promoting a company as a quality company (when the board have just voted in a mass of cheapskate measures) are all examples of incorrect positioning. They're also lies. Leaving moral issues aside, however, promoting messages to these ends will result in a company that appears to be shallow in outlook, brittle in response, and untrustworthy. And the media analysis results will always be disappointing.

Promotional strategies and the associated measurement parameters can be changed at any time. By promoting quality, expertise and a strong international base, a company in a strong second place in a marketplace will give itself every chance of actually attaining market leadership; promoting false leadership through PR will not help it to get there.

All publicly quoted organizations I have had anything to do with have wanted to be seen as successful, and 'financial success' is usually a key message for investors. After a set of poor results, however, companies will always see a dip in the 'financial success' and 'financial stability' scores in the media analysis charts.

A poor set of results is no time to abandon these aspects of the media analysis. It is the job of the public relations team to interpret the results, putting the adverse news into time context, local context and industry context and highlight those areas where the company has been successful in the infrastructure of the statement. The company will have been successful at least in some regard: it's the job of the PR team to communicate this success to investors even when it's thin on the ground, and it's the media analyst's job to tell the team how well they've done it.

CAN GOOD PR COVER UP FOR FAILURE?

Corporate ethics has been a big issue in public relations for some years now, and it's likely to grow as opinion formers within the business close in on an acceptable definition of what PR really is.

Ask a group of public relations practitioners whether PR is 'corporate lying' – as has been suggested by the industry's harsher critics in the past – and they'll hotly deny it. Ask them one at a time, in confidence, how they would handle specific situations, however, and the answers will vary considerably.

Try deciding how you would answer these questions from the media, for example. At least one or two will strike a chord with anybody who has worked in a press office for a busy organization:

1. Why wasn't Mr Okoku invited for an interview?
2. Are all batches tested for *Salmonella* before shipping?
3. Have you had any previous complaints about this?
4. Did Mr Smith know the component could be used to make a nuclear weapon?
5. Had your chairman been drinking before the press conference?

Lying can be very tempting. The core problem is that in some organizations a PR department is expected to lie. The PR professional who would rather offer the truth to audiences is seen as unreliable. The need to lie or put up smokescreens becomes more urgent as communications technology improves and as organizational boundaries become more transparent.

Armed with media analysis, a communications director can hold a mirror up to an organization, demonstrating how the organization is seen from the outside. It can shine a strong light on the big corporate issues, and is a powerful agent for change in the organization, helping to resolve some of these issues internally. An organization which is at ease with itself won't need to ask its communications department to lie on its behalf.

THE ROLE OF BRAINSTORMING TECHNIQUES

Fortunately, a great many of the problems which arise from media analysis don't throw large corporate shadows. They are tough but straightforward PR problems which require creativity and an infusion of new ideas. PR people pride themselves on their creativity and usually relish the prospect of getting to grips with problems of this kind.

Media analysis and brainstorming techniques go well together. As those who have taken part in brainstorming sessions will know, the more precisely a problem can be pinpointed, the easier it is to solve. A poorly described problem ('We need some way of profiling Mr Smith in *Management Today* or he'll fire us!') distracts the creative team, forcing them to concentrate on the periphery of a problem without tackling the core. Why does Mr Smith want to be interviewed in *Management Today*? Why is he going to fire us? Isn't there something else we can do?

It's like going up to somebody and asking them to think of a good idea – any idea. Most people would be stumped and ask for clarification. Ask the person to think of a good idea to make you rich, and you may provoke few suggestions. Ask him or her to give you some suggestions on how to rob the bank on the corner of the road, and the creative juices start flowing – and some of the ideas may be temptingly practical. Media analysis closes down the options in exactly the same way, offering an ideal start point for a brainstorming session.

That start point might be a particular message. Many organizations, especially companies, rely on the creativity and innovation in their business, and need to be seen as innovative by their audiences. If the 'innovation' message is just not coming over in the media it will show up clearly in the charts even though the rest of the messages are turning in good scores month after month. This is a good opportunity for the media relations department to concentrate on this one message and develop some activities which will put the situation right. A request by the manager concerned for ideas on communicating the innovation message will yield so much more fruit than 'We've developed some problems with our client – any ideas?' Or, indeed, 'How can we have Mr Smith profiled in *Management Today*?'

RUNNING A BRAINSTORM

Here are a few suggestions on the running of brainstorm sessions for those who are unfamiliar with the discipline.

1. Decide who will take part. Select a group of between four and ten people: the group should be big enough for people to spark ideas off each other but not too big to be daunting to individuals. They'll each need a writing implement and a pad.
2. Make sure that there is a wide spectrum of people represented. A brainstorm is an excellent way of involving junior people, people in other departments and people used to working in different ways.

3. Appoint a facilitator or chairperson to run the session. That person needn't be the person whose problem it is. The facilitator (or it could be someone else – the 'clerk') has the task of writing the ideas down on a dry marker board or Nobo pad as they are suggested. All the ideas suggested should remain in view by the group as the session continues.

4. The person whose problem it is should introduce the problem briefly, perhaps referring to the relevant media analysis chart. Questions to the problem owner should be discouraged: a question usually means the questioner is considering hiding an idea. Immediately after the introduction, the participants should be asked to suggest ways of solving the problem. Suggestions should be brief. Encourage the use of headlines and short sentences that capture the essence of the idea. These are easy to hear and quick to write down.

5. The clerk should write down all the suggestions. Under no circumstances should contributions be rejected either explicitly ('That's no good – we tried it last year!') or implicitly (negative body language). Otherwise the contributor will think twice before offering a much better idea, later on.

6. When the suggestions are coming thick and fast the quieter members may not be able to air their suggestions easily. They should write them on their own pads to remind them to voice them later when the ideas start to dry up.

7. At the end of the session – which may take only half or three-quarters of an hour – the problem owner will be able to cherry pick from the list of suggestions, and develop one or two of the suggestions into a workable strategy.

Brainstorms are highly enjoyable, especially for those who are naturally uninhibited. But it is often the people who aren't naturally outgoing who have the best ideas. Their ideas are usually prefaced with the phrase 'I know it sounds stupid but . . .'.

Many years ago I ran a brainstorm session to generate ideas for launching a computer with the unlikely name of the Rainbow. During the session we concentrated on making the best possible use of the computer's rather unusual name. Near the end of the session, a junior secretary shyly suggested sending a fresh Rainbow trout to each of the journalists attending the launch – it turned out her cousin was in the fish farming business. We did it – and the press loved it.

At the end of the session it is worth transcribing all the ideas from the board or pad and using them as a memory jogger for the future.

SYNECTICS

Some organizations take the creative process a step further, and use the Synectics process. Synectics is an international management consultancy which specializes in creative problem solving methods and techniques. In brainstorms run by Synectics themselves or by people who are Synectics trained, the rules are more structured.

Questions are barred altogether and participants are encouraged to preface their contributions with the words 'How to' and 'I wish', giving the entire session a more creative and positive emphasis.

Synectics sessions are enlivened by so-called 'excursions'. When the ideas start drying up, the facilitator will invite the participants to include some other totally unrelated element – such as an orange or an aeroplane in their ideas. The excursion often has the effect of removing any creative blocks and getting the ideas flowing again.

Synectics also includes rigorous methods for refining the chosen ideas from the sessions, identifying the advantages and drawbacks of each idea and tackling secondary problems in an additional creative approach to complete the problem solving process. The structure is designed to ensure that actions follow from the session. This overcomes a common criticism of brainstorming – that while it was great fun, none of the ideas were usable.

(Synectics Europe can be found at Fernville House, Midland Road, Hemel Hempstead, Hertfordshire HP2 5BH.)

THE ROLE OF PR CONSULTANCIES IN PROBLEM SOLVING

So far I have tried not to draw too sharp a line between the role of the communications department and the in-house PR team on the one hand and the PR consultancy who may be working with the in-house team on the other.

Different organizations work in different ways: sometimes a consultancy is in the creative driving seat while the in-house public relations department carries out the day-to-day implementation of the programme; sometimes the consultancy (or PR 'agency' as it may sometimes be referred to in these circumstances) is given the implementation work while the creative and management aspects are kept in-house.

A consultancy working outside the client organization, however, has a clear creative edge in tackling message delivery problems highlighted by media analysis. The consultancy's external, unbiased perspective and wide current experience with other clients are of immense benefit when things start to go wrong.

It is surprising and disappointing to many PR firms that they are often called in to carry out strongly proactive work when funds are readily available during the good times, but are shut out when problems arise – times when the consultancy's experience and knowledge can be of most use.

CONCLUSION

In this chapter we have looked at some of the problems which media analysis can reveal. We have examined some of the methods of dealing with them and the people who need to deal with them. We have seen that the media analysis can be part of the solution as well as a method of identifying the problem.

In the next chapter we leave the troubleshooting arena and revisit the media analysis process itself. But this time we focus our attention on influencers and opinion formers – the people who create some of the problems we have been discussing in the paragraphs above. People we need to get on our side.

22 Building an Influencer Database

We've already seen that media analysis isn't simply producing pretty charts. It can also be used to build up fact files about issues, about influences and perhaps most important, about influencers – the people who make the news about your company. The author maps out the structure of a powerful influencer database and gives an example of how it can be used.

The dimensions of media analysis we have encountered so far have primarily concerned messages, target audiences and the direct delivery of one to the other.

But when the financial results coverage has been analysed, the product write-ups have been distributed to the salesforce and the enquiries counted, there remains a further large mass of coverage in which the organization appears, but which only affects the organization indirectly.

Sometimes this coverage concerns the publication of a Government White Paper, or new training requirements for your industry. It might be that the coverage concerns a shortage of electronic components which affects your products, or a three-year drought in South America which deprives you and your competitors of a vital ingredient or raw material. Perhaps a new process has been discovered which will make consumers view your industry, and your company, in a new way.

What is important is that whether you like it or not, you and your organization are involved. Your organization is named in the coverage as a concerned party and, temporarily or permanently, the coverage will change the shape of your media profile.

The way an organization responds to coverage of this type is critical. Not only can issues be fast-moving and unpredictable, but each has the potential of reaching a level of prominence in the media that an individual organization is unlikely to attain. A boycott of agricultural machinery by China would undoubtedly command the front page of the *Financial Times*; an item about a new type of mechanized plough is unlikely to make an appearance at all. And a thoughtful and considered comment on the boycott will change an exporter's reputation in a subtly different way from the changes associated with a product announcement.

Sometimes the big issue is of a strictly temporary nature; occasionally it continues over an extended period. A components crisis lasting a few weeks may need some fast footwork by the PR team and a good on-camera performance by the chief executive: the PR team will be rewarded by seeing a positive movement in the media analysis charts. Media concern about the effects of alcohol on the health of the nation, however, will present a brewer's PR team with long-term opportunities and problems on a very different scale. Such an issue will require a level of management and professionalism that goes far beyond the distribution of a few well-chosen words.

INFLUENCES AND INFLUENCERS

The media don't always think of approaching you and your organization when the big issues arise.

When health matters are at issue, for instance, the media will often go to a local professor of medicine at a nearby hospital, or a leading local practitioner for comment instead. When trade issues are at stake, the media are quite likely to obtain a comment from an MP or the general secretary of a representative trade association. Stockbrokers' analysts are often consulted on financial issues.

Each of these groups of key opinion formers can dictate how an issue is reported. They also hold more than their fair share of influence on whether your organization's profile flourishes or suffers as a result.

So is the big issue out of the hands of the communications department, with the PR team unable to do anything about it? Fortunately, no – and effective media analysis can pinpoint the people who need to be targeted with the appropriate information.

By adding a few lines to the information collected about each cutting or tape, the analyst can enhance the value of the media analysis enormously, giving the organization a new research tool and a response mechanism at the same time. Once the information has been consolidated, the organization has an influencer database at its disposal.

TRAPPING THE INFORMATION

If you are going to build an influencer database, the first thing to remember is to trap the right information: attempt to answer the questions 'Who?', 'What?', 'Where?', and 'Why?' before the analysis is carried out.

WHO?

It will be tempting to prejudge the 'Who?' question by deciding who the influencers are in advance of the analysis and just trapping namechecks of specific people.

If your charity campaign has been fortunate enough to obtain the services of a leading celebrity to attend launches, press conferences and presentations, you will no doubt wish to analyse the coverage to see the extent to which that person has influenced it. As the campaign takes off, however, other celebrities may become involved: try widening the analysis to cover celebrities as a whole.

Perhaps the prime influencer in the campaign is one of the celebrities who joined of his or her own accord because of the early publicity and some personal reason. Perhaps the celebrity's mother has recently died of the disease you are targeting; perhaps relatives may live in the country whose aid programme you are promoting, or they may be already involved in your charity unbeknown to you – personal triggers which may prompt a person in the public eye to get involved.

The same argument applies to Government spokespeople. Don't just analyse for mentions of the Trade minister who gave the keynote speech at your seminar – widen it to politicians as a whole, and you will automatically track the progress of any ensuing media debate in which opposition spokespeople may become involved.

WHAT?

It is important to record accurately the capacity in which the influencer is quoted. Sometimes an influencer will wear more than one hat. A doctor may comment on a recent rise in the number of meningitis cases as a well-informed and authoritative medic living in the area concerned, or as a spokesperson for a medical organization or group.

Beware the supposedly impartial industry spokesperson – perhaps the president of a professional body or trade association who also represents a private company with its own very specific communication agenda. Media analysis will usually identify these links.

It is rare that a newspaper or magazine will give precise attribution. Professor Smith may be referred to as '... of Oxford University' in one publication and as '... of Brasenose College' in another. A cross-check to ensure that Brasenose is in fact an Oxford College is vital.

It is also important to ensure that there are not two individuals sharing the same name. This applies especially to the medical profession: many group practices have married partners and in commenting publicly on a professional issue, they are quite possibly going to have rather different views!

WHERE?

In building up an influencer database, the analyst will need to contact the organization associated with the influencer following publication to ascertain address, telephone number, fax and e-mail number so that direct contact can be initiated and maintained.

Don't expect to be able to gather this information from the editors of the media publishing the item in which the influencer is mentioned. Journalists are highly proprietorial about their sources and while they may be prepared to pass on the details of a well-known organization (which is easy to track down anyway), they are unlikely to be prepared to divulge the private addresses of key personal contacts.

Universities, trade associations and other industry bodies are usually easy to track down through directory enquiry services, especially where the approximate location is indicated in the media coverage. Individuals writing from private addresses are more difficult to track down, especially given the growing tendency for private individuals to keep their telephone numbers ex-directory. Industry directories can be massively helpful, and although they tend to be costly, they can make up for the cost in time saved.

Big issues are often of an international nature, and gathering information about overseas organizations also presents its own range of challenges.

WHY?

An answer to the 'Why?' question holds the key to the whole information gathering exercise.

If it is the intention to establish and maintain a dialogue with the influencers identified, it is likely that the organization will need to track the stance of each individual on specific subjects.

The analyst may wish to track the influencer's personal delivery of corporate, generic or issue-related messages. More likely, the organization will need to establish how the individual stands on a particular issue – for instance pro- or anti-smoking, pro- or anti-Sunday trading, or where he or she stands in the abortion debate. Tracking this data will enable the PR team to target specific information depending on the position he or she has taken.

If individual opinion is to be tracked in media coverage, overall editorial stance of the media sector in which he or she features on the same issue should also be recorded. A comparison between the two sets of data will be necessary to determine the extent to which the individual concerned has changed the editorial content as a whole.

GATHERING AND ANALYSING THE DATA

The following tables are examples of the kind of influencer data which the analyst will need to gather and the kind of simple tabular report which can be computed from it.

We use the example of the short/fat versus long/thin warship debate which was prevalent in the world's national, defence and shipping press some years ago.

		Research type
Cutting no.	23	Assigned
Date	August 1989	Media analysis
Publication	Defence materiel	Media analysis
Word count	380	Media analysis
SW namechecks	–	Media analysis
Spokesperson	Mr Gerard Downs	Media analysis
Organization	Institute of Marine Warfare	Media analysis
Address 1	23 Winchester Square	Telephone
Address 2	London WC9 2J7	Telephone
Address 3	United Kingdom	Telephone
Telephone	0171 299 5000	Directory
Fax	0171 299 4328	Telephone
Stance	Pro	Media analysis

Table 22.1 Influencer data – analysis of a single cutting

Spokesperson	Organization	Numbers of articles		
		Nationals	**Defence**	**Shipping**
G Downs	Institute of Marine Warfare	3	11	0
P Smythe	Institute of Marine Architecture	0	2	8
Lt P Jones	Royal Navy	0	1	0
Capt T Fry	Royal Navy	0	1	0
P Rideout	Tomkins Engineering	0	2	1
S Briggs	Solent Warships	1	0	0

Table 22.2 Table of data produced as a result of media analysis of a particular issue over an extended period

Our organization is Solent Warships (SW) – a fictitious shipbuilder in the short/fat lobby. All the names of companies and people in the list, and the numbers, are fabricated.

In Table 22.1 we create a typical record, and indicate the method by which the information may be obtained:

Table 22.2 shows one of the uses which can be made of the data gathered in research of the type indicated in Table 22.1.

From the data in Table 22.2 we will be able to determine that Gerard Downs of the Institute of Marine Warfare is a key spokesman in the defence and national press, but as far as the shipping press is concerned, Peter Smythe is clearly the man to get on your side.

Solent's Managing Director Stan Briggs has done well to get his letter published in the *Daily Mail*, but has not managed to get his views across in the specialist media. Paul Rideout, Marketing Director of Tomkins Engineering clearly has the ear of the defence and shipping press, and is one of Solent's suppliers: there is a possible co-operative venture on the cards here.... The PR

205

team will need to research some of these names and addresses for the follow-up information campaign.

On some very detailed and complex issues, the stance can be broken down into component positions and messages. For instance, P Rideout's main reason for supporting the short/fat position might be because the construction lends itself to certain types of alloys in which his company has specialist skill and equipment.

KEEPING TRACK OF LETTER WRITERS

Issues attract letter writers the way a honeypot attracts bees. A determined writer of letters to the editor will sometimes copy dozens of letters to various publications and succeed in seeing many of them in print, giving rise to an initial, false impression that there is a swell of opinion on a particular issue. Again, media analysis will help to identify these people so that their views can be kept in perspective.

Stylistic similarities and phrasing will often reveal a letter writing campaign sponsored by a political party, or driven by an active pressure group. Individuals who regularly have their letters published but who are not visibly attributed to an organization need to be flagged separately in the database, and deserve special care when dealing with them – they may be individuals acting independently, but they may be pseudonyms or people acting on the instructions of others.

It's often worthwhile keeping letters to the editor as a separate element of the analysis for these reasons.

METHODS OF STORING THE DATA

Learning a complex relational database system in order to build a workable influencer database is not required. Most modern word processing systems available for the personal computer include a workable list processing capability which will enable the communications team to build and update a list of up to several hundred names.

With such a list held on computer, the communications team will be able to:

● Print a complete updated reference list as required;
● Find all items associated with a particular person;
● Send a personalized letter to all people on the list;
● Identify groups of people who share certain opinions;
● Identify groups of people from the same business;
● Print data tables like the one above;
● Keep certain groups separate (e.g. overseas).

If the list continues to grow, it may be decided to transfer the list on to a recognized database. This can usually be effected easily and automatically once the database is understood and training in the appropriate software has been received.

Influencer databases become more useful as they grow larger over a period of months. By plotting the accumulated data in trend charts, the rise in importance of key issues and the influencers behind them can be charted. The visibility of the issue itself can also be tracked as it rises to prominence, goes off the boil slightly, and re-emerges as a new survey is published or a new fact is uncovered.

But the real value of an influencer database is that it enables the organization to enter into dialogue with the parties who are taking part in the public debate – directly.

USING THE DATA

A letter of support to each of the influencers, an information pack explaining the organization's stance, or a newsletter on the issue concerned will be assured of close attention because the interest of the individual in the subject matter has already been established.

There is no reason why the contents of any correspondence should not be changed according to the views expressed by the influencer in the media. While a factual information pack may be enough to silence an opposer, a warm letter of support may spur a supporter on to more and even more positive coverage.

As indicated in the example, the media analysis may indicate individuals with whom a much closer relationship may be necessary. The gentleman from the Institute of Marine Warfare in our example has clearly built up media contacts in a key press sector over many years, and a briefing on some specifics may be mutually useful.

When the database has grown in size over several months, the organization will be in a position of some considerable power and may be able to convene a meeting of interested parties, circulate a highly influential petition or use the information to bring pressure to bear in some other way.

INFLUENCER DATABASES AND PRIVACY LEGISLATION

A word is necessary here on legislation designed to protect the privacy of the individual – the Data Protection Act 1984 in the UK, and similar legislation elsewhere throughout the world.

According to the Data Protection Registrar in the UK, the recording of information gleaned from newspapers, magazines and broadcast media on to computer media does not fall within the auspices of the Act.

However, when an opinion or information gained through other means is appended to this data, the record then falls within the Act. Storing this type of information on computers is illegal in the UK if that organization is not registered with the Data Protection Registrar. UK organizations wishing to create an influencer database are therefore strongly advised to register under the Act. This in turn means that any individual whose details are kept in these records will be entitled to examine the details held about him or her on the computer.

Readers are advised to check their own country's data protection and privacy laws before proceeding with the creation of an influencer database.

THE COST OF REGISTRATION

Registering under the Data Protection Act is not in itself very expensive, but taken as a whole, media analysis can represent a significant proportion of the media relations budget for an organization.

In Chapter 23, the whole problem of financing media analysis and the importance of making provision for it in the annual budget is considered.

23 Budgeting for Media Analysis

This brief chapter argues the case for allocating sensible budgets for media analysis. A large proportion of the cost of a Titan missile is in its control and guidance system, yet only 5 per cent of media relations professionals spend anything at all on media analysis!

In some of the more sophisticated military hardware, the guidance and control system costs more than the rest of the system put together. Yet when we want to improve the guidance and control system for the perhaps more worthy business of improving corporate communication, many of us are reluctant to spend anything on it at all. Excellence in communication has been unquantifiable, and communication itself untrackable for far too long.

The importance of media analysis will be brought home to the communications industry in exactly the same way that weapon superiority is learnt on the battlefield: those with superior control and guidance systems at their disposal will prove more effective and will prevail over those who don't.

There's no doubt that media analysis will come into much more general use than it is at the moment, but in the meantime someone has to pay for it. We'll be discussing the 'who should pay?' question at more length later in this chapter, but in the meantime the following scenario demonstrates why it's worth paying for it at all.

HOW MEDIA ANALYSIS CAN SAVE PR EXPENDITURE

I hope that earlier chapters have made it clear that media analysis will improve the quality of an organization's communication both via the media and in general. As such, it is well worth investment. But it can also actually save organizations real money in the short term, as can be seen from the following real-life example.

Each year, an organization in the non-ferrous metals industry holds a press conference and briefings for the press on the state of the industry and the outlook for the metal during the next 12 months. The organization was concerned that the amount of money spent on the exercise was escalating uncontrollably, and asked the IMPACT team to analyse the media coverage resulting from the event. The analysis revealed that while the press release issued to coincide with the event was well taken up and effective in terms of message delivery, and the time spent in the one-to-one briefings for the newswires and national media was time well spent, the most expensive item – the press conference – was a waste of time and money.

Although it was well attended, many of those who came to the press conference failed to write an article and the ones who did so failed, in the main, to communicate the detailed messages that the organization was attempting to communicate.

As a result, it was decided to cancel the press conference in future years but retain the briefings and the press release – a saving of over £3 000 for the next year and for following years. The analysis had cost less than £1 500.

This somewhat simplistic example shows a real, short-term quantifiable saving: the benefits that improve targeting, clarify a company's positioning and give real feedback on the successful and unsuccessful elements of a programme are of course of much longer-term value and deeper significance.

HOW MUCH IS MEDIA ANALYSIS GOING TO COST?

The cost of a media analysis programme does not follow any hard and fast rules as different methods incur different levels of expenditure, but they are relatively easy to work out. Broadly speaking, the cost depends on the depth of the analysis and the volume of coverage.

Quantitative analysis (namechecks, volumes, counting cuttings) is easy to carry out and may be implemented by an in-house department without any recourse to an outside consultant or analyst. To carry out an independent analysis for message and issue content will cost more. Depending on the complexity of the analysis, some analysts will levy an initial set-up charge for equipment (for example, computer terminal and modem) and development; for others any set-up charge is recouped over a longer period.

Some relatively small companies, with low communications budgets (for instance charities), nevertheless generate very large numbers of cuttings and tapes. For these, media analysis is likely to represent a large slice of the communications budget. There are other firms (for examples, law firms, consultants and many private companies) who have high turnovers and big PR budgets for direct communications, but who generate relatively little press coverage. For these, media analysis is relatively inexpensive.

To build up an idea of the budget required, filling in a table such as the one shown by Table 23.1 for each company in the shortlist of suppliers you have chosen to look at more closely is a good exercise. The table can apply to both in-house and external media analysis. When assessing the relative cost of an in-house and an external solution, do not forget to take into account the cost of staff

Item	Set-up and equipment	Cost/ month	Cost/ quarter	Cost/ annum
Analysis				
Commentary				
Trend data				
Other costs				
TOTALS:				

Table 23.1 Choosing a media analysis bureau. By completing the whole table, an accurate idea of annual costs can be obtained

time in analysing the coverage – it may be considerable when volumes of coverage are high.

An external service provider will want to know:

1. Number of cuttings, videotapes and audiotapes per month.
2. Frequency of report needed (monthly, quarterly).
3. Form of report – charts only, data on disk, colour etc.
4. Competitive analysis or one organization only.
5. Depth of analysis – messages, issues and media sectors.

The supplier is unlikely to give you a completely watertight budget for the year because volumes of coverage will vary from one month to another and will be impossible to forecast. If you gather all your coverage into a daily, weekly or monthly digest for senior staff or the salesforce as suggested in Chapter 6, send a selection of these to your supplier to give them an idea of scale.

The budget you agree with your supplier will in all likelihood consist of a monthly or quarterly fee and a run-on cost for cuttings or tapes over and above the agreed monthly number estimated. It is wise to set a budget 10–20 per cent above the agreed monthly fee to allow for this excess material. After all, nobody knows when a crisis, a huge order or a contested takeover that will double the monthly cuttings haul is going to occur.

If your organization is in the big coverage/small budget category, the annual sums required for media analysis may prove hard to swallow. In these circumstances, the sampling options we outline in Chapter 6 may provide some legitimate ways of cutting the costs to a reasonable level. I'd unhesitatingly recommend these cost-saving options ahead of any solution involving untrained staff carrying out a volume-only calculation, or the dreaded advertising value equivalents (AVEs) as outlined in Chapter 15.

WHO SHOULD PAY FOR MEDIA ANALYSIS?

Let's face it, nobody thinks they can *afford* media analysis! But who will be persuaded to pay for it? So far, funding for media analysis has tended to come from the public relations budget but there has of late been an increasing trend for the cash to come from companies' market research budget. Those who argue that it belongs with the other research disciplines have a powerful case.

Whether media analysis is truly an aspect of market research, however, is a matter for communications and marketing professionals and the accountants to debate. Earlier in this section we discussed the feedback loop and the two major functions of media analysis. If the analysis is required to analyse the effectiveness of the PR team and its programme, perhaps the funding should be from outside the department; if media analysis is used as a management control mechanism inside the department, then the PR department should fund it themselves.

BUDGETING FOR MEDIA ANALYSIS

There will be no cash available for media analysis unless it's budgeted for. If there is no provision for media analysis in your company, it is worth making a diary note now to put in just such a provision. Clearly, as indicated above, organizations will vary considerably in where the money (or the extra staff) will come from.

When media analysis was in its rapid early growth phase in the early 1990s, the PR industries in the USA and UK were struggling with a global recession and were probably held back a little due to a tightening of PR purse strings all over the world. But with easier trading conditions and increasing interest in quality certificates such as ISO 9000 and its national equivalents, the move towards quantifiable measurements in the communications business is now surely on its way.

Media analysis is worth doing well if you're going to do it at all. If your organization is going to join this important movement, you should ensure you have provided enough funds for the job.

WHY MEDIA ANALYSIS COSTS WHAT IT DOES

Perhaps media analysis seems costly. An explanation of why the costs of high quality media analysis are as high as they are may make the cost issue seem clearer. To analyse the issue content and determine how strongly your messages are being delivered within a newspaper article or television or radio programme, it's essential that the item concerned is read, watched or listened to carefully.

This is no simple clerical function in which copy is merely scanned for names and key phrases; each sentence must be read thoroughly and its meaning absorbed and understood, whether it's in a 2 500 word article in *Design Electronics*

212

or a 250 word news item in *Handelsblatt*. Skilled analysts, whether in-house or out-house, deserve to be paid a reasonable wage for this task. That's why the average cost per cutting of around three to five times the cost of retrieving the cutting is unlikely to be lowered in the near future.

Once media analysis is in place, stand by for more interest in media relations from the purse-string holders themselves in the boardroom. We take the media analysis report into the boardroom in our final chapter and gauge what effect it has on its occupants.

24 Media Analysis and the Board

Some communications professionals have recently taken the brave step of airing media analysis results at board meetings. The results have been seismic. At last, the people whose job it is to guard an organization's reputation have secured a powerful lever of influence within the organizations they represent.

'I'm glad you were able to drop in Michele. I've been meaning to invite you here for some time, but well, as you know things haven't been easy, and I've had quite a number of other priorities since Atkins left us.

'The real reason why you are here is, well, I wanted to ask you about the work you and your colleagues actually do down there.

'It always seems so very busy. I've read your last few reports. You're always on the phone. You sometimes work extremely late – I must say that there have been occasions when I know you've left after me.

'Yet somehow, you know – and please understand I am not criticizing you or your excellent department one jot – somehow I can't help wondering whether all the effort is worth it. Whether perhaps by following the "proactive communication policy" which is I think what you entitled the paper you agreed with Mr Atkins, you've been creating as many problems for the company as you've been solving ...

'But I see you have brought one of your presentation folders with you and I'm almost certainly asking questions you're going to answer in your presentation.'

Michele Delany likes the new chief executive although she's only met him three times before. She quietly approves of the dramatic shake-up in the manufacturing division which followed his appointment by six months.

She notes with concern, however, the past tense in her new chief executive's penultimate sentence and wonders whether her presentation will quite hit the spot. She had not thought he'd have read the reports! But it's too late now. With professional polish, she opens the folder and runs through the PR department's recent record. A quick resume of departmental objectives ... 72 press releases issued in the year ... sponsored seminars in three targeted industries ... support for the Taiwan Junior Soccer league promoted in the local press and television. She is encouraged when he nods vigorously over the national press coverage of the slightly better annual results. There is a wry smile when she ends with the excellent coverage in the *Herald Tribune* and the *Straits Times* of his own appointment the previous May.

She leaves an immense folder of cuttings and transcripts on the table in front of him. He waves them away.

> 'Yes, yes, yes. An excellent performance Michele and please pass my thanks on to your colleagues for their efforts. I do have a few questions however. The most important of them is this: last year we spent £458 000 on public relations. Or thereabouts. What did we actually get back for this? An increase in sales perhaps? Has our reputation improved as a result? Are we finding it easier to do deals in the Far East?'

THE BOARD LANGUAGE BARRIER

We'll leave Michele to worry about her answers for a while. But her problem highlights the situation which communications people have in communicating their performance to their boards. Public relations has grown to the point where it is using up significant percentages of companies' budgets, and boards expect PR people to communicate the results of their work in language other than lists of actions.

A manufacturing director who gives an end-of-year board report based on how many times his chargehands have used an overhead gantry, or how many times the No. 3 furnace has been shut down for maintenance will receive short shrift. Boards are usually more interested in results than activities.

So far, Michele has only talked about activities. The chief executive has asked her about results. The public relations department needs to learn the language of results.

ACTIVITY REPORTS AND MEDIA ANALYSIS REPORTS

Michele probably receives contact reports and/or activity reports monthly from her PR consultancies. She also prepares a monthly report for the board director to whom she reports. These reports traditionally chronicle activities rather than results, and when they do deal with results, they tend to contain phrases like 'the brochure has been well received' and 'there were 25 attendees at the briefing' rather than 'the project resulted in a 50 per cent increase in our media visibility for the month'. Activity reports are written in the kind of language which boards hate.

Compare this with the media analysis report. Media analysis records shifts in visibility and in message delivery – shifts which can be correlated with changes in audience opinion, sales patterns and customer behaviour.

As we have seen in Chapter 20, there are a number of uses which the media analysis report can be put to, depending on whether the information contained in it is used as a feedback control mechanism within the communication function ('We need to do something about our flagging quality message'), or as a method of justifying a communication method or a level of expenditure on media relations. Activity reports, on the other hand, do not have many uses on their own except as minutes.

The board needs to be able to assess the reputation of the company or organization directly as well as decide whether the communication team is doing a 'good job'. It is ultimately the board who have the responsibility for the direction of the organization, and it does not need me to stress that a company's media profile forms an important part of this direction. The media analysis report, again, is ideal for giving the board the feedback they need, while the activity report will merely impress them with the detail of how the results were achieved.

A media analysis report gives the board one of the missing jigsaw pieces, enabling it to see the whole corporate picture a little more clearly than before. Boards need control, and there is no control without good quality information.

PRESENTING TO THE BOARD

It is unlikely that the board will need or want to see the media analysis report in its entirety each month. An executive summary together with selected trend charts will probably suffice.

The board is likely to allocate a relatively short space of time to media relations on their agenda, and the following points may be helpful in deciding what to include and what to leave out.

1. Volume and visibility

Some indication of how visible the organization is, especially comparative trend information, is likely to be of interest. '750 000 words' or '125 namechecks' will not be especially useful to know – they're likely to be more interested in whether the figure is going up or down – and who is gaining and who is losing ground.

2. Messages

Boards vary: if the messages are based on a mission or vision statement or are strongly linked to brand values, they will take a keen interest in message delivery. Again, stress the trends in message delivery rather than the absolute figures which will mean little to those not deeply involved.

3. Correlation

A justifiable correlation between message delivery and a sales figure, or a link between changes in messages delivery and changes in audience perception or behaviour will do two things. First they will make an immediate point about the results achieved; and second, they will make a general point about the importance of delivering positive messages in the future.

4. Line of best-fit

A best-fit straight line on the trend charts, using the graphical capability of any reputable spreadsheet, will tell the board at a glance the overall direction of a message trend. Not too much should be read into heavily smoothed data like this, but straight-line graphs do convey key points across forcefully.

BOARDS' GROWING INTEREST

There are already signs that boards are beginning to take a far keener interest in their media profiles since the advent of comprehensible media analysis, and this must be a positive development for the communications industry.

Many board members often already receive a daily, weekly or monthly slab of 'relevant cuttings' from the press office, but how many read them? How many even skim them? A two-page board report based on media analysis charts once per month can be read on the train or in a taxi and will give the salient points the board are likely to take interest in. A bundle of several weeks cuttings with no analysis probably induces nothing but boredom and guilt.

Media analysis seems to be changing all this. Feedback from clients served during the time when the IMPACT service has been operating indicates that boards are becoming increasingly reliant on media analysis as a means of appreciating how the organization's media profile is evolving – a sensitive indicator and early warning system which has not been available to them in the past.

RETURNING TO MICHELE'S PRESENTATION

Michele confidently flips over another page in her presentation. On this page, rather than the bullet points of the previous pages, is a bar chart tracking volumes of coverage over the past 12 months [Figure 24.1].

> 'I'm delighted you asked me about results, Sir Matthew. I don't often get the chance to tell board members just what we have achieved for you, you know! And I can answer all your questions.
>
> 'This chart shows just how much coverage we have achieved and how rapidly it's gone up. This chart and the equivalent line-of-best-fit chart [Figure 24.2] will save you going through the bundles of cuttings. You'll note that your competitors coverage has stayed more or less the same in one instance and in the other case has actually dropped significantly over the same period. Incidentally, the only reason they were so well covered in March was coverage in the tabloids of the Wiltshire scandal . . .
>
> 'The next chart,' Michele flips the page in the presenter, 'tracks delivery of one of our key messages in the trade and vertical press [Figure 24.3]. The messages – "quality", "customer service" and "innovative approach" are based on the mission statement which you helped to develop last year before you took over as chief executive.
>
> 'You'll notice that the "quality" and "innovative approach" messages have risen significantly since we started tracking them. The "customer service" message isn't

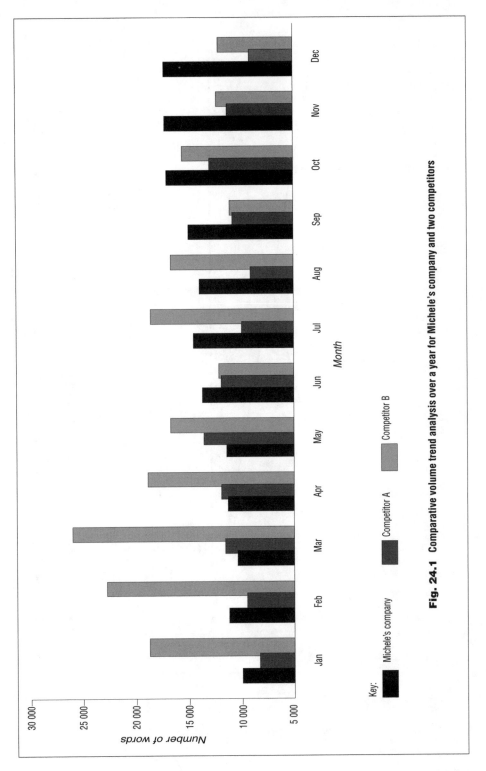

Fig. 24.1 Comparative volume trend analysis over a year for Michele's company and two competitors

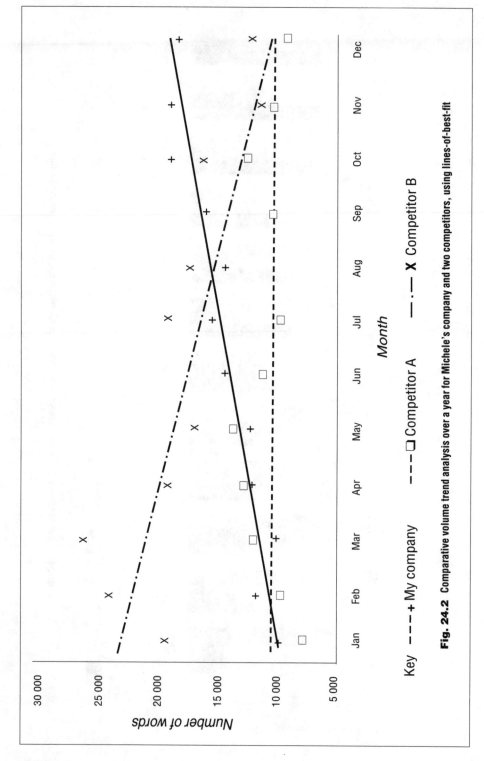

Key - - - + My company   - - - □ Competitor A   - · - x Competitor B

Fig. 24.2 Comparative volume trend analysis over a year for Michele's company and two competitors, using lines-of-best-fit

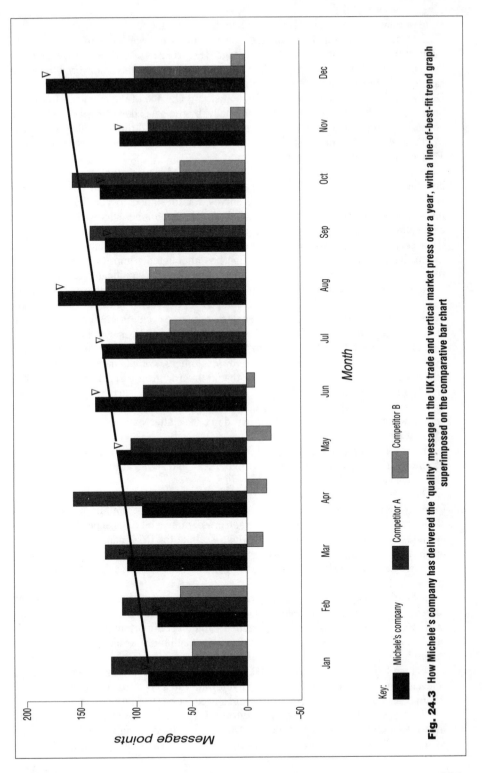

Fig. 24.3 How Michele's company has delivered the 'quality' message in the UK trade and vertical market press over a year, with a line-of-best-fit trend graph superimposed on the comparative bar chart

Key:

■ Michele's company   ■ Competitor A   ▨ Competitor B

quite so rosy I'm afraid, but I'll come back to that in a moment.

'Now look at this next chart, which correlates enquiries received in our sales department with delivery of the quality message [Figure 24.4]. The enquiries peak in September – immediately after the August product launches which delivered this message so effectively. You'll remember that the advertising campaign didn't break until October. It looks as though we can link something like 400 of the enquiries to the PR programme, and this is confirmed, incidentally, by the sales department records. Our conversion rate is running at 30 per cent at the moment, so I think you'll agree...', Sir Matthew was already nodding agreement, '... that we've more than covered our costs. That answers your first question.

'You ask about our reputation. Well, I have some good news on that front too. You will be aware of the Audience Selection survey which we carried out on our key audiences. What you may not realize is that the survey was designed to parallel exactly the messages we are tracking in the media analysis. The September survey shows a 30 per cent increase in the number regarding us as "innovative" and a 26 per cent increase in those regarding us as "a quality company". Again, the increase correlates strongly with the media analysis charts. Your reputation has undoubtedly improved, and I believe there is a good case to be made that the press office played a significant part in this.

'Now for the "customer service" message. Frankly, the media analysis shows there has been a decrease in delivery of this message over the year [Figure 24.5]. And I can't honestly say the survey and the media analysis reinforce each other. We needed to look at the coverage more closely to find why this message hasn't been coming over

'So I have divided the coverage into two groups – the coverage the press office has generated and the coverage generated by customers, complainants, suppliers and others who write about us. You will note that in the first group, the chart [Figure 24.6] shows a high and still rising level of "customer service" delivery, while in the other group we see a negative and deteriorating position. Sir Matthew, there are a number of people writing about us who believe we don't look after our customers very well.' Michele paused for a reaction.

There was a long pause. 'Well, I don't think we do, to be honest. Not always.' Sir Matthew shuffled a little uncomfortably in his seat, and stared at the two charts. 'What articles caused the negative scores?'

'I have them for you here.' Michele passed over a sheaf of five or six pages of coverage from a variety of sources. 'There's no one issue that is at the bottom of this. There's some adverse product coverage in the trade press, quite a bit of local newspaper coverage and of course there's the item in *Computing* about the IBM manager who waited in our Boston reception for an hour while the service manager was out at lunch. That kind of coverage is not really in our power to control, but it still reached 100 000 of our customers.'

Sir Matthew snapped out of his reverie, looking at his watch briefly. 'Michele, you've more than answered my questions. I'm impressed with the professionalism of your approach. But I've kept you from your duties – your very important duties – for too long and I have a meeting with customer service in half an hour – would you mind if I keep these charts and cuttings to show them?'

Michele looked a little disappointed. 'Well, yes of course, although I've shown the relevant ones to them already. But don't you want the answer to your third question? About deals in the Far East?' Sir Matthew gestured for her to continue, briefly.

'Well it seems the key message in Tokyo and Taiwan is "commitment". We're delivering the "commitment" message very hard indeed over there. I can prove it. Do you want to see ...', Sir Matthew shook his head vigorously. 'It's early days though, and I don't

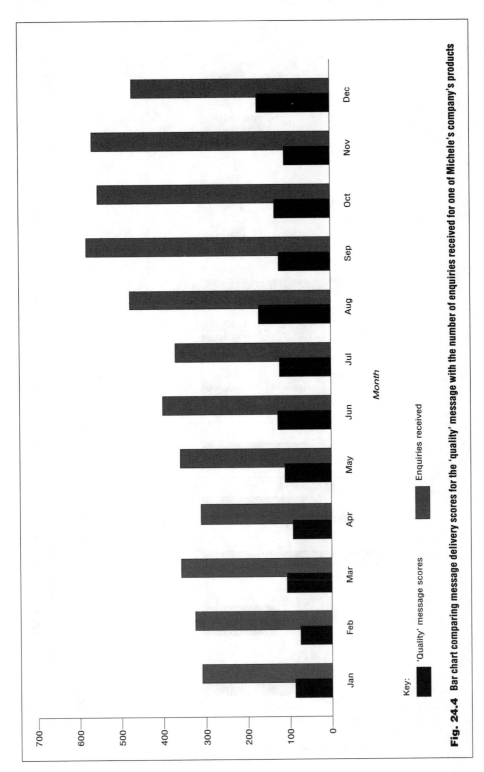

Fig. 24.4 Bar chart comparing message delivery scores for the 'quality' message with the number of enquiries received for one of Michele's company's products

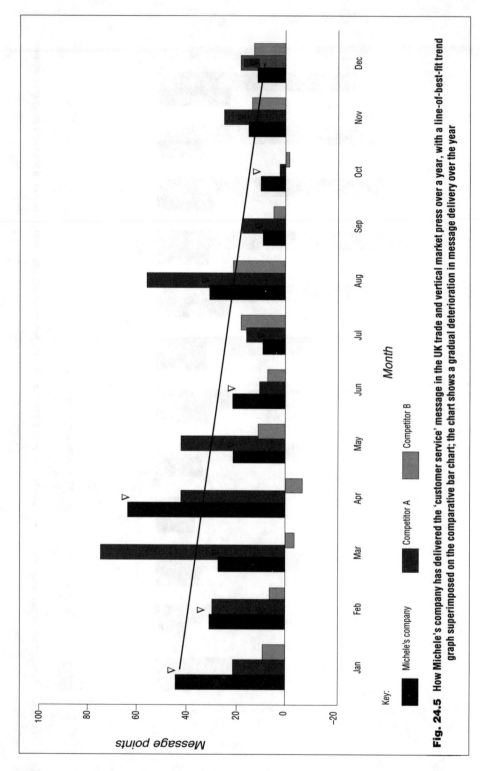

Fig. 24.5 How Michele's company has delivered the 'customer service' message in the UK trade and vertical market press over a year, with a line-of-best-fit trend graph superimposed on the comparative bar chart; the chart shows a gradual deterioration in message delivery over the year

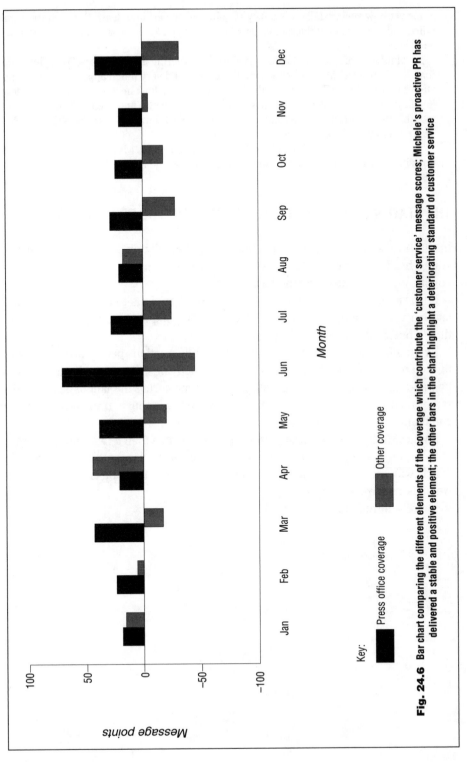

Fig. 24.6 Bar chart comparing the different elements of the coverage which contribute the 'customer service' message scores; Michele's proactive PR has delivered a stable and positive element; the other bars in the chart highlight a deteriorating standard of customer service

Key: Press office coverage   Other coverage

know yet how successfully this policy is going to convert into deals. But both the local office and I feel very confident. Perhaps I could let you know in say another six months and we can review it?'

Sir Matthew had opened the door as she was gathering up her papers. 'Yes, please do that. But in the meantime there's something else – I'd very much appreciate a present-ation a bit like this each month for the board meeting. I don't need you there – just a few headings and some of those charts. You choose which. And please, send the first month's to me rather than circulate them to the board. I want to surprise a few people.' There was a twinkle in his eyes.

Sir Matthew thought to himself as the door shut after her. Maybe she should present the slides to the board herself. I wonder where that would lead?

THE STATUS OF THE PR PROFESSIONAL AND THE PR INDUSTRY

In the brief and fictitious example above, a potentially difficult situation for the young head of a public relations department has been transformed into a good opportunity by astute use of media analysis.

It was a good opportunity for the professional, anxious to defend her position and her department; it's indicative of an equally good opportunity for the rest of the PR business to share with her.

By quantifying the results of their work, public relations people are learning to fight harder for the budget which funds their activities. They are also learning to find and use the levers of corporate power. In mastering the language of results rather than simply reporting on activity, they are beginning to transform their role and their status.

Public relations deserves a more professional status than it has achieved so far. Only in the last decade, however, has it had access to the tools of measurement which will enable it to gain the professional respect from business colleagues which is a necessary first step.

There's nothing holding us back now!

References and Further Reading

Hamilton, S. (1987). *A Communication Audit Handbook: Helping Organizations Communicate*, Pitman Publishing. This short book covers most of the principles of internal communication auditing. It is written from the perspective of the auditor rather than the subject organization, but is a worthwhile read for either party.

Ries, A. and Trout, J. (1986). *Positioning, The Battle for your Mind*, London: McGraw Hill.

Worcester, R. and Downham, J. (eds), (1988). *The Consumer Market Research Handbook*, third edition, London: McGraw Hill, November.

Index

Accountability (in public relations
departments) 5
Acquisitions/takeover situations (effects
on public relations) 165–166
Activity reports 216–217
Adverse media coverage 4, 9, 74, 93, 129,
131–139, 192, 226
anticipating 132–133, 135–136, 141–144
identification of 134–135
Advertising value equivalents 9, 20, 29, 127,
139, 144, 145–150
in adverse coverage 147
Age groups (in target audiences) 38, 39
American Express Travel Services 92–94
Anglian Water 87–91
Article type analysis 117
Audience analysis 28, 31–39, 171–180
costs 180
for broadcasts 154
methods 173
reports 179
role in message formulation 178
see also Target audience
AVEs see Advertising value equivalents
Awareness measurement (in target
audiences) 28
Ayer Directory (USA) 38

Bacon's (USA directory) 38
Bad news see Adverse media coverage
BCBS (health insurance company) 97–99
Behaviour influencing messages 8, 12, 20,
22, 26, 28, 33, 45–47, 48, 102, 137
Behaviour measurement (in audiences) 8,
28, 171–180
Benchmark analysis 5, 17, 56, 109, 110,
133–134, 142, 163
in media relations 183
Beneficial corporate attributes 42
Beneficial/neutral/adverse analysis 85,
110–111
Benn's Directory 38

Bias (in evaluation) 63
BNA analysis 85, 93, 110–111
Boardroom view of media analysis/public
relations 52, 78, 163, 215–227
Brainstorming in media analysis 195–197
Brand profiles 101, 110, 111, 120, 171, 172,
174
low visibility 191
policing 117
Briefs
for analysis/evaluation 67–69, 144, 179
for market research 179
for press cuttings agencies 55–56, 65
British Rail Telecommunications Ltd 83–87
Broadcast media 6, 19–20, 37, 39, 49, 59, 61,
107, 108, 143, 210
analysis of coverage 54, 59, 64
Broadcast monitoring services 59, 65, 151
Broadcast times (effects on message
delivery) 154
Broadsheet national press (UK) 11, 33, 37,
54, 56–58, 107, 108, 126, 151
Brochures 80, 98
see also Company literature
BS5750 (British standard in quality
management) 5
Budgeting (for media analysis) 209–213
Business-to-business market 38, 120, 173
competitor analysis 120

Calculation of audience penetration 38
Causal statements 48
CD-ROM databases 58
Change measurement 177
Circulation analysis 38, 39
see also Readership analysis
Collection of media coverage data (for
analysis) 53–61
Communications
as an industry 181–188
in organizations 6–7, 13, 21, 22–23,
93–94, 190, 209

methods of 74
see also Communications audits;
   Communications strategies
Communications audits 13, 73–82, 97, 178
   by outside consultants 75
   in-house 75–76
   objectives 77
   purpose of 73–74
   report delivery 82
   techniques 78–81
   unrealisable objectives 194–195
Communications directors 64–65, 67, 134,
   164, 190
Communications objectives *see*
   Communication strategies
Communications programmes *see*
   Communications strategies
Communications strategies 3, 6, 7, 12, 13,
   21, 22–23, 28, 30, 33, 39, 43, 48, 51–52,
   53, 67, 73, 75, 76, 78, 82, 91, 98,
   102–110, 144, 165, 172, 173, 176, 178,
   192, 193, 194
   analysis 28, 31–39, 171
   costs 182, 209–213
   feedback 181–188
   see also Communications audits; Public
   relations
Company announcements 134
   see also News releases; Press releases
Company literature 74, 76, 80, 108, 165
   see also Brochures
Comparative analysis *see* Competitor
   analysis
Competitor analysis 17–18, 20, 36–37, 56,
   84, 109–121, 137, 139
Computers *see* Information technology
Connotations (of words) 29, 125, 127
Consultancies (in public relations) 198
Consumer research 174
Corporate attributes (beneficial) 42
Corporate audiences (for public relations
   messages) 35
Corporate ethics 195
Corporate image 11–16, 18, 21, 25, 43–45,
   47–48, 52, 76, 95, 117, 142, 165, 172,
   174, 191, 217
   changing 13–14, 43–45
   defined 12
   effects of crises 143
   ideal images 13
   low visibility 191
   measurement 76
   real images 13
   role in media profiles 14–16
   role of sponsorship 123–129
   see also Competitor analysis; Corporate

profiles; Media profiles
Corporate lying (concept) 195
Corporate objectives *see* Organizational
   objectives
Corporate profiles 101–108, 164, 172, 189,
   217
   see also Corporate image; Negative
   media profiles
Correlation between message delivery and
   sales 217
Costs of media analysis 5–6, 209–213,
   215–216
Crisis coverage 74, 141–144, 187
Critical mass (in media coverage) 60, 192

Data analysis 17, 48, 60, 64, 65, 67
   see also Sampling (of media coverage)
Data Protection Act (1984) 207–208
Databases of influencers 202–208
   data collection 204–206
Definition of objectives (in media analysis)
   23
Delays in starting media analysis 161–168
Delivery effectiveness of messages 16, 20,
   24–28, 33, 36, 64, 113–117, 134, 135,
   149–150, 155, 174, 175, 183, 185, 189,
   190, 191–192, 210, 217, 222

Editions (of newspapers) 152–153
Editorial value *see* Advertising value
   equivalents
Editorial weight (in media analysis) 4
Effectiveness of public relations
   evaluation 3, 6–9, 24–25, 29, 65
Election results (as a source of audience
   data) 176
Electronic mail analysis (in
   communications audits) 79
Enquiry figures (use in audience
   measurement) 173, 222
Ethical aspects of public relations 195
Existing customers (as a target audience)
   32
Expert systems (computer programs) 6
External communications audits 75–77,
   80–81
External media profile/public relations
   analysis services 4, 66–67
   costs 210–211

Favourable media profiles *see* Positive
   media profiles
Fax analysis (in communications audits) 79
Feedback (in communications) 181–188,
   216
Financial press 108

Focus groups 175
  in communications audits 78
Formulation of messages (in public
  relations) 41–52, 73, 80, 178
Foster's lager 125–127
FT-Profile online database 56, 143, 144

Government departments (as a source of
  audience data) 177
Group 4 (security company) 136–137

Handbooks (as a source of audience data)
  176, 177
Headlines (in printed media) 26, 153
Horizontal marketing 36

ICL (company) 94–97
Ideal images (of organizations) 13
Illustrations (use in public relations
  materials) 58, 157–160
  cost factors 159
Image (of organizations) 12–16, 18, 21,
  43–45, 47–48, 52, 165, 191, 217
  changing 13–14
  defined 12
  ideal images 13
  real images 13
  see also Media profiles
IMPACT media analysis service 88, 89, 91,
  95–97
Impact of messages 20, 26, 28, 29, 48
  see also Delivery effectiveness of
  messages
Impressions (in media analysis) 27–28
In-depth interviews (in communications
  audits) 78, 81
In-house media analysis 64–65, 84
Indirect media coverage 201–202
  see also Influencer databases
Industry surveys 77, 81, 173, 175
Influencer databases 202–208
Information (as a resource) 15, 21, 26, 43,
  46–47, 74, 82, 110, 117, 134, 142, 143,
  146, 153, 174, 182, 216, 217
  blockages 76
Information content (of public relations
  messages) 73
Information packs 80, 207
Information superhighway 58
Information technology 6, 56–59, 104–105
  use in public relations 4, 76, 164
Infomercials (in broadcast media) 124
Innovation messages 196
Internal communications (corporate) 52,
  77, 79, 105
Internal communications audits 75–76, 79

International audiences (for public
  relations messages) 35
International media analysis 37
Interviews (as an evaluation technique) 78,
  81, 174, 175
ISO 9000 series (international standards in
  quality management) 5, 79, 212

Key messages (delivery of) 20
Keywords (for press cuttings analysis) 55
Knowledge (in audiences) 43, 44, 102, 173,
  174
  influencing through sponsorship 125
  measurement 173–174

Letters-to-the-Editor 206
Line-of-best-fit analysis (in public relations)
  185–186, 218
Literature surveys (in communications
  audits) 79
Live media coverage 138–139
Local audiences (targeting, for public
  relations messages) 36
Local press 33, 36, 133, 135–136, 144

Management changes (effects on public
  relations) 166
Management information 4, 9, 86–87, 164
Market leadership 17, 22, 166, 194
Market research 8, 28, 38, 63, 64, 81, 146,
  174, 175, 178–179
  costs 179, 212
Marketing 3, 8–9, 20, 35, 82, 99, 110–111,
  145, 171
Marketing audiences (for public relations
  messages) 35–37
Meaning (in signs, text and images) 29
Measurement (in media analysis) 19–30,
  167–168, 176–177
Measurement of change 177
Media (in a causal role) 18
Media analysis 1–9, 15, 16, 17, 18, 21, 27,
  33, 35, 38, 39, 47, 53, 56, 63–69, 82, 164
  adverse media coverage 9, 131–139, 192
  advertising value equivalents 9, 20, 29,
  127, 139, 144, 145–150
  article type analysis 117
  audience analysis 171–180
  board view of 215–227
  brainstorming 195–197
  budgeting 209–213
  competitor analysis 17–18, 20, 56,
  109–121, 137, 139
  concept of 8–9, 11–18
  corporate change factors 161–168
  costs 5–6, 185–186, 209–213, 215–216

crisis coverage 141–144
data collection and analysis 48–52
defined 4–5
delay in starting 161–164
evaluation techniques 83–99
feedback 181–188, 216
in communications audits 76
in-house 64–65
in sponsorship 124–129
indirect media coverage 201–208
influencing role of quality management
   5
international 37
live coverage 138–139
measurement techniques 19–30
open analysis 137–138
pictures 157–160
positional data 151–155
programme management see feedback
raison d'etre 5
reports 216–217
source analysis 113–117
sponsorship coverage 128
subjectiveness 29
techniques 83–99
time factors 6, 161–168
timing (broadcasts) 154–155
trouble shooting 189–199
Media coverage 19–30, 52, 53
analysis 53–61, 65
collecting and sampling data 53–61
costs of generating 148–149, 190, 191
evaluation 8–9, 11, 18, 21, 47, 65,
   113–117, 145–150
quantity measurement 23–24, 192, 210,
   226–227
value of (monetary) 8–9, 13, 20, 29, 127,
   139, 144, 145–150
see also Local press; National press;
   Press cuttings agencies; Regional
   press; Trade press
Media profiles 11–18, 27, 84, 87, 142, 161,
   167, 189, 192, 201, 217, 218
analysis 63–69, 113
negative 14–15
role of organizational image 14–16
trend analysis 17
see also Negative media profiles; Positive
   media profiles
Media relations 3, 9, 35, 36, 38, 47, 54, 63,
   64, 77, 82, 95, 110, 127, 174, 176, 178,
   179–180
costs of 148–149
effectiveness 7–8, 29
feedback 183–185
trouble shooting 189–199

Media sectors (for analysis and
   monitoring) 55, 57, 58
Media targets see Target media
Meetings analysis (in communications
   audits) 76
Memo analysis (in communications audits)
   79
Message density 95–97, 192
Message point readership 49–50, 148, 149
Message pressure (parameter) 50–51
Message strength 16, 20, 26, 28, 146–147,
   155
Messages (in communications) 6, 8, 22–23,
   24–25, 29, 32, 39, 41–52, 65, 74, 81, 89,
   95, 98–99, 101, 103–108, 109, 162,
   191–192
analysis 48–51, 65, 111–117, 121, 126–
   127
audience analysis 172, 178
behaviour influencing 8, 12, 20, 22, 26,
   28, 33, 45–47, 48, 102, 137
changing (in response to changed
   environment) 67
competitor analysis 111–113
correlation between message delivery
   and sales 217
content see analysis
delivery effectiveness 16, 20, 24–28, 33,
   36, 64, 113–117, 134, 135, 149–150, 155,
   174, 175, 183, 185, 189, 190, 191–192,
   210, 217, 222
delivery through sponsorship 124–127
formulation of 41–52, 73, 80, 178
impact 20, 26, 28, 29
in adverse media coverage 131–139
in business-to-business market 120–121
in crisis coverage 141–144
in sponsorship 123–129
negative messages 133
news-hooks 47
opinion influencing 17, 28, 44–45, 47, 98,
   102, 137, 172, 174
reviewing of content 67
role of pictures 157–160
strength of 20, 26, 28, 155
targeting 31–39
Mission statements (corporate) 21–22, 74,
   76, 82, 103–108, 217
Monitoring agencies 54–56, 59, 65, 151
MPR see Message point readership
Multiple messages 48
Mutual understanding (in public relations)
   42

Namechecks 20, 24, 65, 89, 90, 95, 124, 191,
   202

National press (UK) 37, 38, 49, 56, 85, 95, 109, 126, 135, 136, 143, 149, 151, 153–154, 210
  see also Broadsheet national press (UK); Tabloid national press (UK)
National Readership Survey 38
Negative media profiles 4, 14, 15, 129, 133, 189, 192
  see also Adverse media coverage
Negative perceptions (of companies) 14, 15
  see also Negative media profiles
Network analysis (in communications audits) 79–80
New markets (effects on public relations) 166–167
News hooks (in messages) 47
News releases 82, 117, 131
  see also Press releases
Newsletters 80
Newspapers 8, 56–58
  see also Broadsheet national press (UK); National press (UK); Tabloid national press (UK); Press cuttings
Nexis online database 143, 144
Non-advertising media 147–148
Non-profit organizations 22
Numerical sampling technique (in media analysis) 60–61

Objective definition (in media analysis) 23
Omnibus surveys 175, 177
One-way-traffic (within public relations) 42
Online databases 56–58, 143, 144
Open analysis (of media coverage) 76, 98, 137–138, 142, 143, 184
Opinion influencers 202–208
Opinion influencing messages 17, 28, 44–45, 47, 98, 102, 137, 172, 174
  in sponsorship 125
Opinion measurement 28, 76, 171–180
Opinion polls (as a source of audience data) 176
Organizational change 74, 94, 161–168
Organizational communication 6–7, 13, 21, 22–23, 93–94, 190, 209
  see also Communication strategies
Organizational image see Corporate image
Organizational objectives 21–23, 73
  in non-profit organizations 22
Outsourcing (of analysis tasks) 66–67
Overseas media 59
  analysis of coverage 59

Patronage 128

Perceived images (of organizations) 12, 13, 14, 124, 127, 142
  see also Corporate image
Photocopier-reduced press cuttings 23
Photographs see Illustrations (use in public relations materials)
Pictures (role of) 157–160
Pims Directory 38
Policing of product image (in the media) 117
Population data (UK) 51
Position of coverage (in printed media) 151
Positional data 26, 151–155
Positive media profiles 15, 16, 43, 135
Potential customers (as a target audience)
  in horizontal markets 32
  in vertical markets 32
Precision of messages 44, 46
Press conferences 210
Press coverage see Media coverage
Press cuttings 6, 19–20, 29, 49, 53–56, 58, 61, 64, 67, 88, 89, 120, 128, 145, 190, 213, 216, 218
  photocopier-reduced 23
  reading by board members 218
  uses of 54
Press cuttings agencies 54–56, 151
  briefing of 55–56, 65
Press relations see Media relations
Press release distribution services 166
Press releases 47, 60, 74, 80, 84, 101, 113, 117, 166, 210
Privacy laws 208
Problem solving (in public relations) 189–199
Profit motive 22
Programme management (in public relations) 183–188
  see also Communications strategies
Public relations 3–4, 17, 18, 21, 29, 37, 39, 41–52, 53, 63, 64, 67, 69, 73, 74, 80–81, 84, 88–89, 92, 93, 94, 96, 97, 101–108, 110, 117, 128, 131, 139, 163–164
  advertising value equivalents 9, 20, 29, 127, 139, 144, 145–150
  accountability 5
  audience analysis 171–180
  board view of 215–227
  brainstorming 195–197
  comparative studies 109
  consultancies 198
  cost factors 5–6, 149–150, 185–186, 212, 215–216
  coverage measurement 23–24

dealing with adverse media coverage 131–139
dealing with indirect media coverage 201–208
defined 41–42
effectiveness evaluation 3, 6–9, 24–25, 29, 65
effects of growth in the industry 4
effects of organizational change 161–168
ethics 42, 195
evaluation mechanisms 8, 9
feedback 181–188, 216
in acquisitions/takeover situations 165–166
in change of senior management situations 166
message formulation 42–47
motives 42
mutual understanding 42
proactive activity 93
problem solving 189–199
programme management 183–188
role in changing organizational image 13–14
role in communications audits 75
role in remedying adverse messages 195
role of mutual understanding 42
targeting 33–35
trouble shooting 189–199
use of information technology 4
use of pictures 157–160
use of press cuttings 54, 55
use of source analysis 113–117
see also Messages (in communications)
Public wire services 166

Quality management 14, 136
influencing role in public relations 5
Quantity of media coverage measurement 23, 210, 226–227
Questionnaires
in audience research 173
in communications audits 79

RAC 15–16
Radio programmes 8
see also Broadcast media
Ratner, Gerald 11, 14
Readership analysis 28, 38, 39, 49, 153, 155
Reading lists (for press cuttings analysis) 55
Real images (of organizations) 13
Recall (in audiences) 171, 172
Regional audiences (for public relations messages) 36–37, 39, 54
Regional press 33, 37, 39, 107, 108, 128

Regional sampling (of media coverage) 61
Reinforcement process (in communications audits) 80–81, 82
Results of media analysis/public relations 4, 215–227
analysis 63–69, 83–99
Reviewing of media analysis parameters 67
Royal Automobile Club see RAC

Sales see Marketing
Sales figures (use in audience measurement) 173, 176
Sampling (of media coverage) 53–61, 65, 67
Sector sampling (of media coverage) 61
Sector surveys (in communications audits) 77, 81
Semiotics 6, 29, 125
Share price data (as a source of audience data) 176
Sheffield Forgemasters (steel firm) 141–142
Socio-economic groups (in target audiences) 38, 39
Source analysis (of media coverage) 113–117
Specialist sections (in printed media) 152
Sponsorship 19, 20, 21, 101, 123–129
message delivery 124–127
Sponsorship media coverage 128
Spreadsheets (as analytic tools) 185–186
Strength of comment (in media analysis) 4
Sub-messages 48
Subject specification (for press cuttings analysis) 55
Symbolism (in messages) 29
Synectics (problem solving method) 197–198

Tabloid national press (UK) 33, 57–58, 107, 108, 126
Tapes of broadcasts 19–20
Target audiences (for communications/ public relations) 6, 12, 13, 16, 22, 26–28, 31–39, 43, 44, 48, 65, 67, 73, 77, 102, 109, 146, 155, 165, 167, 171, 172
changes in 163
identification of 31–32, 52, 73
in business-to-business markets 121
in sponsorship 128
see also Audience analysis
Target media 27, 33, 35, 37, 53, 55, 56, 64, 65, 110, 137, 138, 167
overseas 59
Technical press see Trade press
Telecommunications 83–87

Telephone call analysis (in communications audits) 79
Telephone research (in media analysis) 98
Telephone surveys 173–174, 175
  in communications audits 79
Television broadcasts 8
  factual content 6
  semiotic significance 6
  see also Broadcast media
Television programmes 8
Time factors (for press cuttings analysis) 55
Time sampling (of media coverage) 61
Timing of broadcasts 154
Timing of media analysis 161–168
Today (BBC radio programme) 147–148
Trade associations (as a source of audience data) 176
Trade press 17, 36, 37, 38, 55, 85, 107, 108, 120, 126, 137, 144, 149, 226
Trend analysis (of media profiles) 17, 185, 217
Trend charts 17–18, 89, 177, 217

Trouble shooting 189–199
Two-Ten Directory 38

Unique selling points (of products) 167
Unrealisable communications objectives 194–195

Value (defined) 8
Vertical markets 33, 35, 36, 54, 120, 137
  overseas 59
Visibility *see* Brand profiles; Corporate image
Vision statements 103–108
Volume measurement (of media coverage) 23–24, 134, 177, 191, 217

Wire services (public) 166, 210
Word count (as a measurement technique) 23, 24

Yearbooks (as a source of audience data) 176